Comparing Legal Cultures

This volume is dedicated to the
incomparable Mrs Isla Dow

Comparing Legal Cultures

Edited by
DAVID NELKEN
Distinguished Professor of Sociology, University of Macerata, Italy and Distinguished Research Professor of Law, University of Wales at Cardiff

Dartmouth
Aldershot • Brookfield USA • Singapore • Sydney

Published by
Dartmouth Publishing Company Limited
Gower House
Croft Road
Aldershot
Hants GU11 3HR
England

Dartmouth Publishing Company
Old Port Road
Brookfield
Vermont 05036
USA

British Library Cataloguing in Publication Data
Comparing legal cultures. – (Socio-legal studies)
1.Sociological jurisprudence 2.Culture and law
3.Sociological jurisprudence – Congresses 4.Culture and law
– Congresses
I.Nelken, David
340.1'15

Library of Congress Cataloging-in-Publication Data
Comparing legal cultures / edited by David Nelken.
p. cm.
"Socio-legal studies series."
ISBN 1-85521-718-X (hb)
1. Culture and law. I. Nelken, David.
K487.C8C66 1996
340'.115—dc20 96–43132
CIP

ISBN 1 85521 718 X (Hbk)
ISBN 1 85521 898 4 (Pbk)

Typeset by Manton Typesetters, 5–7 Eastfield Road, Louth, Lincolnshire LN11 7AJ, UK
Printed and bound in Great Britain by Biddles Limited, Guildford and King's Lynn

Contents

List of Contributors

Erhard Blankenburg is Professor of Law at the University of Amsterdam, Holland.

Roger Cotterrell is Professor of Legal Theory at Queen Mary Westfield College, University of London, UK.

Malcolm M. Feeley is Professor of Law at the University of California at Berkeley, USA.

Eric A. Feldman is a Research Fellow at Yale University, USA.

Maria Rosaria Ferrarese is Professor of Sociology of Law at the University of Trento, Italy.

Lawrence M. Friedman is Marion Rice Kirkwood Professor of Law at Stanford University, California, USA.

Carlo Guarnieri is Professor of Comparative Judicial Systems at the University of Bologna, Italy.

Michael King is Professor of Law at Brunel University, UK.

Setsuo Miyazawa is Professor of Law at the University of Kobe, Japan.

David Nelken is Distinguished Professor of Sociology at Macerata University, Italy and Distinguished Research Professor of Law at the University of Wales at Cardiff, UK.

Carlo Pennisi is Professor of Sociology of Law at the University of Catania, Italy.

Hanne Petersen is Professor of Law at the University of Copenhagen, Denmark.

Brad Sherman is Professor of Law at Griffiths University, Brisbane, Australia.

Acknowledgement

The Law and Society Review is thanked for its permission to reproduce that part of Chapter 3 which appeared in a revised version in 1994.

Comparing Legal Cultures: An Introduction

David Nelken

Given the limited progress which has been made in comparative sociology of law since the writings of Max Weber, little justification is needed for seeking to compare and contrast legal institutions and processes in different societies and cultures. But the task of understanding the 'other' – in a world of ever-increasing contacts and mutual influences – is much more demanding than merely juxtaposing descriptions of the operations of law or attitudes to law in different countries. The contributions in this volume were first presented at a workshop on 'Comparing Legal Cultures' in Macerata University in Italy on 18–20 May 1994, organized by the Department of Social Change, Legal Institutions and Communication (under the auspices of the ISA/RCSL).[1] They discuss central features of law in countries as different (or as similar) as Britain, France, Germany, Holland, Italy, Japan and the USA. But their special concern is with the theoretical *point* of such exercises: the aim of this collection is to consider the possibilities and advantages of using comparative work so as to clarify the meaning and character of *legal culture*.

The attempt to use a comparative perspective to grasp legal culture requires the ability to transcend competing approaches and methodologies which threaten otherwise to oversimplify what is at stake (Nelken, 1995). Some of these alternatives are false dichotomies insofar as they are rarely found in the pure form: this is certainly true for the opposed dangers of ethnocentrism and relativism and, to a large extent, also applies to the choice whether to aim at useful as opposed to strictly scientific types of comparative work. Other dilemmas are more real. What is culture? Should we concentrate on the world system, on national legal cultures or on specific institutions? Should we take culture to be the set of behaviours and ideas of a given population or embrace more post-modern accounts of culture as a constructed flow of images?[2] What about legal culture? Are we interested in the definitions of law used by politicians, legal officials, legal scholars or more in lay or popular definitions of law? How do all these relate to sociological definitions of law? How should we go about studying (legal) culture? Are we aiming to learn more about other cultures or more about what we take for granted about our own? What sources shall we use to make sense of culture? Does behaviour count more than words? Should we rely on what people can tell us, or search for the assumptions that make sense of their world views?

Many (if not all) of these issues are examined here in relation to aspects of legal culture as various as litigation rates (Blankenburg, Nelken); attitudes towards legal institutions (Friedman): crime rates (Miyazawa); assumptions about who should invoke the law (Ferrarese); the practice of prosecution (Guarnieri) juvenile justice (King); lawyers' images of similarity and opposition of municipal law in comparison to other legal systems (Sherman); legal ideologies (Cotterrell); and rights rhetoric (Feldman).

Legal culture as a topic for research raises both conceptual and methodological problems. This volume is therefore divided into two parts so as to group together, on the one hand, those chapters which are more relevant to the theoretical problem of how and when to invoke the concept of legal culture and, on the other hand, those which are more concerned with methodological difficulties in disclosing aspects of given legal cultures. Part I thus seeks to throw light on different uses of the *concept* of legal culture. It focuses in particular on debates concerning the way the term is used in mainstream work by American 'law and society' scholars and by leading European empirical sociologists of law, but then goes on to canvass more radical dissenting views about the difficulties of this idea. Part II seeks rather to illustrate some of the various ways legal cultures can be investigated. The approaches represented in this volume include: looking at one legal culture from the perspective of another; examining the way similar legal institutions develop in different settings, and explorations in the use of quantative and qualitative methodologies aimed at bringing out what is special about given legal cultures and the processes by which they are (re)produced.

In the opening chapter of the collection Roger Cotterrell takes as his target the changing use of the term 'legal culture' in the work of Lawrence Friedman. He argues that the concept, like the notion of culture in general, lacks rigour and is ultimately theoretically incoherent. The variety of meanings given to the term over the years by Friedman makes it of little use to sociology of law because it is difficult to build such a protean term into testable explanations (especially as legal culture is sometimes taken as what needs to be explained and at other times is asked to play the role of explanation). Cotterrell argues that, at least in modern complex societies, it is best to treat legal culture not as a description of existing empirical variability but as an ideal-type category to be used heuristically. In his view most of the work the concept is supposed to do for comparative sociology of law can be better accomplished by using the term 'legal ideology'.

In his reply, Lawrence Friedman admits that legal culture is not a social variable that can be measured with any precision. But, he claims, it shares this quality with most of the basic conceptual building-blocks of social science. Nor is this a reason to criticize it as incoherent. The value of the term, according to Friedman, is that it helps us line up relevant phenomena concerning the relationship between law and culture into one very general category under which we can then subsume other less vague and more measurable phenomena, spurring us to gather more information in particular about public attitudes towards the law and legal institutions. As far as explanation goes, our accounts of legal culture serve, for example, to capture an essential intervening variable in explaining the type of legal changes which follow large social transformations such as those following technological breakthroughs. Finally, as compared to 'legal ideology', the term 'legal culture' is more concerned with a variety of social influences on attitudes towards law, rather than just with the ideas and influence of legal professionals.

In Chapter 3 Erhard Blankenburg draws on his extensive empirical comparative research into litigation rates in Europe in the course of a methodologically grounded search for 'indicators' capable of throwing light on legal culture. The author's view is that our explanatory focus should be on the 'supply side' of legal institutions and the infrastructure of available alternatives to using the courts. He documents this approach in a comparison of the puzzling difference in litigation rates in neighbouring areas of Netherlands and former West Germany which are alleged to be otherwise remarkably similar. Blankenburg argues that the relatively low litigation rate in Holland can best be accounted for by the Dutch infrastructure of filters and alternatives to courts, as compared to the incentives in Germany to make use of the swift and relatively cheap court institutions. He develops his thesis by careful consideration of a wide range of different kinds of legal cases and social disputes.

In his extended commentary on Blankenburg's argument, David Nelken tries to assess the strengths and limits of an approach to legal culture which attempts to explain its variability in terms of measurable differences in legal infrastructure. Nelken identifies in Blankenburg's work a number of controversial claims which relate to the study of legal culture: (1) litigation rates can serve as useful (measurable) indicators of legal culture; (2) legal culture can be studied without reference to meaning; (3) the 'supply side' of legal culture, and in particular the institutional shape of legal infrastructure, is more likely to yield a satisfactory explanation than 'demand-side' factors in explaining patterns of legal behaviour such as litigation rates; (4) 'there is no legal culture outside existing legal institutions': the influence of 'folk' or general cultural mentalities may therefore safely be ignored; (5) we need to open up 'the black box' of legal culture so as to reveal (infra)structural influences on the choice to use law. After discussing each of these propositions in turn, Nelken links Blankenburg's argument to current debates between culturalist and structuralist approaches to legal culture, and suggests why these approaches need to be transcended.

Like Blankenburg, Malcolm Feeley in his thoughts on 'comparative criminal law for criminologists', wants to underline the difference between comparative law scholarship and the enterprise of explanation in the social sciences. But he is, if anything, more radical than Blankenburg. Rather than worrying about the neglect of 'meaning' in the comparative study of culture, as Nelken does, Feeley wants to apply the same protocols to comparative work as would be appropriate in any other sort of empirical investigation. Indeed, for Feeley, all explanations in social science can be said to be comparative – because they are concerned with concomitant variation – which is the functional equivalent of experimentation. He strongly criticizes comparative sociology of law for having made insufficient progress in scientific terms and suggests that the reason for this may be that many scholars persist in combining the rather different exercises of comparative work in law and in the social sciences. What in legal writing is usually a normative, policy-oriented effort at comparison, in the social sciences is an exploration of general propositions geared to explaining variation in social and legal order. After considering a range of contributions to this field Feeley concludes that scholars have not produced a body of research that develops theory, tests propositions and accounts for variation; their writing tends to be descriptive and although this can provide useful insights it does not constitute explanation.

The next two chapters are concerned in different ways with the notions of law employed in studies of legal culture. In Chapter 6, Carlo Pennisi also tackles the work of Blankenburg, but this time from a different angle, claiming that its weakness lies precisely in its failure to develop a concept of legal culture which can be used in empirical sociological research. For Pennisi what is unsatisfactory about the meaning given to the concept of legal culture by Blankenburg (and Friedman) is its insufficient recognition of the need for reflexivity. Where Blankenburg is content to define law by sociological fiat, Pennisi argues that definitions of legal culture must find a way to mediate, on the one hand between the meaning of law to legal actors and the public and, on the other hand, the way the sociologist identifies it.

In Chapter 7, Michael King, writing from a point of view sympathetic to Luhmann's sociological theory of law, offers a theoretical critique of the ideas of law, society and culture which are presupposed by mainstream work in this field. Dealing with the concern raised by Pennisi, he argues that only by adopting a systems approach, such as that of Luhmann, can comparative researchers appreciate that their observation of law is itself a result of socially generated sustained meanings attributable to one or other functionally differentiated systems of communication. From this starting-point King questions the way comparative sociologists of law make the boundaries of cultures coincide with national legal boundaries, whereas for Luhmann a country does not qualify as an autopoietic system. Unless care is taken to define the term 'culture' as a network of communications (and world-constructions), comparative work risks ending in stereotypical accounts of national culture – accounts which are doubly misleading as the effects of globalization increasingly mean that nations cannot isolate their cultures from world society. King concludes that we will learn more by contrasting the way law relates to other systems than by trying to compare legal cultures.

The last chapter of Part I is contributed by Hanne Petersen. She too is highly critical of much work which sets out to compare legal cultures, but this is not so much because of the way it identifies law but rather because of its neglect of the question of how law constitutes identity. For Petersen, a central feature of the legal cultures of modern Western industrial societies is the extent to which they devalue gender and nature. This means that we need to rethink how law constructs the difference between nature and culture by placing in question even the very notions of law and of science – the subject and methodology of comparing legal cultures. According to Petersen the way law deals with women and nature is linked insofar as women are seen as representative of nature and the 'private' realm. The process of transforming nature into 'culture' is one which to a large degree takes place outside the remit of a law which deals with already 'cultured' legal subjects. This sphere is regulated rather by the psychological and other 'disciplines' as described by Foucault, though, as Petersen suggests, the difficulty of coping with AIDS or the new reproductive technologies are now beginning to draw law into this sphere. More generally, as compared to the respect for nature which is central to many non-industrial legal codes, the modern mechanistic world view assumes culture to be higher than nature and this has highly negative effects on law's concern for the protection of nature. Petersen offers an overview of recent critiques of the scientific world view and shows how they are intimately linked with calls for a change in legal culture, including the idea of a revival of some new form of 'natural law'.

The opening chapter in Part II by Maria Rosaria Ferrarese offers an account of American law through Italian eyes. She illustrates one of the most obvious yet useful contributions of comparative sociology of law: the possibility of seeing a too familiar legal culture from a different perspective. Ferrarese outlines the central features of Anglo-American common law as they present themselves to a sociologically trained Continental lawyer. Starting with the philosophy of checks and balances, she goes on to consider the importance given to private law and the mobilization of law by the parties for their instrumental purposes, as compared to state-initiated legal action. She then discusses the adversarial process, the importance of procedure over substance and the possibility of negotiation within the law. Much of what she has to say may well seem 'natural' to a common lawyer; in that very obviousness – of what for her is a surprisingly entrepreneurial conception of law – lies the significance of the account of legal culture which Ferrarese unfolds.

A major issue in comparing legal cultures is deciding which units to compare. A classical method is to look for countries or systems which are assumed to be basically similar but also have known differences in some feature of their use of or attitudes to law (as in the 'experiment' conducted by Blankenburg). In his contribution to the volume, Carlo Guarnieri, a political scientist who specializes in comparative judicial politics, offers another example of this methodology. He compares the organization of public prosecution in France and Italy in order to show what happens to formally rather similar judicial structures which evolve and operate in different political and institutional environments. He is particularly concerned to evidence those differences which can be attributed to the influence of legal culture. This he defines as a set of historically learned responses that disclose not only what is valued in a society but also how institutional problems will be framed and solutions envisaged. He begins by providing a brief historical overview before proceeding to a close point-by-point contrast (informed by interviews with those involved) regarding the extent to which prosecutors actually exercise discretion. He also investigates the location of political responsibility for the decisions taken in each of the two countries compared. He concludes that there is, relatively speaking, greater correspondence between legal norms and actual behaviour in France than in Italy and that, in practice, the formal denial of discretion in Italy may actually facilitate a higher degree of operational discretion. Referring to Nelken's work on trust and criminal justice (Nelken, 1994) he argues that the formal denial of discretion reflects a legal culture which expresses and reproduces a low level of inter-institutional trust. But a paradoxical result of outlawing discretion in the name of a formally impersonal conception of law is that, for even the smallest exercise of power, it is more than ever necessary to gain the (personal) consent or acquiescence of all the other institutional actors concerned.

The low crime rate in Japan, and, in general, the reluctance of the Japanese to resort to law, is one of the most puzzling test cases for theorizing in the field of comparative sociology of law and criminology. In his chapter on 'the enigma of Japan', Setsuo Miyazawa sets out to discuss empirical comparative research on criminal behaviour from a Japanese perspective. He argues that, once we have ruled out the problem of cultural relativism, progress in comparative criminology requires a judicious mixture of quantitative and ethnographic methods. Using the latter approach he dissents from the argument that Japan's anomalously low crime rate is due to what has been described as its preference for 'reintegrative shaming' rather than other forms of punishment (Braithwaite, 1979). He suggests instead that companies and schools operate extremely harsh and exclusionary systems of social control and that Japanese people conform because conformity is highly rewarded while non-conformity costs enormously. Miyazawa sets out his proposal for a cross-national project for investigating crime rates which will also make sense of the Japanese case. Adapting anomie theory to the Japanese situation, he argues that anomie is less likely where there are widespread expectations of a growing economy: in addition, looking at Japan in the light of 'control theory' reveals a society where people have unusually intense bonds to conventional associates, especially those in the company in which they work.

A useful contrast in ways of doing comparative research into legal culture, once again with Japanese legal culture as the topic of study, is offered by Eric Feldman in his chapter on patients' rights and citizens' movements in Japan. He too is interested in explaining Japanese 'difference' and starts from the widely held claim in the literature that the relatively low level of litigation in Japan is linked to the low tendency to assertion of individual rights, especially as compared to American legal culture. But Feldman seeks to show that there is in fact something equivalent to rights assertion in Japan and that this is likely to be an increasing trend. Distinguishing carefully between rights, rhetoric about rights and rights rhetoric (and concentrating on the last of these) he argues that rights in Japan do matter, but they exhibit differences from, and matter in different ways than, rights in the United States. Rather than searching for explanations of variance, Feldman describes the process of 'transplantation' of rights discourse in Japan and the internal debates as to the nature and remit of rights which reveal how and when rights became a real issue in Japanese culture. He examines in particular the struggles of 'new rights' movements in the 1980s, claiming that, though their substantive successes in the face of political and bureaucratic resistance were very limited, their long-term importance was that they began to articulate political claims in the language of rights. The chapter ends with an extended analysis of the movement for patients' rights in medical decision making and in managing the problem of AIDS, as an example of the continuing importance of rights rhetoric in contemporary Japan.

Both Feldman and Brad Sherman, the author of the final chapter in this volume, are interested in legal transplants. While Feldman compares legal cultures by examining the fate of transplanted ideas such as the notion of individual rights, Sherman proposes that we study how the images of other legal systems come to shape the internal development of legal culture. Sherman, however, is interested not simply in tracing patterns of influence but in showing the reflexive influence on legal evolution of the activity of comparative law research itself. Taking as his theme the birth of modern copyright law, he explores the idea that 'the formation of identity is usually a product of denial'; in other words, legal culture is in part a country's idea of how it is different from others. Historically speaking, whether or not an interest in copyright could be protected universally or at least by means of bilateral treaties, raised, as a practical matter, the questions of similarity and difference which scholars examine when studying comparative legal cultures. International copyright treaties presupposed and required a representation of domestic law and this led to a search for common denominators which then helped to constitute the law. Nineteenth-century openness to importing other nations' laws gave way to the belief that the British style of copyright was naturally and inevitably different from the approach adopted in France and Germany. But Sherman shows that it was only after the (re)invention of its law that it became possible to claim that a specific British approach had always existed.

Notes

1 The original papers have all been extensively reviewed and revised for publication. Those included here which were not presented at the Macerata workshop are Lawrence Friedman's, which was commissioned as a response to the critique offered by Roger Cotterrell, and the two papers on Japan (whose legal culture offers a particularly stimulating challenge to comparative sociologists of law). Other papers given at the workshop have been published in D. Nelken (ed.), special issue of *Social and Legal Studies* on 'Legal Culture, Diversity and Globalisation', **4**, (4), 1995). These were: Sergio Lopez-Ayllon, 'Notes on Mexican Legal Culture'; Antoine Garapon, 'French Legal Culture and the Shock of Globalisation'; Tony Prosser, 'The State, Constitutions and Implementing Economic Policy: Privatisation and Regulation in the UK, France and the USA'; and Lucia Zedner, 'In Pursuit of the Vernacular: Comparing Law and Order Discourse in Britain and Germany'. The Macerata initiative, a product of the working group on comparing legal cultures of the Research Committee of Sociology of Law of the International Sociological Association (ISA/RGSL), will be taken further in the form of an ambitious project on comparing legal cultures based at the Onati International Institute for Sociology of Law in Spain.

2 Jonathan Friedman argues that dissolution of ethnographic authority means that culture can now only be defined as 'an enormous interplay of interpretations of a given social reality' (J. Friedman, 1994: 73). Most writers on comparative sociology of law have shied away from the challenges of post-modernism, sometimes even taking refuge in positivism or functionalism to a greater extent than they would if they were writing about their own culture!

References

Braithwaite, J. (1979) *Inequality, Crime and Reintegration*, Cambridge: Cambridge University Press.

Friedman, J. (1994) *Cultural Identity and Global Process*. London: Sage.

Nelken, D. (1994) 'Whom Can You Trust? The Future of Comparative Criminology', in D. Nelken (ed.), *The Futures of Criminology*, London: Sage, 220–44.

Nelken, D. (1995) 'Disclosing/Invoking Legal Culture', in D. Nelken (ed.), special issue on 'Legal Culture, Diversity and Globalization', *Social and Legal Studies*, **4** (4), 435–52.

PART I
INVOKING LEGAL CULTURE: DEBATES AND DISSENTS

1 The Concept of Legal Culture

Roger Cotterrell

Introduction

The search for a rigorous concept of legal culture has obvious attractions for a comparative sociology of law; that is, a sociology of law offering general comparisons of the characteristics of different specific legal systems. A focus on legal culture might, indeed, be seen as a means of fusing the aspirations of sociology of law and comparative law.

Comparative law – the comparison of the different legal systems of the world (Zweigert and Kötz, 1987:2) – offers the example of a scholarly enterprise that has developed explicit conceptual frameworks for comparison between state legal systems. The idea of 'legal families', for example, whatever its difficulties, suggests that different state legal systems, or central elements of legal doctrine within them (including styles of developing and presenting doctrine, and of legal reasoning and interpretation), can be treated as having sufficient similarity to make comparison fruitful. At the same time, it suggests that these comparable systems or system elements treated as a group can be distinguished from others treated, for certain analytical purposes, as qualitatively more remote (see, for example, Zweigert and Kötz, 1987:ch.5; David and Brierley, 1985:17–22).

However, the main conceptual mechanisms of comparative law seem inadequate for the purposes of sociology of law, since what is required for the latter is a conceptual framework allowing comparison, not of legal doctrine as such, but of legal ideas and practices regarded as inseparable from a broader social context. One of the enduring problems of comparative law has been its inability to demonstrate convincingly the theoretical value of doctrinal comparisons separated from comparative analysis of the entire political, economic and social (we might call it contextual) matrix in which legal doctrine and procedures exist (cf. Friedman, 1975:201). Comparative law has seemed unable to provide viable frameworks for comparison of laws or legal systems treated as aspects of or elements within a political society (cf. Damaska, 1986:6–7). Indeed, some writers have suggested that the destiny of a comparative law that solves these problems of comparison is, in fact, to become sociology of law (cf. Hall, 1963:10–15; David and Brierley, 1985:13) or at least 'a composite of social knowledge of positive law' contributing to a humanistic sociology of law (Hall, 1963:ch.2).

The promise held out by the search for a concept of legal culture appropriate to comparative sociology of law is that of an idea that would embrace or recognize all those elements of the contextual matrix that have to be taken into account if comparisons of legal systems and their characteristic elements are to be sociologically meaningful. But the difficulty of any such concept – as of the concept of culture itself – is its imprecision and vagueness, which is a consequence of the demands made upon it and the role in analysis that it is typically required to play.

This chapter is concerned to examine in general terms the theoretical utility of a concept of legal culture. It takes, as a focus for exploring possibilities, the attempt by the American legal sociologist Lawrence Friedman since the late 1960s to elaborate and apply such a concept. The first main section of the chapter examines Friedman's various formulations and applications, over a period of more than a quarter of a century, of a concept of legal culture, and assesses how far his claims for the explanatory power of this concept are justified. Friedman's work is emphasized here because it is, by far, the most sustained effort to work with an explicit concept of legal culture in recent comparative sociology of law and to defend and elaborate theoretically its use.

My claim is that the concept, as developed and applied in Friedman's work, lacks rigour and appears – in certain crucial respects – ultimately theoretically incoherent. This result should be seen, however, less as a fault of Friedman's particular elaboration of the concept of legal culture than as a reflection of general problems in using 'culture' as an explanatory concept in theoretical analysis of law. It may, indeed, be impossible to develop a concept of legal culture with sufficient analytical precision to give it substantial utility as a component in legal theory and, especially, to allow it to indicate a significant explanatory variable in empirical research in sociology of law.

The remainder of the chapter is concerned to ask in what circumstances the concept of legal culture may, despite these problems, be valuable in social studies of law and how far some of the theoretical aims for comparative sociology of law sought by developing the concept of legal culture can be pursued by other means.

Problems of the Concept of Legal Culture

The main problems that the chapter identifies with the concept of legal culture, as developed in Friedman's work, relate to, first, the definition of the concept; second, the varieties of legal culture and their relationships; third, the causal significance and mechanisms of legal culture; and, fourth, the explanatory significance of the concept. While these problems are fundamental, an examination of them also highlights constructively criteria that should guide analytical frameworks for comparative sociology of law.

The Definition of the Concept

In Friedman's most extensive theoretical discussion of legal culture he offers a variety of characterizations: legal culture 'refers to public knowledge of and attitudes and behaviour patterns toward the legal system' (1975:193). Legal cultures may also be 'bodies of *custom* organically related to the culture as a whole' (1975:194). Legal culture is a part of culture generally: 'those parts of general culture – customs, opinion, ways of doing and thinking – that bend social forces toward or away from the law and in particular ways' (1975:15). Thus the emphasis is on clusters both of ideas and of behaviour patterns, intimately related. In later formulations, however, legal culture appears only as ideational: the behavioural elements appear to have been discarded. Legal culture consists of 'attitudes, values, and opinions held in society, with regard to law, the legal system, and its various parts' (1977:76), 'ideas, attitudes, values, and beliefs that people hold about the legal system' (1986:17) or 'ideas, attitudes, expectations and opinions about law, held by people in some given society' (1990:213; and see 1985:31; 1994:118).

The imprecision of these formulations makes it hard to see what exactly the concept covers and what the relationship is between the various elements said to be included within its scope. As long as explanatory significance is not attached to the concept of legal culture and it is used only as a residual category to refer to a general environment of thought, belief, practices and institutions within which law can be considered to exist, no serious problems arise. In some discussions of the concept of general culture Friedman seems to imply this approach. Thus a 'common sense view' of culture is advocated; culture merely refers to the range of individual variations in a certain environment (1990:212, 213); national culture is 'a kind of aggregate, hard to compare with other aggregates' (1975: 209). Culture appears, therefore, as a kind of residue; the contingent, even arbitrary, patterning produced by many specific, diverse and possibly unrelated factors.

This view is, however, clearly insufficient for Friedman's purposes. The patterning is held to reflect something, like a shadow of an unseen object

(1990:196); therefore legal culture has significance as more than just an aggregate. As will appear, for Friedman, it is to be understood as itself a causal factor in legal development (it '*makes* the law, at least in some ultimate sense' (1990:197)) and is therefore an essential component in theoretical explanation in sociology of law. For this reason the concept requires far more rigorous specification than it seems to receive. Yet the variety of meanings of legal culture here is strikingly reminiscent of the variety of meanings of the term 'culture' itself that have often been found in anthropologists' writings (cf. Geertz, 1973:4–5).

The Varieties of Legal Culture and Their Relationships

Friedman remarks that 'one can speak of legal culture at many levels of abstraction' (1975:204; cf. 1994:120). Each nation has a legal culture (1975:209); legal culture can describe 'underlying traits of a whole legal system – its ruling ideas, its flavour, its style' (1975: 15); each country or society may have its own legal culture and no two are exactly alike (1975:199). On the other hand, Friedman writes extensively of what he calls the legal culture of modernity, or modern legal culture, which is a characteristic feature of many contemporary societies (1975:204ff; 1994); elsewhere he writes of Western legal culture (1990:198–9); and even of an emergent world legal culture (1975:220).

Again, however, and especially in his more recent work, he has strongly emphasized the idea of a plurality of legal cultures – indeed, 'a dizzying array of cultures' (1990:213) – within countries or nations. In the United States, for example, there is a legal culture of rich and poor; of blacks, whites or Asians; of steelworkers or accountants; of men, women and children, and so on (1990:213); 'It should be possible to isolate a pattern for any particular group we might select' (1994:120). A complex society has a complex legal culture (1990:96). American legal culture is not one culture but many: 'There are legal conservatives, legal liberals, and all sorts of variants and subgroups. Within specific groups, legal culture consists of particular attitudes which, however, do tend to cohere, to hang together, to form clusters of related attitudes' (1985:98; and see 1986:17).

The concept of legal culture is thus stretched two ways. On the one hand, it points towards broad comparison and the recognition of extremely wide historical tendencies or movements that are certainly not contained by the boundaries of nations or state legal systems. On the other hand, the concept is invoked to recognize familiar themes of legal pluralism as understood in its social scientific sense (cf. Merry, 1988). Up to a point, this catholicity of application suggests a concept of considerable subtlety. Legal culture does not appear as a unitary concept but indicates an immense, multitextured overlay of levels and regions of culture, varying in content, scope and influence and in their relation to the institutions, practices and knowledges of state legal systems.

Looked at in another way, however, the highly flexible idea of legal culture presents serious problems for its theoretical application when specific questions are asked about the relationship between legal culture and particular aspects of state legal systems. If legal culture refers to so many levels and regions of culture (with the scope of each of these ultimately indeterminate because of the indeterminacy of the scope of the idea of legal culture itself) the problem of specifying how to use the concept as a theoretical component in comparative sociology of law remains.

Friedman has consistently described a fundamental duality of legal culture which may in some respects cut across the various levels or regions of legal culture noted above. He distinguishes in a broad manner, reminiscent in this respect of Savigny (Savigny, 1831:28–9), between the legal culture of 'those members of society who perform specialised legal tasks' (Friedman, 1975:233) and that of other citizens. The legal culture of legal professionals, which Friedman considers 'specially important' (1975:194) is 'internal' legal culture. Contrasted with it is what he has variously called 'external' (1975:223; 1986:17), 'popular' (1990:4) or 'lay' (1977:76) legal culture. The relationship between 'internal' and 'external' legal culture remains, however, very unclear. It is not apparent why internal legal culture *must* be regarded, sociologically, as specially important, nor why exactly the behaviour and attitudes of professionals have a great effect on the pattern of demands in the legal system (cf. Friedman, 1975:194). This is a crucial matter given that, as will appear, the concept of legal culture is intended to explain much that is socially significant about the workings of legal systems.

Lawyers' legal thought, according to Friedman, is necessarily bound to its culture and culture determines the limits within which legal thought can change (1975:206). Internal legal culture reflects the main traits of lay (or external) legal culture (1977:79). Nevertheless, in his view, different kinds of professional legal reasoning – if this is taken to mean the formal, authoritative stating of reasons for a legal decision – are socially significant. Legal reasoning may tend towards closure or openness, and towards innovativeness in doctrine or resistance to innovation. Different types of legal system can be classified in terms of the types of reasoning that dominate within them. Such matters as legalism, reliance on legal fictions, the use of reasoning by analogy, and specific aspects of judicial language and style, can be related to these classifications.

It remains unclear from Friedman's discussions, however, just what social consequence these various matters are considered to have, although he clearly considers them to be expressions or products of internal legal culture. Equally, it remains unclear how internal legal culture, in this sense, is to be distinguished from what comparative lawyers think of as the 'style' of a legal system or legal family (cf. Zweigert and Kötz, 1987:68ff). Yet Friedman suggests that the idea of legal families is not useful for sociology of law because stylistic differences between legal families do not necessarily correlate with contrasts in socioeconomic conditions of existence of law. Hence differences between families of law, unlike differences between legal cultures, may be socially relatively insignificant (1975:202; 1977:75–6). If this is because they are based only on arbitrary aggregations of traits, it seems that this may also be a characteristic of legal culture, at least in some of its forms, since, as has been seen, this can also be considered merely as a range of individual variations, culture itself being 'a kind of aggregate'.

As will appear, the lack of clarity in explaining the sociological relationship between internal and external legal culture has serious consequences for the explanatory usefulness of the concept of legal culture. The cause of this lack of clarity seems easily identifiable, however. While, as has been noted above, Friedman emphasizes the diversity and multiple levels and regions of legal culture, ultimately he continues to use the concept of legal culture in a way that implies unities of what may be extremely diverse elements of ideas, practices, values and traditions. Thus the use of the concept of legal culture encourages a view of 'internal' legal culture as a unity set against 'external' legal culture.

By contrast, in, for example, Weber's rich analyses of the relationships between styles of legal thought and the social conditions in which they develop, particular strands of influence are traced without the need to assume any uniform idea of culture or that the infinitely complex historical patterns marking the evolution of ideas, beliefs and values should be conceptualized as more than transient chance encounters between co-present elements from the infinite data of history. Certainly Weber was concerned with unique, historically significant aggregates of intellectual, moral and social conditions – for example, in such complex phenomena as the spirit of capitalism, the rationality of the West, or the social orientations associated with the dominance of certain religions (see, for example, Gerth and Mills, 1948:ch. 11) – but in no case does culture, as such, seem to be employed as a key variable in explanation. It may be necessary to conceptualize cultural 'aggregates' for the purposes of organizing inquiry (and the use of the method of ideal types in doing this is discussed later in this chapter), but the inquiries themselves are almost always concerned with specific, differentiated elements – for example, particular religious, economic, legal or political orientations of intersubjective action – that can be identified and related within these aggregates.

The Causal Significance and Mechanisms of Legal Culture

What is the concept of legal culture for? For Friedman it specifies a vital element in determining the social circumstances in which legal systems operate. Legal culture 'determines when, why, and where people use law, legal institutions, or legal process; and when they use other institutions or do nothing'; it 'sets everything in motion' and is an essential variable in explaining the workings of law; adding legal culture to the picture of law 'is like winding up a clock or plugging in a machine' (1977:76). The causal significance of legal culture is thus unequivocally asserted.

Especially in his 1975 book, *The Legal System*, Friedman has offered a relatively detailed account of the way he sees legal culture acting to affect the working of legal systems. Social forces create an impetus for change but do not work directly on the legal system (1975:15,153; and see 1994:118). Interests have to be turned into demands and demands must be pressed successfully on the legal system to produce 'legal acts' (for example, new laws). Legal culture achieves or permits the translation of interests into demands (1975:150,193) through the attitudes expressed in legal culture that operate to shape demands; and legal culture also determines the manner in which the legal system responds to these demands. In this latter capacity, however, legal culture (presumably both internal and external) operates to build 'structures' (1975:209). These are structures of the legal system itself, such as systems of rules, as well as of power and influence operating on and around it (1975:150). But, while these structural elements operate to resist or accommodate demands, Friedman is anxious to deny the idea that somehow the legal system itself, as a system, responds. 'Real forces, real people' are at work, 'the concrete opposition of interest groups expressed *through* or *in* the legal system' (1975:155). Nevertheless, the legal system – the procedural and doctrinal structures – 'does make some difference; exactly how much we do not know' (1975:156). The analogy of the rope in a tug of war is used. The legal system is the rope; it can be stretched to a certain extent; perhaps its weight and bulk also add some inertia element. But the rope hardly determines who wins the game.

There is, undoubtedly, a great deal of vagueness in the causal mechanisms of legal culture being suggested here, but the general outline of Friedman's view is clear enough. Legal culture controls the pace of production of demands brought before the legal system for specifically legal solutions to problems or protection of interests. And, by more obscure and complex means, legal culture seems also to determine the legal system's responses, partly, it would seem, through the operation of internal legal culture shaping legal structures and partly through 'external' pressures, reflecting social distributions of power and influence, which equally affect the system's responses.

The problem with this account is again the relatively undifferentiated character of legal culture – or at least the difficulty in linking what Friedman has to say about these shaping elements operating on the legal system with the image of an immensely complex interplay of varieties of legal culture, as discussed earlier. The concept of legal culture explains too much. Indeed, it seems to explain everything that happens or fails to happen within the legal system. Yet, at the same time, it explains very little, because the attribution of so much to legal culture, when legal culture itself embraces such an indeterminate array of elements and operates on such an indeterminate set of levels of generality or specificity, fails to identify any particular factors that can be seen to be making a difference to the situation of law in society for the purposes of inquiry in sociology of law.

The Explanatory Significance of the Concept

Friedman disarmingly admits frequently the vagueness of the concept of legal culture; it is 'an abstraction and a slippery one' (1990:95). Statements about legal culture 'rest on shaky evidence at best' (1975:204). Few systematic data on comparative culture exist (1975:209). 'As it is, I can only estimate, interpret and infer' (1990:198). An exposition might be 'less an explanation of data than guesswork about what the data might show' (1994:119). Why maintain a concept that is so hard to pin down? The answer implicit in Friedman's writings seems to be that the concept serves more of an artistic than a scientific function; it allows impressions of general tendencies to be sketched. Litigation enthusiasm may be an aspect of legal culture in certain countries: 'These are, at any rate, strong impressions' (1975:212). And, as the issue of citizens' invocation of law in different countries and especially in the United States has been returned to in Friedman's writings over the years, the idea that the matter is one of legal culture has allowed him to adjust his accounts of the relevant culture to changing interpretations of the sociological reality of variations in the extent and nature of citizens' involvement with the state legal system in different countries and periods.

Thus the idea of legal culture has been able to embrace the notion that somehow law is seeping into more areas of life and that claims consciousness is extending in certain countries (1975:210–11); that there is a growing general expectation of justice and of recompense (1985:43,144; 1986:22; 1990:60); that there is simply more law as a component of social life (1986:20); and that a culture of choice in which people expect to be able to formulate, express and fulfil personal choices and, if necessary, pursue them through law has become pervasive in the United States and elsewhere (1990:74).

Friedman's discussions on these themes are often avowedly impressionistic: like a painter's portrayal of a landscape, rather than a surveyor's measurement of the terrain. The appeal of the concept of legal culture is that it seems to suggest a way of ranging across important but indeterminate matters – relating especially to the significance of general changes in social beliefs, opinions, values and outlooks – that cannot be easily encapsulated in the kind of testable hypotheses about social action that American law and society research has usually sought. Discussion of legal culture is a means of inferring and suggesting rather than explaining in behavioural terms; of describing general impressions where these cannot easily be supported by systematic empirical analysis.

Legal Culture and Legal Ideology

The problems of Friedman's account of legal culture reflect, in the main, general difficulties with the concept of culture itself. These difficulties seriously limit the utility of the concept for a comparative sociology of law aimed at systematic empirical explanation and the development of theory capable of clarifying general causal or functional relationships between social phenomena.

On the other hand, the concept of culture – and perhaps legal culture – remains useful as a way of referring to clusters of social phenomena (patterns of thought and belief, patterns of action or interaction, characteristic institutions) coexisting in certain social environments, where the exact relationships existing among elements in the cluster are not clear or are not of concern. Culture is a convenient concept with which to refer provisionally to a general environment of social practices, traditions, understandings and values in which law exists. Legal culture, in this sense, may have the same degree of significance for sociology of law that the idea of legal families has for comparative law: a means of characterizing in extremely broad and, perhaps, more or less impressionistic terms large aggregates of distinct elements.

Otherwise, the concept of legal culture might best be replaced in most contexts of analysis by other concepts. Much of what legal culture can embrace might be considered in terms of *ideology*. Like legal culture in Friedman's formulation, legal ideology can be regarded not as a unity but rather as an overlay of currents of ideas, beliefs, values and attitudes embedded in, expressed through and shaped by practice. Unlike Friedman's concept of legal culture, however, the concept of legal ideology can be considered to be 'tied' in a relatively specific way to legal doctrine. Legal ideology is not legal doctrine but can be regarded as made up of value elements and cognitive ideas presupposed in, expressed through and shaped by the practices of developing, interpreting and applying legal doctrine within a legal system. One advantage which the concept of legal ideology has over that of legal culture is that a more specific idea of the source of legal ideology and the mechanisms of its creation and effects can be offered than seems to be the case for legal culture.

Legal ideology can be seen as significantly generated and sustained by the professional practices of law and diffused through the impact, in one way or another, of institutionalized, professionally developed and applied legal doctrine on citizens' consciousness. This is not to claim that ideology *originates* in these practices and forms of doctrine; legal doctrine itself necessarily reflects ideological currents which it does not control and which themselves deserve analysis by those wishing to understand the development of doctrine. But it seems important to emphasize the intellectual and institutional mechanisms by which legal doctrine may have power to shape 'commonsense' understandings – forms of taken-for-granted knowledge and belief – outside the spheres of professional legal practice. Hence, although the concept of legal ideology embraces a very broad and somewhat indeterminate range of ideas embedded in practices, a specific link between ideology and doctrine can be theoretically specified.

Legal doctrine in contemporary conditions is typically fragmented, intricate and transient; it is in continuous process of reformulation, supplementation and amendment, especially in the light of changing governmental policies. It often combines highly particularistic regulation with extensive authorization of the exercise of official discretion. Legal ideology, by contrast, can be regarded as the repository of all of contemporary legal doctrine's impossible aspirations: in a sense, the 'opposites' of its technical characteristics. Legal ideology embodies, for example, the sense of legal doctrine as timeless or self-evidently valid principle; of self-sufficient legal logic applicable to solve all legal disputes; of law as a 'gapless', complete code of systematic regulation; or of legal ideas as a coherent embodiment of consistently elaborated values.

The concept of legal ideology provides a focus for important inquiries about the ways in which legal doctrine, transformed in ideological thought, helps to constitute or shape social understandings and structures of beliefs, attitudes and values; and how law as doctrine provides a conduit through which extremely broad currents of thought and belief can be translated into regulatory practices (Cotterrell, 1995:7–14). Another advantage of using the concept of legal ideology is that it seems easy to think in terms of specific ideologies, or currents of ideology, and to recognize that currents of ideology may conflict with each other and reflect different kinds of social experience. Marxist theories of ideology tended to fall into the trap which we have seen as a real one for the concept of legal culture: that of *assuming* unity in what are no more than possibly arbitrarily identified aggregates. But the concept of ideology lends itself, in less constrained analyses, to use in identifying quite specific systems of values and cognitive ideas.

It allows analysis of the way in which values and ideas can indeed be sustained as systems despite contradictions and incompatibilities within and between them; and it also facilitates recognition of the tenacity of these systems of thought and belief, and of their resistance to modification through experience. It inspires examination of the structure of ideological systems, of the role of rhetoric and symbolism within them, and it allows recognition of the ubiquity of conflict between currents of ideology. Perhaps more clearly than the concept of legal culture, the concept of legal ideology emphasizes the link between social power and currents of thought and belief. It focuses, for example, on the way that the professionalized doctrinal production of legal systems exerts social power through its shaping of such currents.

The concept of legal culture, at least in Friedman's formulation, seems to focus most directly on a diversity of elements that exert influence *on* the production of 'legal acts' within legal systems and are held to explain differences in the character and orientation of these systems and their responsiveness to interests and demands; Friedman tends to remain vague or agnostic about the power of professionalized legal practices and doctrine to exert influence on the wider contextual environment in which these exist; he focuses broadly on aspects of the whole environment of culture as a determinant of law.

By contrast, analyses of legal ideology may present a more manageable theoretical task insofar as they explore mechanisms by which law, usually in the sense of the professionalized practices of state legal systems, exerts influence on, or translates and thereby helps reinforce, wider structures of values, beliefs and understandings. The task might seem more manageable to the extent that institutionalized, professionally managed legal doctrine is taken as its specific focus, rather than a potentially unlimited diversity of cultural sources of influence on legal systems.

The Use of Ideal Types

The concept of legal ideology, as sketched above, may not, however, be particularly oriented towards those specific tasks of comparative sociology of law that seem to inspire the use by some scholars of the concept of legal culture. These tasks are to consider the social determinants of specific institutional differences in state legal systems, or differences in practice, style and organization, or patterns of citizen involvement with professionalized law and its agencies. Since the focus is on diversity in legal systems, the inquiry seems to return to that of the interface between comparative law and sociology of law. But, in this context, an approach such as Mirjan Damaska's (1986), which focuses on the interaction of specific variables related to political structure and political ideology in explaining differences in patterns of legal procedure, seems more promising than one that adopts the concept of legal culture as an explanatory tool.

Damaska writes about his variables and their interaction as providing 'models' for analysis (Damaska, 1986:14). Thus the analysis is based on ideal types of governmental structure and procedural authority, on the one hand, and of orientation towards political authority, on the other. These are to be used to explain elements of what Friedman would call internal legal culture, especially the kinds of differences in legal organization and outlook that are often associated with contrasts between common law and civil law families recognized in comparative law. But Damaska denies an intention to make general claims of causation. The presence in the political and ideological environments of specific legal systems of characteristics approximating the explanatory models is considered to 'justify or support particular clusters of procedural forms', but not usually to determine them (Damaska, 1986:14).

Damaska's effort seems to be, in part, to 'disaggregate' what might be thought of as very general differences in legal culture as between common law and civil law procedural systems. (For a detailed discussion, see Goldstein, 1995.) He suggests that the comparative law concept of legal families is inadequate to characterize the distinctive features of procedural systems, first, because of the variety of practices that different systems, even if considered to be within a single family, present and, second, because of the apparent lack of relationships between procedural elements that are clustered together as characteristic of one or other legal families.

In Weberian fashion, Damaska seems to recognize the impossibility of characterizing cultural complexity except in terms of the tracing of specific, more or less unique, clusters of historical developments in particular legal systems. These developments are to be understood in terms of certain underlying ideas which they can be considered to express: that is, 'ideas that are capable of moulding forms of justice into recognisable patterns' (Damaska, 1986:5). The logical relationships between these postulated ideas (about governmental organization, including the organization of judicial systems, and about bases of legitimate authority) produce ideal types of procedural systems that can facilitate comparisons between actual procedural systems.

The use of pure or ideal types (that is, logically constructed concepts deliberately designed not to represent empirical reality but to organize interpretation of it) seems to be one important way to combine two vital research requirements in comparative sociology of law. First, it makes possible a recognition of the myriad of elements that might be referred to as legal culture without falling into the trap of thinking of culture as a 'unity' rather than an 'aggregate'. At the same time, it facilitates comparisons.

The approach has classic origins in Weber's studies of broad cultural aggregates. Indeed, in one sense, the whole of Weber's work might be considered to focus on the characterization of Western culture as a unique aggregate. But the method of ideal types may be the only general method available that makes possible the study of large cultural aggregates without reifying them. An ideal type by its nature assumes, first, that what it designates as a logically unified, self-contained idea created purely for the purposes of intellectual reflection must not be taken to correspond to a logically structured, self-contained empirical reality. Second, it assumes that the empirical phenomena which the ideal type is used to organize are no more than a set of data, selected for the specific purposes of research, from the infinity of historical experience.

The price that must be paid for this valuable methodology is that we recognize that culture (and, specifically here, legal culture) has no empirical existence *per se* as something that is itself to be measured, observed or experienced. Rather, it is an idea that may yield methods of measuring, observing or experiencing specific social, including legal, phenomena. But this seems to be possible only when the idea of 'culture' is radically transformed into sets of logically elaborated ideal types.

The Study of Cultural Aggregates

There may, however, be certain limited conditions under which the concept of legal culture, in something like Friedman's descriptive and empirical sense, gains a more precise utility. In other words, there may be circumstances in which it is appropriate to identify legal culture as an empirical category, rather than to treat it as merely a set of ideal typical constructions.

It may be feasible in certain conditions not merely to abstract from the infinity of data by means of ideal types by which culture can be characterized but to attempt to describe and record, ethnographically, in all its richness and complexity, a cluster or aggregate of attitudes, values, customs and patterns of social action such as might make up external legal culture in Friedman's sense. But this is likely to be feasible only when relevant cultural aggregates are small-scale and isolated, so that no serious problems of differentiating and distinguishing cultures are encountered.

For example, Bronislaw Malinowski's rich, classic ethnography presents what he certainly could regard as the legal culture of the Trobriand Islanders (Malinowski, 1926). The scope of Malinowski's ethnographic study is determined not primarily by the effort to trace specific variables, but by its concern to bring to light social structure, change and continuity and functional relationships in an account of a complex and undifferentiated cultural whole. The limits of the cultural aggregate are here defined, and made manageable for the purposes of ethnographic research, by the geographical isolation of relatively small Melanesian societies.

It should be emphasized, however, that, because the concern is with the cultural aggregate as a totality and with the immensely complex interweaving of diverse elements within it, 'the legal' is necessarily undifferentiated from other aspects of culture, or differentiated only in provisional and variable ways. Hence legal culture is only a certain *aspect* of culture (a point of view on it) as an undifferentiated aggregate. Strictly speaking, there is no legal culture, but only culture seen from a certain standpoint of legal relevance to the observer. Still there are unresolved problems with the scope of culture. But 'Malinowski's rather fuzzy concept of culture' (Firth, 1988:16) avoids these insofar as it refers merely to the totality of ethnographically recorded social life within a geographically (thus, from a sociological point of view, arbitrarily) limited space. Only when efforts are made to theorize this totality as an integrated and distinct unity of some kind (cf. Malinowski, 1944) does the concept become deeply problematic (Paluch, 1988).

These ideas are not irrelevant in considering contemporary large-scale societies, such as those of Europe or North America. The problems of the vagueness of the concept of legal culture and of assessing the causal significance of the numerous layers or regions of legal culture that Friedman indicates as related to change in a legal system might seem less acute in the context of these contemporary societies if the extent of the relevant cultural aggregate could be limited in a manner comparable to that achieved in studies such as Malinowski's. This is sometimes possible when the focus of attention switches from unified or centralized state legal systems and towards a *plurality of regulatory systems* in contemporary societies; the scope of these plural systems mirroring that of the various kinds of legal culture discussed earlier in relation to Friedman's work. Clearly, this possibility of analysis using the concept of legal culture arises not because the concept in such circumstances acquires a more unified content, but – as with Trobriand 'legal culture' – because as a purely practical matter the diversity of elements in the cultural aggregate, being more local, narrowly confined or limited in scale, may seem more manageable: more apparently amenable, for example, to what the anthropologist Clifford Geertz refers to as 'thick description' (Geertz, 1973:ch.1).

The focus on legal pluralism in anthropological studies, as well as in some early work in sociology of law such as that of Eugen Ehrlich (1936), goes along with a relatively sharp sensitivity to cultural variation. In Ehrlich's writing the stress on a plurality of systems of legal ordering beyond the legal system of the state is intended to mirror this variation precisely and to show the complexity with which differences in attitudes, values, beliefs and customs might be directly registered in regulatory diversity. It may be, indeed, that the concept of culture is especially appropriate to ethnographic research that aims to portray the interweaving of cognitive structures, systems of values and belief, patterns of social action and regulatory structures as a relatively undifferentiated complex existing in a limited social locality; a complex aggregate which is of interest *as an aggregate*, as a portrayal (as far as practically possible and, indeed, plausible) of the entire, intricate web of social life.

But, as has been noted above, this approach makes it difficult to retain a differentiated theoretical focus on 'the legal' or on institutional elements that might be treated as equivalent to, or set in the place of, those aspects of social organization that in complex societies would be treated as distinctively legal. To isolate 'the legal' requires an analysis of culture into its components and a specification theoretically of the relation of elements. But this is precisely what the use of the idea of culture as an aggregate seeks to bypass – or, at least, seems to justify bypassing. It seems significant that, as anthropology has developed a concern to study specific regulatory, order-maintaining or dispute-focused aspects of social organization, separating these analytically at least to some extent from other elements of social life, the concept of culture has tended to lack prominence alongside the range of other concepts that the literature has employed (see, for example, Snyder, 1981).

Would it be possible to treat internal legal culture in Friedman's sense – that is, the values, attitudes and perhaps practices (the ambiguity in Friedman's writing was noted earlier) of legal professionals – as a small-scale cultural aggregate? The answer would seem to be generally negative on the basis of the arguments above. Friedman's own uncertainty as to how far internal legal culture can be distinguished from external, and what its independent social significance may be, seems understandable in the light of anthropological approaches to the ethnographic presentation of culture. There seems no obviously satisfactory way of isolating internal legal culture from the larger cultural aggregate within which, insofar as it is to be treated *as* culture, it must be implicated in an immeasurable array of linkages.

Nevertheless, the prospects for using the concept of a cultural aggregate in relation to the analysis of certain aspects of contemporary state legal systems may not be so limited as suggested above. There is some affinity between the use of the concept of culture to synthesize complex aggregates of elements present in small-scale social contexts, and some important recent efforts to develop sophisticated ethnographic accounts of popular legal consciousness in the United States. This work, particularly associated with members of the Amherst Seminar on Legal Ideology and Legal Processes, explicitly adopts the concept of ideology rather than any idea of culture as indicating the focus of its concerns. In accordance with the orientations of analysis of ideology suggested earlier in this chapter, the focus is more obviously on the power of the state legal system to produce structures of social understandings, attitudes and values among lay citizens than on the ways in which these kinds of diffuse understandings, attitudes and values shape the workings of the state legal system. On the other hand, some of this writing is in terms of culture, as well as ideology: 'Legal words and practices are cultural constructs which carry powerful meanings not just to those trained in the law or to those who routinely use it to manage their business transactions but to the ordinary person as well' (Merry, 1990:8–9). And much literature stresses the conflicts, tensions and negotiations between popular or lay legal understandings and those of lawyers and other professionals within the state legal system, or the relative integrity of popular legal consciousness.

In general, as might be expected, this kind of research is at its most persuasive when it looks in detail at a wide range of aspects of relatively limited social contexts: for example, specific towns considered as communities (see, for example, Greenhouse 1986); or social interaction in such settings as lawyers' offices (see, for example, Sarat and Felstiner, 1989), mediation hearings in court (Merry, 1990) or social welfare offices (Sarat, 1990a) where negotiations around the meaning of law take place. These studies acquire much of their explanatory power from their detailed ethnographic recording of entire complex contexts of social interaction. On the other hand, a specific relation to law is maintained because the state legal system and its practices and processes are treated as the background against which social interaction takes place and in relation to which forms of popular consciousness develop or are shaped.

To this extent, it might be said that these studies are directly concerned with legal culture – and especially the interaction of internal and external legal culture in Friedman's terms. They seem to make a virtue of the character of legal culture as an aggregate of many contingent elements. On the other hand, the use of the concept of ideology maintains a clear focus on the relationship between relative social power and the possibilities for establishing or negotiating legal meaning. The popular legal consciousness literature depends on the general conditions for effective ethnography: especially the restriction of focus to *specific* social contexts. It implies the possible utility of a concept of legal culture in those kinds of contexts.

Equally, however, this literature seems relatively unconcerned with the tracing of social causality or the construction of explanatory theory; neither does it usually attempt the kind of comparative projects that this chapter has taken as central to a specifically comparative sociology of law. Ethnographic accounts of popular legal consciousness and its expression in social action seem to aim to set out complex 'thick descriptions' of specific social settings of law. Yet this literature also generally affirms a commitment to sociology of law as social science (Sarat, 1990b).

Conclusion

A general conclusion to be drawn from these reflections on legal culture is that the concept is most useful for its emphasis on the sheer complexity and diversity of the social matrix in which contemporary state legal systems exist. We have noted that legal culture may be understood as a vast diversity of overlapping cultures: some relatively local, some more universal. Yet, in many circumstances, reliance on a general concept of 'culture' also makes problematic the theoretical identification of a specifically *legal* culture.

As social studies in law at present tend to retreat from or reject many traditional understandings of the idea of a specifically social science and adopt, appropriately and necessarily, interpretive methods that deny many positivist implications of the use of the term 'science' in this context, the temptation may be to rely more heavily on relatively vague concepts of culture and legal culture in the interpretation of social phenomena. The argument of this chapter is that this kind of reliance would, except in limited and carefully defined circumstances, be a mistake and that an examination of Friedman's long-term elaboration of implications of the concept of legal culture reveals problems that are probably endemic in its use.

In certain contexts, however, the idea of an undifferentiated aggregate of social elements, co-present in a certain time and place, may be useful and even necessary in social research. This idea is expressed conveniently in the concept of culture. In the study of relatively specific social contexts, the concept of legal culture may also be useful to embrace provisionally an entire contextual matrix in which state law operates.

More generally, it may be appropriate and necessary to refer in terms of culture to clusters of social phenomena whose exact interrelation is not known but whose collective significance is recognizable and requires emphasis. By this means it becomes possible to characterize complex webs of beliefs, values, understandings and practices, which sociological studies employing ethnographic methods may appropriately seek to describe, perhaps as a prelude to more specific inquiries about the ideological significance of legal doctrine and the practices in which it is institutionalized.

References

Cotterrell, R. (1995) *Law's Community: Legal Theory in Sociological Perspective*, Oxford: Oxford University Press.

Damaska, M.R. (1986) *The Faces of Justice and State Authority: A Comparative Approach to the Legal Process*, New Haven, Conn.: Yale University Press.

David, R. and J.E.C. Brierley (1985) *Major Legal Systems in the World Today*, 3rd edn, London: Stevens.

Ehrlich, E. (1936) *Fundamental Principles of the Sociology of Law*, trans. W.L. Moll, reprinted New York: Arno Press, 1975.

Ellen, R., E. Gellner, G. Kubicka and J. Mucha (eds) (1988) *Malinowski Between Two Worlds: The Polish Roots of an Anthropological Tradition*, Cambridge: Cambridge University Press.

Firth, R. (1988) 'Malinowski in the History of Social Anthropology', in Ellen *et al.* (eds) *Malinowski Between Two Worlds*, pp. 12–42.

Friedman, L.M. (1975) *The Legal System: A Social Science Perspective*, New York: Russell Sage Foundation.

Friedman, L.M. (1977) *Law and Society: An Introduction*, Englewood Cliffs, NJ: Prentice-Hall.

Friedman, L.M. (1985) *Total Justice*, Boston, Mass.: Beacon Press.

Friedman, L.M. (1986) 'Legal Culture and the Welfare State', in G. Teubner (ed.), *Dilemmas of Law in the Welfare State*, Berlin: de Gruyter, pp. 13–27.

Friedman, L.M. (1990) *The Republic of Choice: Law, Authority and Culture*, Cambridge, Mass.: Harvard University Press.

Friedman, L.M. (1994) 'Is There a Modern Legal Culture?' *Ratio Juris*, **7**, 117–31.

Geertz, C. (1973) *The Interpretation of Cultures: Selected Essays*, New York: Basic Books.

Gerth, H.H. and C.W. Mills (eds) (1948) *From Max Weber: Essays in Sociology*, London: Routledge & Kegan Paul.

Goldstein, S. (1995) 'On Comparing and Unifying Civil Procedural Systems', in R. Cotterrell (ed.), *Process and Substance: Butterworth Lectures on Comparative Law*, London: Butterworth, pp. 1–43.

Greenhouse, C.J. (1986) *Praying for Justice: Faith, Order and Community in an American Town*, Ithaca, NY: Cornell University Press.

Hall, J. (1963) *Comparative Law and Social Theory*, Baton Rouge: Louisiana State University Press).

Malinowski, B. (1926) *Crime and Custom in Savage Society*, London: Routledge & Kegan Paul.

Malinowski, B. (1944) *A Scientific Theory of Culture and Other Essays*, Chapel Hill: University of North Carolina Press.

Merry, S.E. (1988) 'Legal Pluralism', *Law and Society Review*, **22**, 869–96.

Merry, S.E. (1990) *Getting Justice and Getting Even: Legal Consciousness Among Working-Class Americans*, Chicago: University of Chicago Press.

Paluch, A.K. (1988) 'Malinowski's Theory of Culture' in Ellen *et al.* (eds), *Malinowski Between Two Worlds*, pp. 65–87.

Sarat, A. (1990a) '"The Law is All Over": Power, Resistance and the Legal Consciousness of the Welfare Poor', *Yale Journal of Law and the Humanities*, **2**, 343–79.

Sarat, A. (1990b) 'Off to Meet the Wizard: Beyond Validity and Reliability in the Search for a Post-Empiricist Sociology of Law', *Law and Social Inquiry*, **15**, 155–70.

Sarat, A. and W.L.F. Felstiner (1989) 'Lawyers and Legal Consciousness: Law Talk in the Divorce Lawyer's Office', *Yale Law Journal*, **98**, 1663–88.

Savigny, F.K. von (1831) *Of the Vocation of Our Age for Legislation and Jurisprudence*, trans. A. Hayward, reprinted New York: Arno Press, 1975.

Snyder, F.G. (1981) 'Anthropology, Dispute Processes and Law: A Critical Introduction', *British Journal of Law and Society*, **8**, 141–80.

Zweigert, K. and H. Kötz (1987) *An Introduction to Comparative Law*, Vol. 1, 2nd edn, trans. T. Weir, Oxford: Oxford University Press.

2 The Concept of Legal Culture: A Reply

Lawrence M. Friedman

When we study how human beings act, think and go about their lives, it is very comforting to have concepts or variables that we can measure with some degree of precision. Per capita income is that kind of variable. It has its problems, but in general it works; and it is a useful tool, too, for comparisons across cultures (more or less).

Roger Cotterrell, in his thoughtful though highly critical contribution, quite correctly points out that 'legal culture' is not one of these happy concepts. But of course it is not the only one. Many of the basic building-blocks of social science – fundamental concepts like 'structure' or 'institution' or 'system' – are vague or general, or hard to define or delimit. That fact does not make them necessarily 'incoherent'. In the study of law and society, problems arise even with regard to such (apparently) simple ideas as 'judge' or 'court'. not to mention 'legal system' or 'doctrine', and any such problems even become more acute when the issue before the house is cross-national comparison.

But that is no reason for throwing the baby out with the bathwater. Some concepts – and I think 'legal culture' falls into this category – are useful ways of lining up a range of phenomena into one very general category. And we can subsume, under this general category, other categories, which are less vague or general. The parts can be crisper and brighter than the whole. 'Public opinion' is this kind of general category; 'standard of living' is another. It is not easy to say what a 'standard of living' is; much more down-to-earth is to do a survey and discover how many houses or shacks in some town have toilets and running water. Then we can measure other things in the same community: how many people have radios? How many calories a day do they get? How long does it take for the average worker to earn the cost of a pair of shoes? How many telephones are there? Out of all these, we can put together a meaningful concept of 'standard of living'.

In principle, one should be able to do the same thing for 'legal culture', although I would be the first to admit that it is not so easy to draw up a catalogue of subcategories. But we may be getting ahead of the story. It is reasonably clear what a standard of living means; but what is a 'legal culture', and what is the concept supposed to do for us? I will restrict myself to the term as I have used it. There is no copyright protection on phrases and a number of scholars have used the term 'legal culture' in ways that are quite different from my use of the term. A prominent example is Erhard Blankenburg.[1]

Legal culture, as I have defined the term, refers to ideas, values, expectations and attitudes towards law and legal institutions, which some public or some part of the public holds. Like 'public opinion' (a not unproblematic idea itself), legal culture refers to measurable phenomena; indeed, it is an umbrella term to cover a range of measurable phenomena. I say 'measurable' – which is not the same as 'measured'. In fact, we have, for almost every society, precious few data about legal culture, because we have never bothered to gather them.[2]

Of course, no two people have the same ideas and values about law (nor do they have the same political views or, for that matter, the same taste in music or films). But there surely are patterns in the distribution of these ideas and values. And it is likely that such patterns follow the fault-lines of other categories, so that it may make sense to talk about the legal culture of any identifiable group, from stamp collectors to French women over 65. Some of these patterns are no doubt sharper and more interesting than others.

What is so important about legal culture? In my view, legal culture is an essential intervening variable in the process of producing legal stasis or change. Everybody will admit that new inventions (birth control pills, the atom bomb, computers, air conditioning, jet aeroplanes) make a big difference in society; and the same is true of new situations (an earthquake, a war, a plague, a revolution). All of these external events and situations generate changes in law. But *how* do they do this? Somebody invents the motor car and later we see modifications in tort law, and a massive pile of new regulations: on drivers' licences, rules of the road, drunk driving, air bags and so on. The stork did not bring these about: people did; they were the result of political and legal processes. What sets these processes in motion, or determines their shape or their outcome, are the pressures that are the direct result of changes in legal culture.

It is not enough, in other words, that something changes in the world. The change, if it is important enough, brings about changes in attitudes, expectations and desires; and this in turn creates a situation in which people may put new demands, or modify old demands, on legal systems and the legal order. Probably some reaction or change in the legal order is inevitable, once you have the car or a war or the invention of birth control pills; but precisely what this change will be can rarely be predicted. After all, legal culture is itself the product of a complicated interaction, so that the same plague or the same invention has a different impact in society A as compared to society B.

To put it another way, any equation which takes the form social change *X* leads to legal result *Y* is simplistic and unsatisfying. A better form would be: social change *X* leads to a change in legal culture *Y*, which results in this or that kind of pressure on legal institutions, and what comes out is legal result *Z*. In other words, 'legal culture' is a generic term for states of mind and ideas, held by some public; these states of mind are affected by events, situations and the like in society as a whole, and they lead in turn to actions that have an impact on the legal system itself.

These states of mind are, in principle, discoverable empirically, but this is no easy task, even if we try very hard to discover them, which mostly we do not. Attitudes are never particularly easy to measure and some (towards sex, for example) are especially hard. Sexual *behaviour* is hard to measure, for that matter. Yet nobody would argue that these attitudes and behaviours are just not there; or that they are not measurable in principle; or that concepts of sexual behaviour and attitudes are 'incoherent'. No doubt in the course of many years of writing about legal culture and the like I have been guilty of a certain sloppiness in language, and I may even have changed my mind here and there, but I think the core of the concept remains about the same. I have to say I fail to see what is so wrong with the general idea.

Cotterrell feels we cannot 'use' the concept as a 'theoretical component in comparative sociology of law'. I am not sure what he means by this. There are daunting problems that stand in the way of *any* comparative sociology of law, especially at the level of whole cultures or whole societies. But there may be little pieces we can profitably compare, including pieces of legal culture. If I did a survey and discovered that French women were afraid to call the police to complain about sexual harassment, but Italian women were not, that would be an interesting though very fragmentary bit of information, and a fragmentary but interesting contribution to the comparative sociology of law, and it would be, among other things, a finding about legal culture. If we added more societies, and more questions and more situations, we might conceivably reach a point where we could say something much more general, and significant, about comparative legal cultures. Nonetheless, the Franco-Italian survey might itself have considerable value; it might lead us to ask what it was about police behaviour in the two countries, or about women's attitudes in the two countries, that led to such different results.

Cotterrell raises a point about the distinction between internal and external legal culture. Why, he asks, must we regard the internal legal culture as 'specially important' sociologically? I think he puts too much weight on a rather minor phrase in something I wrote. All I meant was this: lawyers and judges in many societies constitute an elite and powerful group. The legal culture of business people is 'specially important', too, compared (say) to the legal culture of the homeless, or of small children. Besides, the *public* accords to lawyers and judges, or may accord them, a special role. Would it be such a wild idea to suggest that the attitude of doctors towards diseases and illness, towards health care plans and the like, has an importance in the politics of medicine, or in 'medical culture', beyond that of a random sample of the population?

In another passage, Cotterrell mentions my suggestion that the 'idea of legal families is not useful for sociology of law', because the 'stylistic differences between legal families' do not necessarily go along with 'contrasts in socioeconomic conditions' in the component countries. This is because the classification into families is based 'only on arbitrary aggregations of traits'. But is this not, he asks, equally true of legal culture, which 'can also be considered merely as a range of individual variations'? I am somewhat baffled by this argument. I do think that the conventional classifications in comparative law are sociologically useless and are, in some ways, 'arbitrary'. The conventions used to classify legal systems into 'families' such as the common law and the civil law do not distinguish between living, vital aspects of a legal system, on the one hand, and legal fossils, on the other. By what criteria can we say that the (living) legal systems of Haiti and France are very closely related, but that the legal systems of England and France are 'unrelated'? I know what these criteria are supposed to be, and they are mainly historical, formal and technical. But the criteria do not seem very important to me, at least if the goal is to illuminate the nature and operation of the actual legal order in this or that country. Conventional comparative law is strongly, obsessively influenced by little tricks and quirks of formal law, which law professors treasure, but which have no established connection to the working system. Hence one *might* call the elements they compare and classify 'arbitrary'.

But how does this objection apply to 'legal culture'? What is studied under the heading of 'legal culture' is by definition a formative element of 'living law' rather than book law. That legal culture can be 'considered … as a range of individual variations' does not distinguish it from any other social phenomena: social phenomena are usually a 'range of individual variations' but they are very often not random and certainly permit aggregation and generalization. Height and weight also exhibit a 'range of individual variations', but there are limits, and also patterns (some ethnic groups are taller than others, on average; men are taller than women; and so on). There *may* be such a thing as 'French legal culture', even though admittedly it could be 'considered … as a range of individual variations', just as there is such a thing as the French language, though no two people speak it the same way. On the other hand, it may be that research might show that there are *no* general patterns such that we could speak of 'French legal culture'. We would, in other words, have to disaggregate. This is, in my book, strictly an empirical question.

Cotterrell says that the concept of legal culture, as I use the term, 'serves more of an artistic than a scientific function'. This is because it allows 'impressions of general tendencies to be sketched'. There seems to be some implicit definition of 'science' here that I do not necessarily accept; concepts, general terms, ideal types and similar constructs are not 'scientific' in themselves, but they are or can be useful building-blocks in a scientific enterprise. That is, they can suggest approaches, hypotheses, modes of explanation and other propositions which are less 'artistic' and more 'scientific'. That was certainly my aim in writing about legal culture. Cotterrell refers to my work on the culture of choice and on the general expectation of justice.[3] The ideas I suggested in these books were not intended to be 'artistic', or, for that matter, to be purely theoretical. I was trying to explain trends in modern law, and in a way that suggested testable propositions – perhaps propositions that are extremely difficult to test (and which might turn out to be totally wrong), but propositions nonetheless.

Cotterrell thinks sociologists of law would do better if they dropped 'legal culture' and took up instead what he calls 'legal ideology'. Legal ideology is not 'doctrine', but is made up of 'value elements and cognitive ideas' which come out of doctrine or the process of applying doctrine. Legal ideology, he explains, is 'generated and sustained by the professional practices of law and diffused through the impact … of … legal doctrine on citizens' consciousness'. This strikes me as an entirely different notion, and one that rests on quite a different set of assumptions. Basically, 'legal ideology', as Cotterrell defines it, conceals a hypothesis about where legal influences that shape society come from. It is a hypothesis that asserts that 'institutionalized, professionally developed and applied legal doctrine' has a very powerful effect on legal consciousness.

Cotterrell goes further; he tells us a lot about the content of this ideology: the ideology treats doctrine as 'timeless or self-evidently valid'; assumes that legal logic can 'solve all legal disputes'; that law is a 'gapless', complete 'code of systematic regulation', and that legal ideas are a 'coherent embodiment of consistently elaborated values'. Of course, this is not legal ideology in general, but a *particular* legal ideology;[4] and it is, I believe, an empirical question whether anybody believes in this ideology and, if so, who; and what the impact of this ideology is on the public, or the functioning of the legal system or anything else.

I am intrigued by the fact that Cotterrell finds this conception so attractive (and the concept of legal culture so unattractive). The two terms strike me as equally vague and general. One of the obvious things that separates them is their centre of gravity. Someone who studied legal ideology would pay very close attention to doctrine, to scholarly work theorizing about the nature of law, and to the ways in which doctrine and its apologists help to bamboozle the public. The study of legal culture has its centre of gravity outside the world of doctrine and professional practice. It finds *its* centre of gravity in the thoughts, wishes, ideas – and ideologies – of those members of the public in some particular society who are the pushiest, wealthiest, most influential, or all of these.

Cotterrell specifically mentions the work 'associated with members of the Amherst Seminar on Legal Ideology and Legal Processes' and their efforts 'to develop sophisticated ethnographic accounts of popular legal consciousness in the United States'. I certainly have no wish to criticize the Amherst group or their work. But I think the passage quoted shows one of the sources of Cotterrell's difficulties. Ideology would be quite an appropriate element in any study of 'popular legal consciousness'. 'Popular legal consciousness' is certainly an element of legal culture. It may be, in a given society, an extremely important element. It might, in some given society, be powerfully shaped by something like 'legal ideology'. But legal culture is, as a concept, intended to be rather broader than 'popular legal consciousness', if that implies the ideas of 'ordinary people'. Non-ordinary people have a 'legal culture': bankers and ranchers, heads of corporations – yes, and lawyers as well. All of these are worthy of study, perhaps some more than others. It depends on the purpose of the study. I can imagine studies which would want to explore what bank robbers think about the legitimacy of law, and others which would try to tap attitudes of bank *presidents*.

I certainly do not want to deny any utility to 'legal ideology' or the study of 'legal ideology'. It does seem to me that some scholars tend to exaggerate its importance. The curious thing about 'legal ideology' is that it tends to focus attention on doctrine, and on 'mandarin' materials of legal scholarship. How these in fact contribute to the mystification of the public, or what these materials have to do with 'popular legal consciousness, is rarely explained.[5] What the theory of legal ideology lacks, for the most part, is any explication of a *mechanism* which makes the impact of legal ideology on society more plausible. It is perfectly possible that the public, or some part of it, does in fact subscribe to an ideology; that this public, or some part of it, looks on certain arrangements (including legal arrangements) as necessary and inevitable, when in fact they are contingent and time-bound. But I would rather not assume that we know where these ideas come from, and how. That remains to be proven and shown.

The temptation to prefer 'legal ideology' to 'legal culture' is easy to understand. Academics are, after all, intellectuals; this is what they are good at. An academic may not be able to paint a picture or fix a broken stove, but many academics (not including me) can get through ten pages of Hegel without a migraine headache, and this is no mean achievement. As a consequence, there is a natural tendency to overrate the importance of purely intellectual, or drily formal, elements of culture. My own preference is to start from the outside, not the inside; from 'legal culture', not 'legal ideology'. Although I say 'preference', I do not mean this as an arbitrary choice. It flows naturally from my assumptions and presuppositions. And, I want to repeat, I do *not* claim that 'legal ideology' is a meaningless concept; or that it is not worthy of study.

Not everyone will share my assumptions and presuppositions, of course; and that is fine. There is a lot of room in the house built by law and society scholars. Let a thousand flowers bloom. I do think 'legal culture' ought to be one of these flowers. It is a useful concept, despite its failings; and I would hate to have to give it up.

Notes

1 See, for example, the essay by E. Blankenburg and J.R.A. Verwoerd, 'Prozesshäufigkeiten in den Niederlanden und in Nordrhein-Westfalen 1970–1984', in Erhard Blankenburg (ed.), *Prozessflut?* (Cologne: Bundesanzeiger Verlag, 1988), p. 257.

2 Legal culture does not, of course, have to be directly measured. It can be *inferred* – from other sorts of materials; and indeed, much of my work consists of drawing inferences about legal culture from scraps of data and from general social phenomena. That these inferences are not, and cannot be, rigorous does not mean that they are not worth making.

3 The references are to *Total Justice* (Boston: Beacon Press, 1985); and *The Republic of Choice* (Cambridge, Mass.: Harvard University Press, 1990).

4 It has, it seems to me, a striking resemblance to the traits Weber described as 'formal rationality', though it is not exactly the same.

5 This criticism applies much less to those members of the Amherst group whose methods are (broadly speaking) ethnographic.

3 Civil Litigation Rates as Indicators for Legal Cultures

Erhard Blankenburg

Indicator Comparisons for Legal Cultures

In scientific as well as everyday talk there is some folklore about the growing litigiousness in many countries. The penetration of legal rules and procedures in all walks of life (Habermas, 1981) allegedly finds its expression in overcrowded court calendars and parties using any and all possibilities of 'forum shopping' and appeal procedures to the extreme. Much of this folklore, however, turns out to refer to a specific area of regulation, or the generalizations are based on a few highly visible cases. Hardly ever do they hold true for the judicial system as a whole and very often there are balancing factors reducing some of the activities which courts used to be engaged in, while others are indeed growing. In the United States, Galanter (1983) discussed the limited validity of claims about an American 'litigation explosion'. Like so many issues in public policy, court reform is a better topic for the media the more these can scandalize spectacular cases. Liability litigation in the United States is a perfect issue for scandalizing: there are so many stories around extraordinary liability cases in the United States that one tends to overlook how uncontentiously most *potentially legal conflicts* are handled inside as well as outside courts.

The phrase 'potentially legal conflicts' already indicates the theoretical tradition in which this contribution is going to be placed. Cases which are litigated are the result of a very selective process. Most of the conflicts which would potentially lend themselves to being decided by a judge in court are being resolved between the parties out of court, either by threat and one-sided action or by negotiating, mediating and settling by taking them to alternative forums, or by one of the parties 'lumping it', leaving the social relationship altogether and possibly avoiding future conflict situations of the same kind altogether.[1] The social impact of litigation is to be sought in avoidance just as much as in court decisions.

Avoidance is not simply an individual choice; it rather comes as a result of cultural patterns as the data of a comparative litigation study show.[2] This is a study on which a working group of a research committee[3] from five countries has been working during recent years, comparing litigation frequencies over the years 1970 to 1984 in five European countries and relating them to a study of 100 years' time series for a great number of countries.[4] In this summary of some of our results I also include references to Japan. All of the countries which I am dealing with here belong to the civil law tradition; comparison with countries in the Anglo-American tradition would require an additional set of variables and considerations.

While in the last two decades litigation has been growing rapidly in all of the countries under study, in none of them do we find a continuous growth of litigation, if this is related to the size of the population. We can even speak of a general tendency of a decline in economically related litigation *relative to* indicators of economic growth such as frequencies of credits granted or contracts entered. Similarly, compared to indicators of consumption, there is a *relative* decline of litigation. On the other hand, novel types of civil procedures are entering the courts, many of them being related to the increasing patterns of social and geographical mobility. Break-ups of relationships, whether a dismissal from work, moving out of a home or moving in, or breaking up family ties, all form patterns of mobility which are litigation-prone.

Historical time series of litigation frequencies show sharp increases and declines within rather short periods, especially during the turbulent history of the European countries: economic crisis usually leads to a sudden increase in court cases, war to a standstill of judicial activities altogether (see Rottleuthner, 1985). Apart from such short-term 'explosions' and 'implosions' of litigation we find long-term waves: the increase in marriage break-ups has flooded the courts in many countries not only with divorce procedures but also with post-divorce conflicts over children and support long after the family has been divided. After less than a generation of dramatically increasing divorce frequencies, however, we observe, that many of the litigious issues which kept divorce courts busy are in the process of being routinized. In many countries divorce procedures are being referred to negotiating outside courts, leaving to the judge in many cases only a notary function and thus relieving the need to litigate for a majority of divorce cases altogether. Simplifying divorce procedures, 'do-it-yourself divorce schemes' and uncontentious divorce registration, which are feasible in a few litigation avoidance cultures, were recently put on the agenda of law reformers in many countries.

A similar tendency to remove conflicts from the court calendars can be observed with respect to cases caused by traffic accidents. For almost a generation of rapidly increasing road traffic, attributing fault and thus determining liability has kept the civil courts in some countries busy, penal courts in separate procedures handling the implicit traffic offence. Litigation avoidance cultures again introduced no-fault schemes in order to avoid the procedural costs of attributing fault in what is essentially a zero-sum conflict, or – even more effective with respect to reducing litigation costs – the insurance companies agreed on internal regulation instead of involving external institutions such as courts, lawyers and an entire group of expert professionals.

As such provisions specific to some area of law tend to converge towards overall patterns of legal cultures, I have introduced the term 'litigation avoidance cultures', as compared to legal cultures which are more 'litigation-prone'. The comparison of legal cultures from which our data are drawn permits a characterization of what allows some countries to develop patterns of litigation avoidance and of what makes other countries especially litigation-prone. The remarkable fact about these patterns is that historically they tend to be stable over long time periods, although also this fact needs to be stated with some caution and clarification.

Litigation frequencies make sense only by social conflict areas. We can interpret them comparatively only if we know something about the baseline of conflicts from which they are selected. I have therefore chosen a very special category of litigious conflicts: that of civil liability claims after a serious traffic accident. Haley (1978) compared such figures in the United States with those of Japan and, while he criticizes the general view that Japanese society is conflict-avoiding, he does show that few of those conflicts which in the United States are taken up by lawyers and brought before courts are the subject of litigation in Japan. The Japanese culture offers a plurality of conflict forums which help avoid litigation in courts. Thus, while in relation to every fatal road accident in Japan we find four liability cases in court, there are twice as many cases in the courts of California. Clearly, this fits the general image of Americans living in a litigious culture. Our European comparison, however, shows that there are cultures which are even more litigious: in the Federal Republic of Germany, 16 serious traffic cases per fatal accident are heard before a civil court and, in Belgium, twice as many. On the other hand, the immediate neighbour of these two countries, the Netherlands, surpasses even Japan in avoiding litigation: here roughly two cases per fatal accident are taken before a civil court. It has to be admitted that such computations have to grapple with not altogether comparable accident statistics, as well as with judicial data based on only small samples of court files, but the data fit a pattern of litigation proneness on the one hand and court avoidance on the other, so that we can take them at least as an indicator for further questions on the explanation for such vast differences of national litigation frequencies.

First of all, a small area of litigation such as civil liability after a traffic accident is not necessarily indicative of the litigious pattern of a legal culture overall. The regulation of traffic accident damages is largely dealt with by the insurance companies. They have a similar common interest in avoiding conflict costs in any country, and on the European continent they are even transnationally involved with each other because of the high traffic density across the borders and because of the international oligopoly which the big insurance companies form. Why should they accept a much more expensive pattern of conflict handling in Belgium than in West Germany? Why do they not turn to the Dutch avoidance pattern in all of the European countries, which must clearly be the cheapest for them? That such cost considerations do play a role we can conclude from the French study in our comparison: while almost every kind of civil litigation increased in the 1970s, traffic liability decreased, from almost 10 per cent on the court calendars to a tiny fraction. Apparently, the French insurance companies have now managed to handle their regulation internally and to avoid court and lawyer costs.[5]

Litigation avoidance is frequently portrayed as a development of this sort – as private regulation taking the place of legal rules or negotiation and arbitration taking the place of judicial decision making. What Teubner (1983) called 'reflexive law' carries that notion: leaving conflict regulation to the social institutions concerned and considering law and legal institutions as a last resort only for those cases which resist self-regulation. However, historical examples for the idea of reflexive law – at least the examples forwarded by Teubner himself – have more often resulted in the reverse: the self-regulation of collective agreements in industrial relations or the handling of consumer complaints by informal easy-access institutions are in fact attempts to formalize formerly unregulated areas of conflict in a quasi-legal framework simply because legal regulation has been met with too much resistance or too many barriers to access. Informalism seems to me in these cases to be a stepping-stone to further judicialization in the course of a historical time perspective rather than examples of delegating a legal framework to self-regulation. But if we look at litigation developments in such a longer time perspective, we also discover patterns of growing avoidance which amount to *dejudicialization.* No-fault insurance as well as self-regulation of liability after traffic accidents, no-fault divorce and the simplification of family court procedures are examples of this effect; the management of mass consumer crediting and automatic debt enforcement[6] is another example which at least explains why ordinary civil litigation does not grow at the pace of economic growth.

There are other institutions which help avoiding litigation – in some countries more, in some to a lesser degree. Conflict handling by public agencies rather than courts can be one of the means, as is the case with most divorces in Denmark (or in Japan). While most Western countries require a judicial procedure to regulate the conditions of divorce, Far Eastern countries and, in our European comparison also Denmark, allow for separation to occur before an administrative agency similar to a marriage registration. Avoidance of litigation in these countries does not mean lack of regulation but may rather be an indication of the contrary: if public bureaucracies regulate the break-up of social relations, rather than the parties involved themselves, they may do this with regard to more authoritative norms than a judge. Judicial procedure may be an indication of emancipation of the private parties' autonomy from public rules rather than a 'legalization' of areas of private autonomy. Litigation avoidance in those cases would point to a particularly high degree of regulation.

There are other forms of out-of-court regulation of conflicts, however, which we are used to see as less formal 'alternatives' to litigation. Social fields with many mediation and arbitration institutions indicate an avoidance culture with respect to normative third-party intervention: industrial relations in many countries have for a long time stuck to anti-legalistic traditions, the British Industrial Relations Act of 1970/1974 forming the most prominent example of the process of transforming a traditionally autonomous field of social regulation, introducing industrial tribunals, developing case law and increasing the pace of legislation. Nevertheless, litigation in labour relations is still kept at a much lower frequency in Britain than it is in France, Belgium and Germany, with their much older tradition of labour courts, and, among the five European countries which we compared with respect to their litigation patterns, there is on the one hand Denmark, which still handles all labour conflicts in a scheme of corporatist negotiations, and on the other hand the Netherlands which allows for a dismissal as a rule only after this has been licensed by the public labour exchange bureaus. Semi-autonomous regulation is here combined with an administrative procedure. Both Denmark and the Netherlands allow the parties to go to civil courts as a last resort, but in fact litigation frequencies in labour cases are extremely low in both countries.

Mediation, informal complaint procedures, consumer tribunals, ombudsmen institutions, rent commissions – there are numerous conflict institutions in both these litigation avoidance cultures, while in the more litigious legal cultures of France and of (West) Germany their equivalents are difficult to establish, have to work under restrictive conditions or did not get off the ground at all. At first sight one might put forward the hypothesis that litigation avoidance would be related to the smallness of a country: however, Belgium in our comparison belongs to those countries which are most litigation-prone, and so do small countries such as Austria and Finland, while a populous country such as Japan forms the prime example of a litigation avoidance culture (see Table 3.1).

Unfortunately, overall statistical indicators show only insufficiently the impact of such extra judicial alternatives. The main reason is to be found in summary procedures, most prominent among them those for debt enforcement. In some of the most litigation-prone countries (like Austria and West Germany), summary debt enforcement has efficiently taken over the task of enforcing uncontested debts which in other countries fill court calendars. In some of the litigation avoiding countries, however, they are dealt with in the adversary procedure, even though largely terminated by default of the defendant. That is why litigation rates in Denmark are rather high, even though adversary decisions are rare. Appeal rates are a good additional indicator to show the variation of *internal alternatives*: West German courts are most efficient in dealing with part of their caseload in a summary procedure, allowing for high appeal rates (with respect to court-avoiding cultures), but not as high as the most litigation-prone countries (like Austria

Table 3.1 Civil litigation per 100 000 inhabitants (1984)

	Civil procedures including summary debt enforcement	Adversarial procedures, first instance	Appeal court rates
Legal cultures which are litigation-prone			
Austria	10 800	5 020	430
Belgium	–	4 800	536
West Germany	9 400	3 561	251
Legal cultures which avoid litigation			
Italy	2 400	1 640	145
Denmark	–	4 800	64
Netherlands	1 600	1 430	37
Japan (incl. summary/ family courts)	–	500	15

Sources: Wollschläger (1989), Blankenburg (1989), Pelligrini (1990).

and Belgium). While Denmark leaves the courts with the task of debt enforcement, but avoids using the courts for the rest, the Netherlands and Japan stand out as avoiding courts altogether.

Clearly, avoiding litigation does not mean absence of conflicts. In our comparison of highly developed countries litigation avoidance is achieved by a plurality of out-of-court institutions, specific for social fields of regulation. They can involve the parties concerned in more authoritative control, as is usually the case with administrative regulatory agencies, and they can offer informal alternatives to a more formal judicial procedure. Such 'alternative' institutions may be out-of-court, helping to avoid the resort to litigation altogether, but they may also be built into court procedures as an offer to the parties to 'exit' after filing a court case. Pre-trial handling and court-annexed arbitration are typical of such procedural avoidance offers: they are the plausible counterpart of the adversarial and highly formal Anglo-American trial procedure. Continental procedure leaves much more discretion to the judge and thereby reduces conflict between the parties and between their lawyers. The plausible procedural 'alternative' here is the in-court settlement (see Röhl *et al.*, 1983), which is attractive especially as it precludes the losing party from going to appeal before the next higher instance which, in contrast to common law trials, is usually provided for in civil law systems. Litigation avoidance, on this understanding, is not only handling conflicts *out of court*; it can also mean choosing an early exit *while in a court procedure*. We do not have the necessary data on a sufficient number of countries to judge how litigation avoidance before court proceedings is generally related to procedural avoidance, but in the following two-country comparison of the Netherlands and West Germany, the result is quite clearly cumulative: the Germans, who are highly litigation-prone to begin with, also avail themselves of the possibility of going to the higher instance courts more often than the neighbouring Dutch, who normally avoid litigation and also choose *exit* more often once they are before the court.

The Infrastructure of Avoiding Civil Litigation: Legal Behaviour in the Netherlands and West Germany

A comparison of these two neighbouring countries with very similar legal traditions and social and economic conditions can be considered as something like a natural experiment. It offers an ideal case for comparisons of legal cultures, because a number of factors which are usually held responsible for people being especially litigious are kept constant.[7]

We apply the term 'culture' to the set of all interrelationships on three levels: that of substantive law and procedural codes, that of the institutions such as the courts and the legal profession, and finally the level of legal behaviour and attitudes towards the law. Each of these levels might form a complex pattern of itself, but only the relationship of all of them can lead to a comparison of 'legal cultures'. It should be evident that comparing them is a much more ambitious undertaking than the comparison of 'legal systems' which is devoted mainly to understanding the differences of law as far as it is in the books. In looking at litigation frequencies we try to approach 'cultures of law' from an opposite angle to that usually chosen by comparativists; in gathering indicators on litigation, courts and lawyers we try to discover different characteristics of *legal action*.

Measuring the set of all interrelationships on three levels remains a crude attempt, especially as data for country comparisons restrict the availability of empirical indicators even more than they would be within any one legal

Table 3.2 Registered attorneys and judges per 100 000 of the population (1970–90)

	Judges[1]			Attorneys[2]		
	1970	1980	1990	1970	1980	1990
Netherlands, absolute	850	1 024	1 490	2 063	3 600	6 381
Rate per 100 000 pop.	6.5	7.3	9.9	16	26	43
West Germany, absolute	12 954	16 657	17 392	23 798	37 312	59 446
Rate per 100 000 pop.	20	27	29	36	60	94

Notes:
1. The number of judges in the Netherlands includes the full-time equivalents of part-time judges. Functionally equivalent to German judges in some respects would be legally trained secretaries ('griffiers') who assist professional judges in preparing their cases to a degree which in Germany would be considered professional work. As they do not take responsibility for decisions, however, they are not included in our figure.
2. The strictness with which the lines of the profession are drawn differ somewhat: about one-third of registered advocates in Germany hardly do any court work; in the Netherlands our estimate is about one-tenth. On the other hand, German advocates enjoy a monopoly for legal advice, while in the Netherlands a number of membership associations, legal cost insurance and legal aid offices render legal services. In both countries attorneys account for only part of the legal profession; what in North America is called 'lawyers' would here adequately be translated as 'jurists', including law trained employees and civil servants. Cf. Berends (1992).

Source: Statistics of the national departments of justice and bar associations.

tradition. So far we have come up with indicators such as size and personnel of judicial staff and litigation frequencies.

Only a few law and society studies[8] have so far ventured to measure litigation differences between countries, let alone to explain them in relation to other empirical indicators. Our example offers a very obvious challenge: in Northrhine–Westphalia at the end of 1984 there were 12 500 lawyers admitted to the bar, in the Netherlands only 4800; in Northrhine–Westphalia about 4700 full-time judges were employed and in the Netherlands 762. This means that, for every 100 000 of the population, there were 73 attorneys and 28 judges in West Germany, compared to only 33 attorneys and a mere five judges in the Netherlands.[9] Both frequencies have increased considerably since and continue to increase in both countries (see Table 3.2). Because growth rates are similar, they do not, however, alter their relative frequency.

The differences in size of the legal profession correspond to those on litigation (Table 3.3). Whichever type of lawsuits we look at, there is a considerably lower level of litigation in the Netherlands compared to West Germany. West German courts were invoked 25 times more often for summary procedures of debt enforcement and two and a half times more often for civil procedures than in the Netherlands.

For anyone who would like to use litigation frequencies as indicators for the degree of regulation which prevails in society, our Dutch–German comparison must be a puzzle. The Netherlands are known for their elaborate

Table 3.3 Litigation rates (first instance)

	Netherlands			West Germany		
	1970	1980	1990	1970	1980	1990
Civil courts	109 025	146 645	228 480	1 206 750	1 671 089	1 948 151
Rate per 100 000 pop.	779	1 047	1 550	2 010	2 770	3 120
Labour courts	[a]	[a]	(9 471)[b]	201 166	302 602	325 969
Rate per 100 000 pop.			63	335	503	520

Notes:

a. no labour courts, cases in civil courts;

b. There are no special labour courts in the Netherlands. However, in dismissal cases there is a special procedure which, since the late 1980s, has been registered separately in the judicial statistics. Until then the volume of cases seemed too insignificant to register nationally.

Source: National judicial statistics, population statistics.

welfare state, they developed detailed regulations on housing and town planning; they enacted statutory rules for tenant protection, labour protection and consumer protection – in short, theirs is rightly considered a highly regulated political, social and economic system. As a rule, we would expect a large profession of legally trained personnel and a high volume of formal litigation as a result thereof, in public law as well as in private law. And indeed, within the Dutch legal community, the impression prevails that litigation is on an ever increasing growth trend. However, our data on the legal profession as well as on litigation show that, among the European countries which we can compare, the Netherlands still rank lowest in size of the advocacy, the judiciary and the caseloads of civil courts. While the number of lawyers and the flood of litigations rise in all countries, they do so at distinct and long-term stable levels of litigation frequency.

Conflict Potential and Frequency of Litigation

The riddle of litigation frequencies could hardly be presented more sharply than by taking our two countries which also on social and economic grounds are very much alike. To keep social and economic factors constant and render the differences of the cultures of legal behaviour even more convincing we compared the Netherlands and its neighbouring German state of Northrhine–Westphalia.[10] They are similar in size: the Netherlands, with a population of 15 million and a land area of 35 000 square kilometres, almost matches that of Northrhine–Westphalia, with 17 million inhabitants and 34 000 square kilometres. Both countries are known for their highly industrial, but at the same time decentralized, metropolitan areas (the 'Randstad' with Amsterdam, Rotterdam and The Hague in the Netherlands and the Rhein–Ruhr area in Northrhine–Westphalia). Both comprise thinly populated, agricultural regions around the metropolitan areas. Both countries have seen an influx of foreign workers in the last 20 years, the Netherlands from its former colonies as well as the Mediterranean, the Ruhr area mainly from the Mediterranean. Economically, the two are symbiotic: Rotterdam being the seaport for the heavy industry of the Ruhr area, there are numerous ties of trade and multinational entrepreneurship. Consequently, if the Ruhr industry experiences a recession (as has been the case in the recent past), unemployment figures in the Netherlands go up.

The social and economic similarities make it easier to test the most plausible hypothesis which comes to mind when observing such different patterns of mobilizing courts as we have in our case: might it be that the occurrence of those conflicts which can possibly give rise to litigation is vastly different in the two countries? In order to test that hypothesis, we have been looking for indicators of the *baselines* of social conflicts which have the *potential* to lead to invoking the courts. Evidently, such baselines have to be gained from specific areas of law: divorce rates served as an indicator in family law, traffic accidents in tort law, the rate of dismissals in labour law and the percentage of rented houses versus home ownership for real estate conflicts as a baseline for landlord–tenant cases. Lacking better indicators, we also resort to relating litigation figures to population in some cases. This results in computing rates of involvement of courts in similar, potentially litigious social relationships. This potential we subsequently compared to the statistics of the respective departments of justice; in case there was no sufficient breakdown by subject matter, we coded court files in a number of places which we considered representative of the whole country.[11]

The usual difficulty of comparing litigation rates and similar legal indicators between countries is that we do not know enough about the baseline of all conflicts which might lead to invoking lawyers and courts. As we know, cases filed in court represent only a small fraction of all those which would potentially be legal conflicts. Computing litigation rates by relating them to the size of population seems a very crude basis for comparison (taking only the adult population would be even more crude and, for many types of cases, no more adequate). We would have to know how many serious accidents people suffered in traffic as well as other circumstances, in order to evaluate the relative litigiousness of tort regulation in a legal behaviour culture; we would have to know the baseline of all dismissals in order to evaluate the litigiousness of employment protection and we would have to know something about numbers of credits given and predominant modes of paying in sales and service contracts in order to assess the level of debt enforcement. The problems of obtaining sufficient statistical data for baseline comparisons render most social–cultural comparisons between more distant countries unfeasible. The Netherlands, however, and the German neighbouring state of Northrhine–Westphalia are so much alike in size, economy, social structure and mentality of the population that in general we might assume that the baseline of conflicts which potentially give rise to litigation are about equal. Nevertheless, wherever we could obtain indicators for baseline comparisons we did so.

We started by breaking down overall litigation figures by basic areas of social relations and their respective legal regulation. Not only the jurisdictional differences, but also the varying scale of the differences in litigation frequencies from one area of regulation to the next render it nonsensical to compare overall rates of civil or criminal cases without further specification. The main factors which determine the selectivity among all potential conflicts are specific to the respective areas: for example, the degree to which mediating institutions provide a filter of pre-court dispute resolution, or the degree to which attorneys and legal aid facilities access or provide out-of-court alternatives. A number of areas of social relations and legal regulations are characterized by specific institutional infrastructures, the most apparent of these being labour relations, where courts cannot function independently of industrial relations set-ups, trade unions and employers' associations. Divorce and, especially, post-divorce conflicts may be handled by social administration and by family counsellors rather than lawyers. Landlord–tenant relations are highly sensitive to the amount of public housing administration and rent control; consumer complaints depend on representative action by consumer boards; and the number of tort cases before courts depends on the amount of discretion which insurance companies apply in regulating claims.

We tried to differentiate the institutional conditions which mitigate conflicts before they might become litigious by breaking conflict areas down into very specialized 'fields of law'. We stopped short of further specialization whenever we had the impression that a more crude differentiation would provide us with a sufficient explanation of major statistical differences, leaving more refined and detailed comparisons to specialized research (which should in our opinion also include more refined comparative law analysis). Our comparison can direct attention only to the gross differences in the level of litigiousness and to their overall legal cultural explanation. It gives ample suggestions for more specialized research on 'fields of law' and on 'semi-autonomous fields' of social relations.

The Civil Litigation Filter

There is no straightforward explanation why the Germans should produce one of the highest rates of *civil litigation* on the European continent and the neighbouring Dutch by far the lowest. The most readily available factor would be some vague notion of greater 'litigiousness' in the mentality of the Germans as compared to the Dutch; however, first-hand impressions in both countries would not suggest such a hypothesis; if the folklore were comparing people from the Rhineland and Westphalia to their immediate Dutch neighbours, intuitive knowledge would rather suggest their differing from Bavarians or Prussians, rather than from each other. The fact is that within both countries we find remarkable urban–rural differences in the level of litigation, but, keeping those constant, we find no further differences from one region to the other. Much more plausible, therefore, would be hypotheses about economic and social variables which might be litigation-prone: economic activity in general has been shown to be related to the use of courts; job mobility and divorce rates might be suspected to contribute to the use of courts; and certainly in Western Europe the level of welfare provisions will be a factor – the more elaborate the system of collective insurance policies, the less often individual claims have to be raised in courts. However, with respect to any of these factors which in general can explain the frequency of civil litigation, the two countries which we compare are remarkably similar.

Social and economic similarities, in any case, would lead us to expect an equally high volume of legal problems to be solved. Also substantive regulation in both countries shows more resemblance than difference. Even procedural law and the organization of courts differ only slightly, and as for 'legal consciousness' factors, such as the willingness of people to risk an open conflict, we do not see any difference in general attitudes between the Dutch and their West German neighbours which could explain the observed differences in propensity to litigate.

What else could explain the observed differences in litigation, if neither the law in the books nor demand factors of litigiousness nor social and economic conditions provide a ready explanation? Instead of looking for a single explanation for the remarkable differences in the litigation rates of the two countries (see Table 3.4), we have to look at *patterns* of legal institutions and the ways that they are used. In our case we find explanations more often on the *supply side* than on the demand side of legal behaviour: the conditions of access to lawyers and courts, the institutions which handle litigation and possible 'alternative' institutions which might help to avoid it. The supply side of the legal culture consists of sets of institutional arrangements and patterns of professional interaction which apparently escape the

Table 3.4 Litigation rates per 100 000 inhabitants for selected conflict areas (1982–4)

	Netherlands	West Germany
Summary debt enforcement	705	9 118
Debt enforcement litigation	650	1 570
Landlord–tenant disputes	200	458
Traffic tort	15	247
Labour law cases	69	586

Note: All data are taken from court file studies: in Germany statistics of Northrhine–Westphalia; the volume in those years is equally high all over the Federal Republic and may therefore be generalized. See Blankenburg and our comparative report on litigation in five European countries: Blankenburg and Verwoerd (1989), pp. 257–329.

Source: Blankenburg (1989).

attention of academic comparative lawyers because they are nowhere laid down in writing. Nevertheless, these patterns of interaction provide an explanation of our riddle: cultures of legal behaviour include sets of institutions which remain 'in the shadow' of the legal system, because they help to *avoid* procedures rather than to *invoke* them.

The first set of factors can be found in the infrastructure of the lawyer profession. There are a number of rather detailed statutory differences as to how attorneys' fees are regulated: German attorneys follow a strict fee scheme and they can rely on the rule that 'the loser pays all costs': while in the Netherlands hourly fees are charged, which renders litigation for small amounts unattractive and the costs in general somewhat unpredictable. This makes a Dutch litigant as well as Dutch lawyers look more carefully for 'alternatives' before starting a formal court procedure.

Furthermore, the German bar enjoys a monopoly for giving legal advice which in the Netherlands is open to all. This gives rise to a number of Dutch membership organizations (such as trade unions, automobile clubs or consumer groups) providing legal advice. It also permits public legal aid offices to work on a subsidy scheme entitling about half of the Dutch population to free legal advice. All of these advisors may represent their clients in lower courts; attorney representation is required only before district courts which are competent for civil law cases involving higher stakes (currently at a value above 5000Hfl.) and divorce.

One might expect such free access to legal aid to stimulate litigation, and in fact the subsidy scheme is being criticized in this regard by welfare state opponents. The comparative evidence on legal aid in several European countries,[12] however, suggests that the free competition of legal services helps to avoid some types of litigation as much as it stimulates others. Which types of cases are stimulated, and which are avoided thanks to the Dutch infrastructure of access to the courts has to be sought out in each area of law separately. As a rule, we find institutions which facilitate judicial remedies side-by-side with 'alternatives' to avoid formal procedures. Avoidance is part of the art and advice of attorneys in Germany as well as in the Netherlands, only the Dutch culture of legal behaviour offers *more* 'alternatives' and *more* pre-court conflict institutions than the German. The final volume of litigation is to be explained by the specific mixture of facilitation and avoidance, which varies according to the kind of problem and the social relationship involved in the underlying conflict.

Debt collection This is the single quantitatively most prevalent issue in civil courts of both countries. Both legal systems at the time of our research offered a summary procedure (the Dutch *betalingsbevel* was taken over from the German *Mahnverfahren* during the Occupation of 1941). It allows the creditor to file an allegation without presenting more evidence than a contract and a statement that payment is overdue. Court clerks under (formal) supervision of a judge screen the forms for correctness and issue a summons. If the debtor contradicts, a formal litigation procedure may be entered; if not, the payment can be enforced with the help of a bailiff (comparable to a US marshal). Table 3.4 shows that summary debt collection is used on a massive scale in West Germany, but rather modestly in the Netherlands. The same holds true for the follow-up: little more than 10 per cent of the summons are protested and subsequently litigated in court, thus a considerable part (about one-third) of the difference in general civil litigation is caused by fewer debt claims reaching the litigation stage in Dutch as compared to German courts.

The lesson to be drawn here is even more illuminating if we go back a few years in procedural history. Before 1984, when Dutch court fees were raised, summary debt enforcement was used somewhat more frequently; since then privately operating bailiffs refuse to use the summary court procedure altogether, maintaining that they can enforce small debts more quickly and more cheaply on their own authority. At the same time, frequent users of debt enforcement increased their efforts to eliminate bad debtors from their delivery lists and to automate their own reminders and subtle threats by increasing the costs of late payment. Computer technology helped even small companies, craftsmen or doctors to organize the early stages of debt enforcement in-house.[13]

To ascribe the downward trend of summary debt enforcement in the Netherlands to the rise in court fees alone would be to overestimate the effect of litigation costs as a single factor. In contrast to their German counterparts, Dutch bailiffs do not need a court-issued title to act on behalf of the creditor; they enjoy the professional privilege of judging the legal validity of a claim on their own. Asking for a summons by court is only one of the means at their disposal, while for the German bailiffs it is a precondition of action. Therefore Dutch bailiffs have never used the court summons as frequently as the Germans; they rather see the possibility of free access to that procedure as competition to their own services. They argue not only that their own professional standards provide the debtors with sufficient guarantee of due process, but that they can also negotiate terms of payment far better in direct contact with the debtors than a court which issues its summons in the absence of the parties and, if it decides in adversarial procedures against debtors, it does this mostly by default. Recently, the bailiffs even achieved legislative success with their argumentation: the latest amendment to the Dutch procedural code in 1992 did away with the 'betalingsbevel'. European harmonization of civil procedural codes, however, may force them to reintroduce a similar procedure in the near future. It is easy to predict the consequences of a European regulation: if summary procedures function effectively, they offer easy access and quick decisions; in a small number of cases they also lead the way to full-fledged litigation by mere contradiction of the summons. The more courts offer such quick and easy access, the more they will also be used for subsequent adversarial litigation. The higher they set the threshold of access, the more they will stimulate out-of-court alternatives; and the more these are professionally regulated, the better they can guarantee standards of due process comparable to those of courts of justice.

Consumer complaints Looking at the other side of trade and service relationships, we see that consumer complaints are almost everywhere treated by informal institutions first. This raises the principal dilemma in terms of public interest that each individual case might be too trivial to risk litigation costs, whereas collectively they would be of great significance for everybody. Controlling product standards, sales practices and fair pricing is best done by organized interest representation using information and consultation with consumers, handling complaints, lobbying and occasionally engaging in litigation towards producers and distributors. In both the Netherlands and West Germany consumer associations were initially organized by trade unions, partly subsidized by public funds, and they are aided by publicity in the mass media. They set up complaint boards for industries with specific troubles (such as for travel agencies, cleaners, the textile industry or car repair shops) jointly with the respective industries. Pre-court institutions take up almost all such cases. While these organizations ease the access for small claims, they at the same time filter out a few more serious cases and occasionally take a test case before the court.

Again, the two countries show the same institutional pattern in principle, but the Dutch consumer organizations are relatively more active, better funded and handle a higher caseload. In this case, however, there is no argument that they prevent the same complaints from being otherwise litigated. Consumer complaints usually are not worth fighting individually in court. More likely, there will be (relatively) fewer test cases in German courts, simply because the basis of collective interest representation is weaker. The lesson is: out-of-court forums for consumers are no 'alternative' to litigating; they rather provide the only basis representing the collective interest, including occasionally seeking access to the courts.

The construction industry Rather frequent consumer problems involving big stakes arise in the construction industry. Problems between builders and contractors are inherent in the long duration and complexity of the job: contractors have to work with a number of subcontract firms which may be hard to coordinate; time schedules are regularly neglected; materials may not be delivered in time and have to be replaced; changing conditions and new requirements make it necessary to adapt the contract; thus renegotiating is the rule. In the end the most beautiful construction will still entail dissatisfactions which the client expresses by withholding part of the price. The saying is: 'Take a lawyer before you build a house' – and, indeed, legal cost insurers in Germany refuse to cover risks arising from construction work because they fear people might take out an insurance policy because they are sure there are risks. (They do not refuse clients who buy a car or engage in a marriage, however.) In German civil courts, construction conflicts are among the most cumbersome proceedings: the court has to reconvene more often than in any other kind of procedure; evidence has to be taken more often; frequently, expert witnesses have to be called in, so that the duration is the longest of all kinds of civil procedures; finally, there are also more than the average number of appeals.[14]

In the Netherlands building contractors hardly ever see the courtrooms. They always include in their standard contracts a clause to the effect that conflicts will be heard by the 'Council for construction firms' (*Raad voor de Bouwbedrijven at Den Haag*), an arbitration service set up by the industry. Parties may choose an arbiter among the architects and engineers of the council, a law-trained secretary ensuring procedural fairness. The arbiters decide in first and last instance; their decisions can be executed formally if registered with the president of a district court. A monthly journal, *Bouwrecht*, publishes all novel decisions and is used as a reference like an exhaustive compilation of case law.

Arbitration Similar regulations exist in a number of industrial sectors. Most national arbitration boards have their seat in Rotterdam; they usually provide industrial experts as arbiters. A statutory arbitration code ('Arbitragewet', book 4.1 of the civil procedural code of 2.7.1986) regulates the procedure. It affords a possibility of appeal to the civil courts if the procedural code is not followed: substantive appeal is possible only if parties have agreed upon its admission beforehand. Publication of decisions is not mandatory, but is often suggested in order to build up a body of precedents. The bimonthly *Tijdschrift voor Arbitrage* publishes all decisions which seem of principal relevance to it. In the course of time it has successfully built up its 'code of arbitration' which is generally considered as a binding source of law.

Conflicts between landlords and tenants Returning to cases which have the potential of appearing in civil courts, a sizable volume is provided by landlord–tenant disputes. Contrary to the expectation that rent law is first and foremost designed to protect tenants' interests, such cases are mostly initiated by the economically stronger party, the houseowner, claiming unpaid rent and often asking for eviction of the tenant. More often than in consumer cases, the tenants mount counterclaims for maintenance or protest rent rises; in a minority of cases they are the ones who initiate the procedure. In both countries tenants' organizations represent the collective interest and provide legal aid to their members. They usually provide conciliation in commissions together with the houseowner associations. In the Netherlands, however, these commissions are given official pre-court status. Before being admitted in court with a plea against raising the rent, a Dutch tenant has to put the claim before a landlord–tenant commission. The procedure before the commission leads to a recommendation and the data gathered by it may serve as evidence in court. If the advice is not challenged by either party within two months, it becomes binding. The Dutch commissions handle many more complaints than their voluntary counterparts or even the courts in West Germany; only about 1 per cent of them are taken to court after the commission has given its advice. Again, the availability of informal procedures before the commissions eases access for tenants to the making of claims; at the same time it effectively filters out tenants' complaints which in West Germany lead to litigation in court.

Protection of employers and employees Employment protection provides a similar lesson. Employers in the Netherlands need permission from the local labour bureau if they want to dismiss an employee for reasons other than manifest misconduct. The procedure before the labour exchange bureau gives the employee a chance to protest, and very often the terms of the dismissal are reconsidered. The dismissal is effective only after the licence has been given. Compared to ex post procedures before German labour courts, this has advantages for both sides: when the licence is given, the employer does not have to fear extensive ex post claims on the basis of unfair dismissal (which are often raised in German labour courts) and the labour side have had a chance to object and question the validity of redundancy or dismissal arguments.

The administrative procedure saves the Dutch from installing labour courts such as exist in Germany and most other European countries. While there is no appeal against the commission's decision in the strict sense, parties can resort to civil courts. As in other countries, in the labour court this is mostly done to challenge a dismissal ex post, especially by those who fall outside the licensing regulation (for example short-term contract workers who are dismissed for misconduct). Few claimants resort to this, so that the judges have to handle less than 10 per cent of the comparable caseload of their German colleagues.

Traffic accidents The regulation of traffic accident damages provides our final example. In both countries most accidents are routinely handled out of court. Apart from cases where the amount of damages is in question, traffic tort comes down to a distribution conflict among different insurance companies. They have every interest in keeping conflicts down: their spokesmen emphasize that an estimated 95 per cent of all German traffic accidents are regulated by insurance agents without attorneys or courts being involved; 'only' about 2 per cent lead to litigation in the court. The same insurance companies, when operating in the Netherlands, however, involve an attorney in less than 1 per cent of cases and the litigation rate of all traffic accident damages is around 0.2 per cent. On the other hand, the volume of these tiny fractions is sizable enough to account for 10 per cent of the caseloads in German civil courts, with less than 1 per cent in Dutch courts.[15]

In this case the difference cannot be explained by a single 'alternative' institution. It is rather the result of an institutional cluster consisting of at least the following elements. Liability insurance in both countries is often sold together with a legal cost insurance. The insurance companies operating in Germany pay all attorney costs in case of consultation as well as conciliation or litigation; the same companies in the Netherlands, however, run their own legal consultation service (which in Germany would be outlawed according to the statutory attorneys' privilege); and while German attorneys point at research showing that 70 per cent of all traffic accidents in their files are settled out of court, the Dutch legal insurance regulators reach a settlement in between 96 per cent and 98 per cent of all conflicts (which, it should be remembered, are only a fraction of all accident damages). Furthermore, expert assessment of damages is routinely initiated in the Netherlands before repair work has started, while the German regulation relies mostly on the car repair shop which does the work. On the other hand, assessment of fault in Germany is often carried out by experts who are invoked by attorneys as well as by the courts; in the Netherlands, police reports are more easily accessible and are usually relied upon by both sides. Altogether, the Dutch practice is clearly more geared towards avoiding conflict, while the German infrastructure of attorneys, experts and even legal insurance companies (after all, more Germans buy legal cost insurance, because everybody runs a higher risk of legal conflicts occurring) has a common interest in holding up its rather costly system of handling (and even encouraging) conflicts.

Finally, a comment should be added about *alternatives within court procedures*. Divorce procedures in both countries illustrate their relevance: both

West Germany and the Netherlands require a court decision to dissolve a marriage.[16] Dutch family law, however, allows for decisions by default, if both parties agree and no children are involved. About one-third of all divorce procedures are decided this way, reducing the role of the judge to that of a notary. Attorneys may suggest and prepare such a 'do-it-yourself' divorce, but so may 'divorce consultation bureaus' which have been set up experimentally by social workers and psychologists together with law-trained colleagues. Initially subsidized by the Department of Justice, they met with resistance by the organized bar. Enjoying a monopoly of representation in district courts (where divorce has to be filed), the bar had the stronger cards. Nevertheless, divorce attorneys also met the competition by setting up their own divorce mediation, supported by the bar, which offers training in settlement skills especially geared for divorce consultation. If ever legislation nullified the attorneys' privilege of representation in first instance (or even allowed for divorce before a notary), it is safe to predict that divorce litigation would largely become 'privatized'.

The Infrastructure of Access to and Avoidance of Courts

Civil litigation is said[17] be like a market because parties have to invoke the court themselves and also because the course of the proceedings largely rests with actions of both parties. Many welfare-state legal systems, however, have moved away from purely formal equality of parties in the direction of compensating for social weakness by substantive as well as procedural law. Freedom of contract is restricted in many areas, such as in tenancy and employment relations. Typical of such areas of compensatory substantive legislation is the concomitant supply of informal institutions and procedures which help to deal with conflict cases out of court. Tenants' rights, employment protection and also consumer complaints are typically dealt with by pre-court institutions which filter away the bulk of the cases, but always leave the possibility of invoking a formal court procedure if informal 'alternatives' have been exhausted. In the Netherlands much more than in West Germany, such filter institutions are effectively taking away some of the potential court caseload by at the same time providing an easy access for (more) cases in a pre-court conflict arena. Dutch consumer complaint boards are more active than their German counterparts. Dutch bailiffs take over debt enforcement cases which in West Germany are treated by court procedures and Dutch rental conflict commissions handle landlord–tenant cases. Dutch labour exchange bureaus check on dismissals which in West Germany will more likely end up in courts. Compared to the costs and duration of litigation in the Netherlands (and this would certainly hold even more with respect to American trial courts), West German courts are so much more efficient that there is less reason for the (legally experienced) parties to try to avoid them; on the other hand, the German courts thereby attract a high caseload of petty cases which in the Netherlands are handled by 'filtering institutions'.

Nevertheless, the extent to which parties to civil disputes in the Federal Republic and the Netherlands invoke courts and, furthermore, the degree to which they make use of legal advice and assistance varies widely from one type of case to another. In both countries in lower courts many parties proceed without being represented by a lawyer; the informality of Continental procedures (in comparison to adversarial trials) and the discretionary powers of the judges render this feasible. Furthermore, court and lawyer fee waivers for litigants with moderate means of income take away some of the financial barriers of access to lawyers and courts. In the Netherlands, about 60 per cent of all private households are entitled to legal aid assistance and court fee waivers in excess of a minimum own risk; in the West German system, the entitlement ends at considerably lower income levels (in legal aid assistance at about twice the social welfare minimum).

However, in neither country do legal aid recipients account for a large segment of court caseloads. Only in divorce cases is a major part of court and lawyer fees compensated by legal aid schemes. In all other cases the economically weaker party is usually the defendant: for them, financial obstacles are usually not a main consideration as the legal aid scheme takes care of most of the financial costs of litigation. Apart from financial cost considerations, however, there remain sufficient reasons to try to avoid getting involved with lawyers and courts: no legal aid scheme will remove the social considerations which keep individuals from actively resorting to lawyers and courts.

There is no single factor explaining why the Dutch handle far fewer conflicts by litigation than the neighbouring Germans. We observe a recurring pattern, however, which is due partly to the institutions filtering access to courts and partly to 'alternatives' which help to avoid them. Part of the 'infrastructure of avoidance' is facilitated by the multitude of forms of legal consultation which is available within and outside the bar. Legal advice is not an attorneys' monopoly, which allows legal cost insurance companies automobile clubs or trade unions to compete with law firms. On the other side, there are individual as well as institutional government subsidies for legal aid which (since the mid-1970s) have enabled 'social advocates' to offer low threshold legal services. Amazingly enough, the abundance of legal advisors fits into a culture of especially low, rather than high, litigation frequencies. In a number of conflict constellations where the law protects the socially weaker parties against the more powerful ones (for instance, consumer protection, tenants' rights and employment protection), 'alternative' institutions attract a high number of cases which would not find any forum in a more litigious culture. At the same time as they effectively filter out recurrent routine cases, thus relieving the court caseload, the infrastructure of legal aid offers a chance of exemplary litigation in strategic test cases.

Quite a different constellation prevails in those areas of law where repeat players are disputing. Insurance companies, mail order houses and banks have a high stake in reducing the conflict costs in everyday transactions. Their strategies are mainly anticipatory; if they have to enter a conflict, they prefer internal settlement to external dispute; if they risk external procedures, they try to withhold their stakes so as to shift the burden of mobilizing lawyers and courts to the opposing party. If they are grievances on the part of customers, they mostly manage to deal with them by using in-house complaint procedures; in sectors which are especially grievance-prone (such as insurance), industry-wide boards serve as appeal instance. The 'alternative' of invoking courts of justice is reserved as *ultimum remedium*.

In Germany, on the other hand, courts seem too efficient and, for the plaintiff, too cheap to provide incentives for avoiding them. In civil courts half of the plaintiffs have their decision within half a year; one-third within three months. Summary proceedings are even quicker. It is mainly the business community who profit from having a quick and effective instrument for collecting debts, regulating accidents and threatening tenants with eviction: as they usually win their cases, the defendants pay all of the fees. In cases where mostly private individuals are the plaintiffs, as with labour courts, social and administrative courts, chances of winning the entire case are empirically small; litigation here is often a means to win advantages outside the verdict: regular examples are in labour courts where employers as defendants buy off the harassment of litigation by a settlement, and in administrative courts where plaintiffs without any substantial chance of success are glad to pay the price of court and lawyer fees in order to win some time.

In our comparison of two countries which in their general cultures are so much alike, we need no explanation on the basis of mentality to account for litigation behaviour. The choices of plaintiffs in using or avoiding the courts are based on similar strategic rationalities on both sides of the border. What is different are the incentives which the legal systems offer. It is access provided by infrastructure on the supply side as well as alternatives to courts which determine the conditions of invoking or of avoiding them.

Legal Culture as Institutional Supply

Comparative law research has a long tradition of analysing the different ways by which legal systems have regulated functionally similar problems. It has arrived at a classification of 'families' of legal systems partly based on substantive, partly on procedural law issues. Unfortunately, it is rather arbitrary which criteria such classification is based on: if Continental European law is compared to Anglo-American traditions, formal and procedural aspects such as the 'inquisitorial' versus the 'adversarial' style of procedures are mostly taken as a token of differentiation. If the comparison is restricted to systems of Continental European law, substantive law issues usually take the lead in identifying 'kinship' and 'family'. This may result from the assumption that in procedural law we would not find much relevant difference among the European legal systems. Relating to the law in the procedural codes this seems true; indeed, between the two legal systems which we are comparing here, those of the Netherlands and of the Federal Republic of Germany, there are many communalities in the way civil and penal courts and procedures are regulated.

Throughout their legal history, the Netherlands and West Germany have had many experiences in common. In the nineteenth century, German codification as well as Roman Dutch law used as a model the French Code Civile which had undergone judicial and administrative reforms under and immediately following the Napoleonic occupation. The French influence in both cultures superseded a practice of rather decentralized local legal cultures. These established many communalities among the northern German states and the Low Countries which, among Dutch legal scholars, were seen as 'the traditional law' versus the French codifications. Transferrals went on throughout the period of the national codifications which came to the Netherlands somewhat earlier than to the German Reich. But cultural and legal communalities were strong enough for Dutch legal scholars to continue orienting themselves towards German scholarship as far as dogmatic refinements were concerned. Many Dutch judicial institutions form a compromise between the French and the German tradition: all of them have a two-tier jurisdiction of civil courts of first instance. They provide the civil litigant with two courts of first instance, the local courts handling small claims up to a set amount in controversy as well as all matters of landlord and tenant law, and in Germany of family matters; and district courts handling matters with higher values at stake, and in the Netherlands all family matters. To each of the two first instance courts there is an appeal instance which treats cases *de novo*, and the uniformity of decisions on legal issues is guarded by a High Court of appeals ('Bundesgerichtshof', 'Hoge Raad') treating cases exclusively on their legal merits.

Any similarities between the two legal systems, however, hold up only if we compare the law as it is in the books. Dutch scholars as well as legislators have always looked to the legal doctrines of the bigger neighbouring countries before drafting their statutes; the practitioners in courts and in the advocacy have not. With a very similar legal system in the books, they have developed amazingly different legal cultures in action. Apparently, the gap between doctrine and practice is so great that even comparativists who have studied both systems in detail have been surprised by most of the differences which are unveiled by looking at frequency indicators. Substantive law, and even procedural codes, might be alike from one country to the next, but they are bad predictors as to how the law is handled. Indicator comparisons lead us not to restrict comparative law to the analysis of legal systems, but to extend it to 'cultures' of legal behaviour.

This terminology deviates from what many law and society scholars have agreed upon. They define 'legal culture' as comprising 'attitudes', beliefs and values with respect to law'.[18] It was a useful definition as long as studies were concerned with popular as well as professional ways of going about their legal system; normative expectations, trust in legal institutions and attitudes towards using (or avoiding) them certainly shape the practice of law. Often such an underlying 'belief culture' will be taken as a source of law, and regularly it will shape the institutions which make it work (or just prevent it from working). In comparing legal systems, however, a misleading connotation comes with this definition. It is commonly assumed that legal rules are rooted in social norms and that the legal system expresses the notions that a dominant group in society has about what is 'just'. Unfortunately, however, the reality of such an assumption is hardly ever tested. It would take a very sophisticated combination of qualitative interviews and survey technique to do it in a meaningful way. Legal scholars as well as judges have therefore developed a practice of assuming what the general public might consider as 'true justice'; by that venerated method they not only project their own 'sense of justice' as being the general one, they also legitimate a highly sophisticated moral dogmatic as representing a public belief.[19] Thus, even though it is already 'occupied' in various ways, the term 'legal culture' is used here for polemic reasons: many authors assume that national differences of law which are not to be found in doctrine must be attributable in 'folk mentalities'. Attitudes alone, however, do not explain the data which we found but rather their interrelationship with law, institutions and behaviour patterns.

For reasons of complexity, no developed system of law could possibly claim such a 'bottom-up' basis. A body of law grows over long periods of time, it is made sophisticated by precedents and differentiated by its own internal logic until it is well beyond the comprehension of popular beliefs. It needs a *profession* to be formulated and institutions to be administered. Ordinary people hardly know how they work. The 'legal cultures' which we discuss in comparative law when trying to characterize 'civil law' as against 'common law', the American as against the Canadian or the English as against the Scottish legal culture will inevitably be those of the professionals and not those of the general public.

Thus, if comparative lawyers use such a definition of 'legal culture' as the sets of 'attitudes, beliefs and values', they are talking about 'internal' cultures of the self-understanding of professionals. They largely reproduce what they have learnt: having been trained in the institutions of their legal system, they follow its inherent set of beliefs, sometimes with more critical distance, sometimes in a more enthusiastic way. Their perception is shaped by what they find, and any attempt at innovation will be marginal to the system in which they act. Professionalism itself is a set of institutions which shapes the perception. We do not know how they relate to the many 'popular legal cultures' of the public, neither do the professionals themselves. As far as survey data have been generated they indicate a very general level of trust or distrust in institutions about which the respondents know little. That is to say, 'legal culture' is as much the product of the system as it is its generator: there may be many normative expectations of the general public, but there is no 'legal culture' outside existing legal institutions.[20]

Notes

1 See the discussion between Felstiner and Danzig and Lowy (1975).

2 See Blankenburg (1989).

3 International Sociological Association Research Committee (Sociology of Law). B.M. Blegvad and A. Wulff, Kopenhagen; H. Ietswaard, Paris; *F.* v. *Loon and E. Langerwerff*, Antwerp; I Verwoerd and Blankenburg, DenHaag/Amsterdam.

4 Hellmut Wollschläger (Bielefeld, 1989).

5 Ietswaard (1989).

6 See Kagan (1984).

7 The results of this comparison have also been published in *Law and Society Review* **28**, (4), 1994, 789–808.

8 However, see Fitzgerald (1982) who followed the entire funnel of 'naming–claiming–blaming' for a number of areas of civil dispute in Australia compared to the United States. Even though he finds Australians significantly less litigious than Americans, much bigger differences would bc found in comparisons of other countries which might in socio-economic respects be rather similar to each other). A lead to fruitful hypotheses might already be found in a comparison of rather crude indicators which Johnson *et al.* (1977) assembled. Galanter (1983, 1992) made some brave attempts to establish rank orders of legal indicators for several countries, but the clearing up of misinterpretations of some data from a number of countries is still necessary. Unfortu-

nately, such attempts have raised more criticisms of the validity of indicators, such as 'what are "courts"?' (Clark, 1990), 'what are "cases"?' (see Ietswaart, 1990) and 'who is the "legal profession"?' (Berends, 1992) than contributions to overcome the obvious incomparabilities of institutions in different countries. While it is evident that 'lawyers' and 'courts' have different functional boundary definitions from one country to the next, there is no other way than to start from indicators of their activities, if we ever want to describe precisely how their functions differ. The comparison of legal cultures which I propose tries to overcome incomparability with a multilayered concept of 'legal culture' while keeping socioeconomic factors constant as far as possible.

9 Blankenburg and Verwoerd (1989); Blankenburg (1985).

10 A number of studies of our own demonstrate that we may generalize from court data of Northrhine–Westphalia to those of West Germany. See Bundesrechtsanwaltskammer (1974) as well as our predictions of future litigation developments (Prognos, 1989) where we have repeatedly shown that there are significant urban/rural differences, but no regional variations in litigation frequencies in West Germany. Insofar as it is representative of German urban/rural relations, Northrhine–Westphalia mirrors exactly the per capita litigation rates of the whole country; in the eastern states of the former German Democratic Republic we at present observe considerably lower litigation figures, mainly due to the development lag of legal institutions (Prognos, 1993).

11 One of the by-products (which helped to finance the study) was that we were able to advise the departments on which categories to use in their official statistics.

12 See Blankenburg (1993).

13 See Raken and Otto (1987).

14 All data taken from our court file study on the basis of Baumgärtel's data: Bundesrechtsanwaltskammer (1974) vol. 2, tables 3.20ff.

15 Dutch frequencies are even lower than those of Japan, the German litigation rate after traffic accidents even higher than in California; the explanation of conflict regulation by internal institutions which Tanase (1990) gives for the Japanese avoidance pattern holds also for the Dutch. See for an in-depth study of German and Dutch insurance practice, Simsa (1995).

16 The higher divorce rates in Germany are most likely due to a difference in court registration: it often occurs that a procedure has to 'rest' for some time before the parties actively pursue it. In Germany this may lead to registration of a new procedure: in the Netherlands it may be continued under the same file number. To the extent that this explains the difference, it would simply be technical.

17 Black (1973).

18 See Friedman (1975) who introduces institutional variables by making the useful distinction between popular attitudes as opposed to those of the legal profession (which he calls 'internal legal culture').

19 Even Savigny based his often quoted 'volksgeist' theory on this notion. Remarkably enough, however, he thought he would find the German *Volksgeist* of his time in the *Geist* of the Roman law.

20 Many German authors use the term in a normative sense as a desired (that is, 'cultured') way of dealing with law (cf. Max-Planck director, Dieter Simon, in a number of recent interviews). I use the term in a non-normative way, but extend it to institutional as well as behavioural patterns in relation to the 'legal system' as it is understood in legal doctrine. While in other contexts the American or German usage of the term might be preferable, it would miss the point in explaining the differences of litigation patterns.

Bibliography

Abel, R. (1982), 'The contradiction of informal justice' in *Ipso, The Politics of Informal Justice*, New York: Academic Press, 267–320.

Berends, Mieke (1992) 'An Elusive Profession? Lawyers in Society', *Law and Society Review*, **26** (1), 161–88.

Black, Donald (1973) 'The Mobilization of Law', *Journal of Legal Studies*, **2**, 125 ff.

Blankenburg, Erhard (1985) 'Indikatorenvergleich der Rechtskulturen in der Bundesrepublik und in den Niederlanden', *Zeitschrift für Rechtssoziologie*, **6**, (2), 255–73.

Blankenburg, E. (ed.) (1989), 'Prozessflut? Studien zur Prozesstätigkeit europäischer Gerichte' in *Historischen Zeitreihen und im Rechtsvergleich*, Köln Bundesanzeiger.

Blankenburg, Erhard (1993) 'Private Insurance as a New Wave of the Legal Aid Movement', *Windsor Yearbook of Access to Law*.

Blankenburg, Erhard, Hellmut Morasch and Heimfried Wolff (1974) 'Tatsachen zur Reform der Zivilgerichtsbarkeit', ed. by Bundesrechtsanwaltskammer, Tübingen: J.C.B. Mohr.

Blankenburg, Erhard and Jan Verwoerd (1988) 'Prozeßhäufigkeiten in den Niederlanden und in Nordrhein–Westfalen 1970–1984', in E.R. Blankenburg (ed.), Cologne: Bundesanzeiger Verlag.

Bundesrechtsanwaltskammer (ed.) (1974) *Strukturanalyse der Zivilgerichtsbarkeit*, 2 vols, Tübingen: J.C.B. Mohr.

Clark, David (1990) 'Civil Litigation Trends in Europe and Latin America Since 1945: The Advantage of Intracountry Comparison', *Law and Society Review*, **24**, (2), 549–70.

Danzig, Richard and Lowy, Michael (1975) 'Every Day Disputes and Mediation in the United States: A Reply to Prof. Felstiner, *Law and Society Review*, **9**, 675–94.

Felstiner, William (1974/75) 'Avoidance as Dispute Processing: an Elaboration', *Law and Society Review*, **9**, 695–706.

Fitzgerald, Jeffrey (1982) 'A Comparative Empirical Study of Potential Disputes in Australia and the United States', dispute processing program working paper 1982–4. Madison, Wisconsin.

Friedman, Lawrence (1975) *The Legal System: A Social Science Perspective*, New York: Russell Sage Foundation.

Galanter, Marc (1983) 'Reading the Landscape of Disputes', *UCLA Law Review*, **31**, 4–71.

Galanter, Marc (1992) 'The Debased Debate on Civil Justice', Dispute processing program working paper 10–10, Madison Wisconsin.

Habermas, J. (1981), *Theorie des Kommunikativen Handelus*, Frankfurt.

Haley, J.O. (1978) 'The myth of the reluctant litigant', *The Journal of Japanese Studies*, **4**, 359–90.

Ietswaart, H. (1989) 'Die Entwicklung des Geschäftsanfalls an Amtsgerichten in Frankreich' in Blankenburg (1989), 159–230.

Ietswaart, Heleen (1990) 'The International Comparison of Court Caseloads: The Experience of the European Working Group, *Law and Society Review*, **24**, (2), 571–94.

Johnson, Earl, Steven Block, William Felstiner, E.W. Hansen and Georges Sabagh (1977) *A Comparative Analysis of the Justice System of Seven Industrial Democracies*, Los Angeles: University of Southern California.

Kagan, R. (1984) 'The routinization of debt collection: an essay on social change and conflicts in the courts', *Law and Society Review*, **18**, 323–73.

Pelligrini, S. (1990), *Il problema sociologica della litigiosita processuale*, Bologna: Tesi laurea soc. diritto.

Prognos (1989/1991) 'Mögliche Entwicklungen im Zusammenspiel von außer- und innergerichtlichen Konfliktregelungen', Basle, partly published in *Speyrer Forschungsberichte* 88/1990.

Raken, A and M. Otto (1987) 'De betalingsbevelprocedure in Amsterdam', *Justitiële verkenningen*, **2/87**, 36–55.

Röhl, H. *et al.* (1983), *Der Vergleich im Zivilprozebt*, Opladen: Westdeutscher Verlag.

Rottleuthener, K. (1985) 'Aspekte der Rechtsentwicklung in Deutschland', *Zeitschrift für Rechtssoziologie*, **6**, 206–45.

Savigny, Friedrich Carl von (1840–48), *System des heutigen römischen Rechts*, Berlin: Veit.

Simsa, Christiane (1995), Die gerichtliche und aussergerichtliche Reguliernung von Verkehrsunfällen in Deutschland und den Niederlanden, Diss. VU Amsterdam.

Tanase, Takao (1990) 'The Management of Disputes: Automobile Accident Compensation in Japan', *Law and Society Review*, **24**, 651–92.

Teubner, G. (1983) 'Substantive and reflexive elements in modern law', *Law and Society Review*, **17**, 239 ff.

Wollschläger, C. (1989) 'Die Arbeit der europäischen Zivilgerichte im historischen und internationalen Vergleich, Zeitreihen der europäischen Zivilprozesstatistik seit dem 19. Jahrhundert' in Blankenburg (1989), 21–114.

4 Puzzling Out Legal Culture: A Comment on Blankenburg[1]

David Nelken

> Litigation rates unfortunately are at best an ambiguous measure of almost anything, including legal culture. (Hamilton and Sanders, 1992:189)

The major problem facing the student of legal culture is how to distinguish, conceptually as well as empirically, the interconnected categories of law, social structure and culture so as to develop 'theories and concepts that can highlight the distinctive role or significance of cultural factors' (Rokumoto, 1995). One promising route (though not the only one) to understanding legal culture is to examine it in comparative perspective. The search for similarities and differences in the meaning, significance and behaviour of law in different settings should make it easier to clarify what sense we should give to the term 'legal culture' and the role it could play in our explanations. But following the route of comparative enquiry is not without its special difficulties (Nelken, 1994; 1995). What are we comparing when we compare cultures or legal cultures? Should our unit of comparison be single institutions, communities, countries, the world society? What about cultural differences within countries – between areas, age groups, classes and genders or classes? How does legal culture relate to wider culture? Is comparison a question of explaining or of translating? Last, but not least, how far is it possible to avoid our definition of legal culture being already marked by the culture of the observer so that it reflects the situation in some societies better than others?

Blankenburg's Puzzle

Many of these problems are raised by the writings of Erhard Blankenburg, which are amongst the most important recent contributions to the field of comparative sociology of law in Europe. This chapter will mainly be offering an extended commentary on his contribution to this volume,[2] though it will also make use of his valuable work on Dutch legal culture (Blankenburg and Bruinsma, 1991; 1994).[3] In Chapter 3, Blankenburg describes what he calls a sort of 'natural experiment' in which differences in wider cultures are reduced to the minimum so as to demonstrate the (measurable) difference made by distinctive legal cultures. His puzzle, as he puts it, concerns why Germany should have one of the highest levels of litigation in Europe, whereas Holland has one of the lowest. The two regions of Holland and Germany which he compares offer an ideal set-up for socio-legal comparison because of their social similarities and legal commonalties. By eliminating as far as possible differences in legal rules and social structural factors – as well as gross differences of general culture – it becomes possible to see the specific influence of *legal* culture in relation to the use of legal institutions.

Blankenburg offers us a careful, detailed analysis of the special factors which apply to different types of legal business in each country, paying special attention to what he categorizes as 'filters' and 'alternatives to litigation'. His major empirical claim concerns the importance of what he calls the 'supply side' as the key to legal culture. The relatively low litigation rate in Holland can best be explained by the way legal institutions and actors are organized so as to encourage a preference for avoiding or finding alternatives to the use of courts as dispute resolvers.

This chapter considers the implications of Blankenburg's arguments for the comparative study of legal culture (and so it will not be concerned with the details of his painstaking analysis of patterns of litigation in neighbouring regions of Holland and Germany). Unfortunately, however, to a large extent the target of his attack seems to be the taken-for-granted protocols of comparative law scholarship rather than the discipline of the sociology of law itself. He well demonstrates the importance of the 'law in action' by showing the great variation in court use in two civil law countries which have very similar traditions of substantive and procedural law, and trenchantly criticizes the neglect by many comparative scholars of 'infrastructural' institutions which lead only a fugitive existence in the written record. Interesting as they are, however, these points would not count as controversial within the sociology of law. Instead, the following are taken to be the main implications of his study for the comparative sociological study of legal culture:

1 litigation rates can serve as useful (measurable) indicators of legal culture;
2 legal culture can be studied without reference to meaning;

3. the 'supply side' of legal culture, and in particular the institutional shape of legal infrastructure, is more likely to yield a satisfactory explanation than 'demand-side' factors for patterns of legal behaviour such as litigation rates;
4. 'there is no legal culture outside existing legal institutions': the influence of 'folk' or general cultural mentalities may therefore safely be ignored;
5. we need to open up 'the black box' of legal culture so as to reveal (infra)structural influences on the choice to use law.

After examining each of these propositions critically we will relate Blankenburg's approach to legal culture to current debates in the comparative sociology of law. As will be seen, in general, our uneasiness with Blankenburg's contribution arises from the fear that his focus on empirical measures of legal culture may distort our understanding of the relationship between legal culture and culture more generally. As Blankenburg himself shows in his book-length study of Dutch legal culture, not all that counts about culture can itself be counted. This considerably reduces the sense and the purposes for which litigation rates can be used as indicators of legal culture, unless we are already familiar with the cultures under examination.

Litigation Rates as 'Indicators' of Legal Culture

What does Blankenburg mean by 'legal culture'? How can rates of litigation serve as indicators? Blankenburg (1994b) proposes that we should think of legal culture neither in terms of codified law nor as the mentality of legal actors, rather we should treat it as a 'multilayered concept'. Our aim should be to study the interrelationship between such different levels (of analysis) as legal norms/law in the books; the characteristics and behaviour of legal institutions; legal consciousness amongst legal professionals and the public; and their behaviour in creating, using and not using law. The point of Blankenburg's intervention in the debate over legal culture may also be better appreciated by seeing those positions he opposes. On the one hand, he is critical of Lawrence Friedman's influential approach to legal culture which focuses on social attitudes and the way social interests are translated into law (see, for example, Friedman, 1975; 1985; 1990; 1994) because it allegedly gives too much importance to the 'demand' side in shaping the behaviour of legal institutions. On the other hand, Blankenburg is also out of sympathy with those approaches which argue that law constructs its environment by reproducing its own elements, such as Luhmann and Teubner's theorizing of law as an autopoietic system; he is not interested in describing how the law 'thinks' (Teubner, 1989). What he wants to explain is how the supply of legal institutions shapes the social environment of demand for their services.

Blankenburg claims that his comprehensive concept of legal culture is the one which is most appropriate for comparative work; other definitions of legal culture (such as Friedman's) might be more appropriate, he suggests, for studying the phenomenon of legal culture *within* a given society (Blankenburg, 1994b). But in Chapter 3 of the present volume, Blankenburg is *not* in fact interested in characterizing the way different cultures fit together. On the other hand, Friedman's definition of legal culture can lend itself just as well also to comparative enquiry (see, for example, Hamilton and Sanders, 1992).

This creates some potential for confusion. Do we want to find legal culture at the end of our investigation or use it as a means of explaining something else? It could certainly be argued that, in principle, the concept of 'legal culture' would play one role where it is taken as a (separable) variable which can be used to explain 'variance' in social behaviour between one or other cultural setting, but quite another where it is itself seen as something to be explained or described hermeneutically, as an aspect of the way different elements of a given culture fit or 'resonate' together. In this latter case, 'legal culture' is less an explanatory term and more the name we give to the patterns we find or invoke. There is no reason why the goal of explanation in one investigation could not itself serve as part of the explanation in a different inquiry. But, as Cotterrell argues in this volume, confusion can easily result from combining such different uses of the term 'legal culture'. In any case, what Blankenburg is most keen to attack is any concept of legal culture which identifies it with the idea of *general cultural mentalities*.

This alternative definition is still very much alive. For Rokumoto (1995: 14), for example, legal culture is 'rather than the sum total of the characteristic features of a society's legal system, legal machinery, legal behaviour and legal consciousness, what gives certain common systematic features to them'. The problem is to know what methods we should adopt to discover the secrets of culture. We can of course conduct interviews with selected members of the society (see, for example, Hamilton and Sanders, 1992). But whose views should we set out to interpret?[4] And why should our respondents be assumed to know the secrets of culture (Sperber, 1985), especially if these depend on comparative reflection? Another strategy is to direct our attention to key, almost 'untranslatable', terms and phrases – as in Rokumoto's examples of Japanese notions of law and its place as expressed through specific concepts of obligation, contract, dispute sincerity, right, harmony, consultation and consensus (Rokumoto, 1995), Nelken's comparison of *fiducia* and 'trust' in comparing criminal justice in Britain and Italy (Nelken, 1994), Zedner's exposition of *innere sicherheit* as the clue to German thinking about law and order (Zedner, 1995) or Blankenburg's own discussion of *beleid* (Blankenburg and Bruinsma, 1994: 63–75) as a 'peculiarly Dutch' concept. But this solution may only fudge the methodological difficulties insofar as it allows us to impose our interpretations without asking who uses such terms, when and for what purposes.

Blankenburg does make some gesture even in the present volume towards characterizing total cultures (when talking of 'high litigation avoidance' or 'low litigation avoidance' cultures). But he describes the hermeneutic approach as insufficiently 'scientific' (Blankenburg, 1994b) for the purpose of explaining what lies behind the pattern of litigation in each of the countries he compares. Because he is so firmly committed to explaining, as opposed to merely interpreting or translating, other legal cultures, his real concern here is to find 'indicators' of legal culture. Only by using 'indicators' and confining himself to objective variables (behaviour and not 'consciousness') will it become possible to measure differences in culture. But because his definition of legal culture is so broad his argument is not free from ambiguity. It is not clear, for example, whether legal culture is the *explanation* of the filters and alternatives which Blankenburg sees as characterizing Dutch 'law in action', or merely the name we give to such patterns of litigation and avoidance (in which case it would be tautologous to use this as part of any explanation).

Indicators, for Blankenburg, both hint at and constitute legal culture. But the boundaries between these roles are not always made clear. On the one hand, he is surely right to argue that we can and must search for measurable indicators of legal culture if we are to use this concept in empirical research. Evidence of levels of crime, of litigation, of alternative means of settlement, of delays before trial, of the numbers of lawyers and the numbers of people in prison may all be relevant to arguments about legal culture. On the other hand, however, the problem of finding reliable cross-cultural criteria for isolating and identifying such variables for the purpose of demonstrating similarities or differences in legal culture is not merely technical. Such variables as rates of crime or litigation are already the product of (unknown) cultural processes which make it misleading to use them to explain cultural differences. Thus it would be mistaken to use differences in crime rates in different societies as measures of trust (assuming that high crime rates signalled lack of trust in society) if that factor was also instrumental in shaping the level of reporting of crime to authorities in the first place, so that where there was less trust less crime was reported. Likewise litigation rates, unless we have other means of interpreting them, cannot provide a reliable indicator of culture (Hamilton and Sanders, 1992: 192ff).

To this type of objection, Blankenburg replies that indicators are always of value for heuristic reasons; if we come up against apparent 'incommensurabilities' in cultural definitions of law, lawyers, courts and so on, it is exactly this which should provoke us to further enquiry. The problem, of course, is how to know in advance whether our indicators are valid. Blankenburg wants to use litigation rates as indicators but he also finds them of interest because they are puzzling. Perhaps we should say, then, that litigation and other measures of legal culture are puzzling (but ambiguous) indicators. Blankenburg has shown us that one of the places to look to resolve such puzzlement may be the pattern of legal infrastructure. But others might say that he has only given us one more reason to confirm our suspicions that litigation rates may not represent a reliable measure of litigiousness. He has not shown that this is always the right place to find the key to legal culture, nor even that litigation rates can be used to explain culture, rather than vice versa. Deciding the suitability of a given indicator, or the equivalence between indicators in different cultures, requires considerable tacit knowledge of the cultures being compared. Once this tacit knowledge (or assumption of equivalence) is brought out into the open, comparison is again forced to become a matter of interpretation rather than measurement. The competition between positivist and hermeneutic methodologies remains open.

Culture Without Meaning

Blankenburg's argument relies on an eclectic mix of the mainstream approaches to explanation which are employed in the empirical social sciences;[5] it combines in particular elements of behaviourism, positivism and functionalism. Choosing methods which are favoured by these approaches allows him to conduct a 'natural experiment' which measures culture with an empirical specificity and concreteness contrasting sharply with the common vices of vagueness or even circularity in discussions of culture. But this strategy also has severe drawbacks in capturing the nuances of cultural meaning. If these approaches to culture enhance the possibilities of measurement, by the same token they stumble when it comes to unmeasurable aspects of cultural ideas and meanings.

Blankenburg's project in Chapter 3 is to search for the key to legal culture through the explanation of different rates of *legal behaviour*. To what extent does this make him a behaviourist? Donald Black, an out-and-out sociological behaviourist, depicts culture quite broadly as the 'symbolic aspect of social life' which includes 'expressions of what is true, good or beautiful, ideas about the nature of reality, ideology, morality, law and aesthetic life'

(1976: 61–83). In order to adhere to his epistemology, however, Black is obliged to examine culture somewhat mechanically in terms of levels of complexity, scales of conventionality and unconventionality, and cultural distance. Culture, he argues, exists apart from the way people experience it, it appears in every social setting and it varies in quantity and style from place to place. Because 'it behaves' it is possible to predict and explain it, and to explain social life with culture and any one aspect of culture with another. Blankenburg's interest in explaining patterns of litigation has some similarity with Black's ambitions, but his allegiance to behaviourism is by no means as extreme. He does not, for example, follow Black's reductive definition of law as 'government social control', but rather treats law as a variety of actions directed towards or by legal institutions. Given the importance of measurement to Blankenburg's argument, however, it would certainly have been helpful to have more clarification of what counts as legal behaviour and what counts as avoidance (when does avoidance count as a supplement and when as an alternative to law?). If we compare his approach to that of Black it is uncertain, for example, whether the avoidance of litigation represents *more* or *less* government social control. Blankenburg normally writes as if he shares Black's view that the fewer steps taken towards a court solution the less law. On the other hand, he also sometimes concedes that the low use of litigation in Holland may be explained by the high level of government social regulation which makes it unnecessary to use the courts to vindicate rights: thus low litigation rates could be correlated with more rather than less law.

Despite his use of the word 'behaviour', Blankenburg is well aware that social life consists of *action* rather than mere behaviour. In seeking to explain *legal action* he does refer to the motives of social actors in using or avoiding court, just as he sees legal provisions and procedures as altering the structure of incentives of rational actors' behaviour. But he tends to imply that actors' rationalities can be deduced from the incentives available (Chapter 3 reports no actual attempt to ask actors the reasons for their use of the law). In general he chooses to prioritize behaviour over ideas or, at least, action over words. Blankenburg rightly argues for the importance of studying legal behaviour (especially that which is not recorded in documents and which refers to paralegal activity) because it is a neglected aspect of legal culture which can only be recovered by empirical sociology. But his focus on behaviour is not merely a matter of tactics. More generally, he wants to get right away from any approach to culture which sees it as a coherent 'system of beliefs' shaping the law. Thus, in attacking Friedman's approach to legal culture, he makes the surprising assertion that 'there is no evidence [*sic*] that the legal system expresses the notions that a dominant group in society has about what is just' (Blankenburg, 1994b; cf. Blankenburg, 1994a:791).

The prioritization of legal behaviour seems to rest on the assumption that 'actions speak louder than words': that we should give more credence to what people do than to what they say. But this 'realist' definition of law begs the question whether or not law does 'behave' and avoids questioning the limits of such a philosophical and sociological conception of law (Benda-Beckmann, 1983). In general, there is a sense in which culture could be said to be more about normative expectations than about behaviourist descriptions.[6] But the correspondence between norms and action also varies by culture. For some legal cultures, for example those of Latin America, Blankenburg's stress on legal behaviour would be particularly misleading (see, for example, Lopez-Ayllòn, 1995; Rosenne, 1971). What is held to be of most importance in these legal cultures may often be found only in words rather than practice; and this just because it does not (yet) have a place in the world of practice! Blankenburg's approach cannot help us understand the way culture binds words and deeds together, even or especially where they are inconsistent or contradictory (cf. Garapon, 1995).

Some of the disregard of culture as meaning in Blankenburg's argument which we have been characterizing as behaviourist could equally well be said to be merely a result of his faithfully following the scientific prescriptions of positivist methodology. The influence of positivist thinking in Blankenburg's work is reflected in a number of features of his argument: his starting-point of seeking to explain the stability (or alleged stability) over time of different patterns of litigation; the device of conducting a 'natural experiment' to solve the 'riddle' of such differences; and the way he freezes the meaning of terms such as 'dispute' or 'potentially litigious conflicts', as if such 'social facts' could be anything other than ambiguous and reflexive measures with insecure cross-cultural validity. As with all positivist writing, the scholar is presented as if he or she is without culture, offering 'a view from nowhere'. By limiting his main comparison to two countries (Holland and Germany) he knows well 'from the inside', Blankenburg avoids the more obvious howlers that one gets in cross-cultural comparison of disparate countries (Nelken, 1994). But criticism *can* be made of his wider discussion of litigation rates in expounding the too all-embracing category of 'legal avoidance cultures'. His claim that Denmark and Netherlands, on the one hand, combine general trust in judicial institutions with an infrastructure of less formal, alternative procedures, whereas 'in the Latin countries of southern Europe avoidance is interpreted as a reaction to the mistrust of politicized and inefficient courts', makes one wonder *who* 'interprets' legal behaviour in this way. Blankenburg's investigation obviously is not and cannot be free from domain assumptions shaped by his national and academic culture(s). Is it safe to assume that economic growth necessarily leads to an increase in litigation?[7] Why does he concentrate on explaining (away) Dutch litigation rates? Why does he not find it as, or more, strange that in Germany *so many* cases do go to court? How far does this attitude to expected litigation rates reflect the academic culture of the 'law and society' movement with its American bias?

The fact that Blankenburg concentrates on behaviour does not mean that he can actually avoid attributing meaning. In particular, he assumes that a means–ends, instrumental attitude to litigation is shared by the members of each culture whose behaviour he is explaining. Thus he rejects explanations based on 'folk mentality' by arguing (rather than showing) that different levels of court use are rational once we take into account the different structure of 'incentives' and 'deterrents' for using or avoiding the courts. If it is difficult to reconcile this reductivist approach to motivations with the variety of possible reasons for using and avoiding courts even in Holland and Germany it is still less plausible as the key to other legal cultures.

The third approach which Blankenburg employs is functionalism. Those who engage in comparative work often find it convenient to assume that legal institutions have identifiable functions and that the aim of comparison is to identify which other institution in the other society is acting as its 'functional equivalent'.[8] This often goes together with some vague idea of an equilibrium: societies may be said, for example, to require a certain amount of social control – an increase in formal social control therefore tends to accompany a decrease in 'informal social control' (Black, 1976). Blankenburg, too, presupposes that every society of a certain economic complexity is bound to generate a certain number of disputes. He is puzzled about the use of courts in Holland, not just in comparison to Germany but also in its own terms. How is it possible, he enquires, that the lawyers and an extensive welfare state do not generate high levels of litigation? His answer is that the infrastructure of the filters and alternatives, which for him characterize Dutch as compared to German legal culture, has the *function* of replacing the need to resort to court litigation.

The assumption of 'functional equivalence' is particularly insidious in this study because it is never spelled out. It is sufficient for Blankenburg to claim that the level of demand for courts must be treated as a constant as between these countries for it to follow that the alternatives to court processing in Holland must be functional alternatives to litigation in Germany. But the assumption of functional equivalence across cultures (whatever institution is concerned) is always questionable; what counts as an alternative or 'supplement' is itself culturally contingent. We could just as well say that it is the *different* function of the court in Holland which means that the availability of lawyers and welfare legislation leads to less litigation. In another society (including Germany) the alternatives which Blankenburg in explaining the low rate of litigation in Holland could easily refer to lead to greater litigation.

However apparently plausible, the differences which functionalist accounts purport to explain in terms of the presence of alternative institutions may often be better seen as a result of historical developments. Avoidance of law may not always signal the presence of satisfactory 'informal' alternatives – it can instead represent a deliberate choice to avoid legal procedures which have been experienced historically as an oppressive force (Shapiro, 1976). Even in the present case study comparing Holland and Germany, the relative absence of an infrastructure of alternatives to courts in Germany may be partially explained as the effort to reject the excessive resort to extra-ordinary forms of legal arbitration which characterized the Nazi period (Marsh, 1946/1992). Other changes which crucially affect the use of the courts, such as trends towards 'juridifiction' or in favour of 'informalism', are more the result of social and political struggles than they are of self-adjusting functional requirements. Crucially, they are often 'imported' as a result of intellectual fashion, from other countries where the level of use of courts may be quite different. The belief that countries must find 'functional equivalents' to deal with their similar problems thus underestimates the power of culture to shape whether problems are recognized as such and what will be taken to count as 'solutions'. This point is all the more telling when we consider how much Blankenburg's own argument seeks to underline the power of the 'supply side' to condition legal culture.

Supply and Demand in the Explanation of Legal Culture

Blankenburg wants to do more than simply draw attention to the necessity to examine the role of legal infrastructure in explaining the considerable difference in rates of litigation between neighbouring regions of Germany and Holland. His central argument is that this variable is *sufficient* to explain the difference between the two countries; legal behaviour is essentially 'conditioned' by the supply of possibilities, what he calls 'the sets of institutional arrangements and patterns of professional interaction'.

Blankenburg asserts rather than documents the basis for this claim. The irrelevance of the demand side is *presupposed*, Blankenburg simply *dismisses* rather than actually disproves the counter-hypothesis that differences in demand could actually be the explanation for the variation in litigation rates.[9] There is 'no reason to think', he says, 'that there is greater willingness to litigate on the part of the Germans as compared to the Dutch, so we must therefore look to the *supply* side of legal culture'. His 'natural experiment' is set up to exclude demand-side factors; it starts from the presupposition that there is no reason to consider that there could be a difference in willingness to go to court between German and Dutch citizens living in adjoining and economically interdependent territories. We are given no evidence about the *potential* rate of litigation apart from reference to the inevitable incidence in modern industrial societies of similar events such as car and industrial accidents. But this in itself proves nothing – it would only be a plausible starting-point if we were already convinced of the unimportance of legal consciousness in translating grievances or disputes (what he calls 'potentially litigious conflicts') into legal claims or controversies. Given that we know that highly developed countries such as Japan do not necessarily have litigation rates which parallel their level of industrial activity, all this is rather begging the question.

This also means that we cannot be certain how far Blankenburg would apply his argument to other societies beyond the two compared in his case study i.e. societies which do have differences on the demand side. But his 'natural experiment' would certainly lose much of its point if its implications were limited to legal behaviour in Holland and Germany. There are also other reasons why his is not an easy argument to put to the test. Whilst it is undeniable that the choice to litigate is likely to be influenced by court structures and alternative routes to settlement, this is far from proving that it is the supply side as such which creates legal culture. It is also unclear how the contrast between supply and demand relates to the better known contrast between 'internal legal culture' (that of the professionals) and 'external legal culture' (that of the lay public, including individuals, groups and organizations). Blankenburg is not proposing simply to reverse the relative importance which Lawrence Friedman (1975) assigns to 'external' as opposed to 'internal' legal culture; he seems more concerned to examine the way the two cultures interact. For the purposes of argument, however, given his frequently expressed disagreement with those who privilege the demand side of legal culture,[10] it seems reasonable to take him as arguing that legal culture (at least in the narrow sense of legal behaviour) is predominantly shaped by supply rather than by demand.

There is much to be said in favour of putting the emphasis on the 'supply side' of legal culture in explaining differences in litigation rates. Rates of crime, litigation and so on inevitably represent measures, in the first instance, of the activities of legal agencies which produce them, and only indirectly describe what is going on in the wider culture (though, just for that reason, they may prove crude indicators of the 'interrelationships' between 'supply' and 'demand' and require supplementation by other evidence). There is also considerable evidence that litigation rates are affected by problems of access and the cost of going to court. For example, it has been argued that the much lower level of tort cases which go to court in England as compared to Western Germany, despite the roughly similar levels of economic activity and welfare provision, is due to the fact that

German courts are more plaintiff-oriented and 'user-friendly' (Markensinis, 1990). Blankenburg has valuably enriched this line of argument with his examination of filters and alternatives to court in the Netherlands.

On the other hand, unlike Blankenburg, scholars who focus on litigation rates usually also try to factor in the part played by variation in demand. Markensinis, for example, commenting on the current growth in medical negligence cases in Britain, suggests that 'the national reluctance to sue, where it exists, may be weakening where there is greater activity by pro-consumer groups and easy access to legal aid' (Markensinis, 1990: 262–3). Though Blankenburg wants to confine Friedman's assertions concerning the importance of the demand side in shaping legal culture to the United States (Blankenburg, 1994b), Inge Markovits, another acute observer of comparative legal culture, has no difficulty in equating American and German legal culture in terms of the importance of the demand side in *both* countries: 'Americans and Germans', she argues 'whether represented by lawyers or assisted by judges, "go to law" to defend their interests. Both countries are saturated with law' (Markovits, 1989:1327). In the United States, scholars of 'everyday justice' have increasingly come to stress how even lower-class groups make strategic use of courts (Merry, 1990; Sarat and Kearns, 1993; Silbey, 1992; Yngevesson, 1993). The question remains why Blankenburg should obstinately insist on seeing differences in the use of courts as only reflecting supply-side factors.

Blankenburg presumably insists on drawing a clear line between the demand and supply sides of legal culture so as to be able to reject explanations of differences in litigation rates based on differences in national character or 'folk mentality'. But reading Blankenburg's own accounts of Dutch legal culture reveals many ways in which the distinction between supply and demand breaks down. He argues at some length, for example, that different explanations are required for types of cases such as landlord–tenant disputes, debt collection or traffic accidents which are processed by insurance companies. In part these differences do relate to the supply side. Litigation is used less for collecting debts in Holland because there bailiffs are trusted to follow their own methods. Building construction cases are organized in Holland so as to avoid court cases. Landlord and tenant cases are sidelined there to filtering processes of mediation. Traffic accidents, the vast majority of which avoid ending up in court in either country, are less likely to be taken to court by insurance companies in Holland than in Germany because of the different incentive structures. But the same points could as well have been discussed in terms of demand. In general, those who go to court rarely, those whom Galanter calls 'one-shotters' (Galanter, 1974), can be simply sidelined to alternative institutions, but Galanter calls 'repeat players' (such as insurance companies) *choose* the cheapest and most effective methods of routinizing their cases. Even in his own terms, Blankenburg's contrast between supply and demand must therefore be modified to find a place for this acknowledgement of the importance of the relative power of the parties.

Even Blankenburg admits that legal professionals in Holland and Germany have different attitudes to the use of law, but he would have us believe that this is not so amongst the general or mass public. Since legal professionals, presumably, constitute part of the supply side of the equation, this should not affect his argument. But why should private lawyers, acting for their individual or corporate clients, not be seen as much as part of the demand side? Perhaps it will be said that the client has little leverage compared to the power legal and other professionals have to define the role law plays in social disputes. But this surely must depend in part on client assertiveness and their consciousness of rights. Even Blankenburg has to concede that organized groups (or the lack of them) influence institutional possibilities. Speaking about Dutch criminal justice in his book on Dutch legal culture, for example, he concedes that for a long period an elite succeeded in maintaining a tolerant stance to crime because 'no public pressure pushed them towards a more punitive policy' (Blankenburg and Bruinsma, 1994:55).

Thus the presence or absence of such demand-side pressures always needs to be *accounted for* rather than defined out of the concept of legal culture. To do this we also need to distinguish the different levels of supply and demand influences. The supply-side explanation may be appropriate if at the highest – hegemonic – level it has proved possible to gain the consensus or at least acquiescence of a sufficient proportion of the population to shape their demands in the appropriate forms and forums. For example, if bailiffs are allowed to enforce debt collection in Holland (but not in Germany) without passing through the courts, as much as reflecting supply-side differences (the existence of alternatives to court procedures), as Blankenburg argues, this may betray the remarkable willingness to trust authorities on the part of Dutch citizens (a demand-side factor). In general, if Dutch political elites have succeeded in mobilizing consensus to the type of legal system that exists, could it not be said that this is because they have in part incorporated relevant features of the demand side?

A final problem with trying to establish the relative importance to be given to either side of the supply and demand equation is the way this focus on efficient means of resolving disputes tends to shift attention from the more fundamental question of the extent to which *this way* of looking at law *is also part of the legal cultures being examined*. We would need to think carefully about the considerable cultural variability that could limit the applicability of such a perspective in comparative work. There are some relevant differences in the philosophies and practices amongst civil law and common law countries in European systems insofar as they endorse an instrumental or party-controlled approach to litigation as an ideal (see Ferrarese in the present volume). Further afield, it is highly doubtful that the way courts are so often used to perpetuate rather than resolve conflicts in India or in South East Asia can be well analysed in this framework (Baxi, 1979).

Legal Culture versus General Culture

The largest claim that Blankenburg makes on the basis of his comparison of litigation rates in Holland and Germany has to do with the lack of connection between legal culture and cultural consciousness more generally. This thesis is certainly the one which has the greatest potential implications for the comparative sociology of law, but it is also the most difficult to accept.

Once again, there is room for disagreement over what Blankenburg is arguing. Put at its strongest, the message of Blankenburg's comparison seems to be that paying attention to legal infrastructure makes it *unnecessary* to resort to talk about general culture in explaining legal culture. Once we trace differences in the infrastructure of legal culture, he argues, we can make sense of the greater or lesser resort to litigation on either side of the German–Dutch border, even if we rule out all cultural variation. We can simply assume that actors are using what he describes as 'the same strategic rationalities' in weighing up the decision to go to court. General culture is of secondary importance in shaping legal behaviour as compared to the institutional fabric of supply-side considerations. As he puts it, 'there is no legal culture outside existing legal institutions'; the key to litigation frequencies will not be found in 'folk mentalities', or even in an effort to establish 'what powerful people think is just' – the place to look must be the organization of these institutions themselves.

Others have also taken Blankenburg to be setting out to make such a large claim, even if they put the point slightly differently. The editor of the *Law and Society Review* (in which the larger part of Blankenburg's chapter recently appeared), summarized his study as follows: 'we have been too quick to assume that legal behaviour (such as litigation) is a direct expression of general culture. He argues instead that a variety of institutional forms are compatible with a particular culture and can have a pronounced effect on legal behaviour' (Munger, 1994: 726). Here, rather than assuming that Blankenburg is arguing for an essential gulf between general culture and legal culture, Munger takes him only to have shown that legal behaviour is not a 'direct' expression of general culture. What is not clear on this reading is in what way legal behaviour is only an indirect expression – and why it should have such relative autonomy. As Munger puts it, infrastructural variation can have important effects on 'legal behaviour' but he does not go as far as Blankenburg clearly does in identifying such behaviour as itself an indicator of legal culture. Finally, Munger talks cautiously of drawing the lesson that different institutional forms are 'compatible with' a particular culture, but he does not specify what he means either by 'compatibility' or by 'culture'.

Munger seems (understandably) uncertain about the exact counter-hypothesis concerning legal culture and general culture which Blankenburg's dismissal of folk culture explanations is intended to rebut. It is difficult to know what weight to assign to general culture when Blankenburg *chooses* to compare two countries which, he claims, have similar cultures. Once again, Blankenburg offers us a clever experiment in which the differentiating role of general culture is allegedly ruled out *a priori*, forcing us to look elsewhere for the explanation of variations in legal culture. But treating culture as a constant makes it more difficult to establish the type of relationships which potentially obtains in other situations. In fact, even in Holland and Germany, the influence of general culture may be extremely important in (directly) shaping a series of assumptions about the role and meaning of law in these countries, *as compared to assumptions existing in other countries* (even if it is unable to account for the difference in litigation rates between them). If Blankenburg's claim about the indirect importance of general culture only applies to the countries compared in his case study because of their similarity in general culture,[11] why does he choose to concentrate on such anomalous cases? Arguably, a more fruitful method which he could have used to establish his point would have been to choose a sample of widely *differing* cultures so as to examine whether (or how far) the factor of legal infrastructure nonetheless proved determinant in explaining legal behaviour.[12]

Leaving these perplexities aside, does it make any sense in principle to drive a wedge between legal culture and general culture? Just as legal culture would surely form part of any definition of the wider culture, so it is difficult to imagine any extensive project of comparing legal cultures which did not also show the way they were directly and indirectly shaped by larger political, economic and intellectual aspects of the culture(s) of which they formed a part. Blankenburg cannot really be denying this (or was his 'natural experiment' designed to solve a puzzle at the expense of creating a conundrum?). What is he really asserting about the nature of the relationship between general culture and legal culture? Certainly, he has avoided the tautology of explaining cultural variation by itself (as in arguing that the Dutch have low litigation rates because they belong to a 'non-legalistic culture'.) But does he merely fall into the opposite error of reducing culture to strategic action in institutional contexts?

The question of the relationship between general culture and legal culture obviously takes us well beyond the issue of whether 'folk culture' offers a satisfactory explanation of litigation rates. The fascinating account Blankenburg himself offers us in his book on Dutch legal culture is the best evidence of the way legal behaviour cannot be separated from a wider consideration of culture. He has no difficulty in that book in describing law as a (more or less) direct expression of culture. He is quite explicit, for example, concerning the need to treat the changing face of civil and criminal justice in Holland as a dependent variable of much broader political developments tied to the 'pillarization' and 'depillarization' (i.e. the breakdown of the established system of power-sharing between vertically integrated political, social and religious groupings) of Dutch society. He talks generally of the 'Dutch culture of muddling through from compromise to compromise', arguing that 'the Dutch tend to be pragmatic: they use law to solve problems, not to create additional ones. If applying the rules would lead to serious disadvantages they try to find ways round them' (Blankenburg and Bruinsma, 1994: back cover). Moreover, his analysis of key terms of Dutch legal consciousness, in particular his exegesis of the term *beleid*, straddles the divide between general and legal culture. *Beleid*, he claims, reflects behaviour which is widespread in Dutch society as well as being also a technical term which has a special meaning for legal culture. Like many other crucial cultural concepts, it is neither fully translatable nor necessarily internally coherent. Broadly speaking, however, *beleid* refers to a praxis which combines paternal decision making with the effort to reach decisions by consensus. In other words, this term reflects and constitutes exactly the sort of cultural magic which allows Dutch legal culture to give the impression of reconciling supply and demand as part of its regulatory strategy.

Blankenburg has given us no good reasons to accept the irrelevance of general culture to the shaping of litigation rates. But there can of course be great variability in the extent to which legal culture does reflect general culture. Comparative sociology of law certainly needs to study cultural differences in the acceptance of alternatives to law, which probably relates to more fundamental differences in the role and rule of law. Paradoxically, however, it may be that Holland and Germany are societies which are particularly free of disjunctions between legal culture and general culture. The existence or otherwise of a wide gulf between legal and general culture is *a further important fact about the general culture*. Some cultures are more legalistic, others more pragmatic. Under the influence of religious traditions or philosophical idealism, law may sometimes be treated as more of an aspiration than a blueprint for guiding behaviour (as in some civil law countries); other societies may model their law more closely on what is already considered reasonable behaviour by the wider culture (as in some common law jurisdictions). Distance between law and other norms may reflect previous foreign domination, the crumbling of empires or the imposition of foreign models of law. But each case will have its peculiarities. In Italy, for example, the frequently observed distance between legal culture and general culture corresponds to that between the official rules and the unwritten agreements which constitute the ties that bind the members of civil society (Olgiati, 1985). Though this, too, is in part the consequence of a heritage of assorted foreign rulers, it has by now become a constitutive part of a political culture in which the capacity to translate paper rights into effective benefits provides leverage for a series of political mediators from local politicians to organized criminals (Nelken 1996a; 1996b). In Japan, on the other hand, the reluctance to reinstitutionalize customary rules as legal rules reflects an ambiguous approach to the cultural implications of legal modernism (Hamilton and Sanders, 1992: 32).

Opening up the 'Cultural Black Box'?

Faced with the different possible interpretations which can be given to Blankenburg's study of litigation rates, it may be helpful to try to rethink what he may have been aiming to achieve. Why does he try to contrast legal culture and general culture? Why does he not just argue that general culture *expresses itself* through the institutional structures and infrastructures on which he would have us concentrate? (What is gained and what is lost by defining the infrastructure itself as legal culture?) We may come nearer to answering these questions if we reconsider Blankenburg's proposal in relation to current developments in comparative sociology of law (rather than as a critique of comparative law scholarship). The most relevant discussions for this purpose (some of which are cited by Blankenburg) are found in the continuing debate over what represents the best interpretation of *Japanese* legal culture, and in particular whether or not institutional and structural explanations for the low rate of Japanese litigation are to be preferred to older explanations which appealed to 'cultural mentalities'. The founders of sociology of law in that country initially argued that Japan's low rate of litigation was due to a *cultural* disposition to avoid conflicts (Kawashima, 1963[13]). Taking aim at this conventional wisdom, John Owen Haley argued that the low use of courts in Japan was a result rather of *structural factors* which included deterrents built into the legal structure, the procedures of the courts and bureaucratic and government policy (Haley, 1978; 1991). Haley denied that Japanese people had a special legal consciousness which included traits of reluctance to litigate or a preference for informal mediated settlement. According to him they rationally calculated the costs and benefits of suing; it was the behaviour of the judicial system which had failed to persuade Japanese people of the utility of using it. Blankenburg's examination of the differences between Germany and Holland thus seems to take up this same theme of structure versus culture. He clearly comes down on the side of the structuralists, strongly rejecting alternative explanations based on 'folk mentality'. What somewhat obscures the link to this previous debate, however, is the way he then goes on to call these *structural* features themselves indicators of 'legal culture'.[14]

One way of capturing the contribution Blankenburg wants to make to the debate about legal culture could be to borrow the language of Patricia Steinhoff in her review of writing about Japanese legal culture (Steinhoff, 1993). Praising the classic Japanese observation study of the police by Setsuo Miyazawa (1992), she argues that its careful analysis of the way the police go about their investigative tasks helped to 'open up the cultural black box and understand the institutional realities that constrain the choices people make. This approach does not treat people as cultural ducks following imprinted values but rather as thoughtful agents who create, reproduce and transform their culture in a dynamic and complex fashion' (Steinhoff, 1993: 829). Blankenburg chooses to call such 'institutional realities' an aspect of legal culture, rather than treat them as a competing explanation for legal behaviour. But his stress on the strategic rationality of decisions to litigate and his rejection of folk culture as an explanation of behaviour is in substantial keeping with Steinhoff's critique of resort to culture as the explanation for social action (a critique which goes back at least to Malinowski's attack on Durkheim: Malinowski, 1926/1962).

If this is what Blankenburg is getting at, it may be helpful to see what has been said (or could be said) on the other side of the argument.[15] An important issue here concerns what it means to talk about behaviour as shaped by culture. Is this necessarily the opposite of strategically rational instrumental action? How far does it carry overtones of non-rational, irrational or at least 'altruistic' behaviour?[16] Pointing to culture does suggest that the behaviour in question is shaped by past collective experience rather than chosen afresh. And there are those who would remind us not to underestimate the influence of such experience. David Bayley, for example (one of those whose work was reviewed), replied to Steinhoff's criticism by claiming that 'appealing to legal culture is not always unintelligent reductionism, socialisation does make a difference to the behavioral propensities that people carry into situations' (Bayley, 1994: 963–4). But it should also be added that it is not only 'dopes' who follow the rules of culture. It is perfectly possible that under most conditions this is also the most strategic line to take.

One of the most thorough discussions of the culture – structure debate is found at the end of Hamilton and Sanders' comparative study. They too remain unconvinced by the attack of the structuralists. But more specifically, they particularly criticize the tendency to try to build accounts of legal culture by confining attention to litigation behaviour rather than looking more widely. According to them, 'a focus on litigation rates fundamentally biases the legal culture/legal structure debate' because it forces us to look at culture in the narrow context of individuals' decision to sue, and at court structure as the environment in which such a decision is made. This tends wrongly to equate culture explanations with micro processes (= decisions) and structural explanations with macro processes (Hamilton and Sanders, 1992: 192). By studying attitudes to law at the point where something has gone wrong and not where things are going smoothly, we miss the chance to see that people might *prefer* (and not merely endure) a system which discourages the assertion of individual rights against the collectivity where other methods of settlement are possible. In terms which turn Blankenburg's conclusions on their head, they therefore go on to insist that 'the discussion of legal culture must move beyond litigation and litigation rates to a larger set of attitudes, beliefs and values. The boundaries of legal culture are not encompassed by a micro-process concern about whether Japanese litigants behave as economically rational individuals when they litigate' (Hamilton and Sanders, 1992:195). Their own comparative investigation of popular conceptions of the responsible actor in the United States and in Japan was intended in fact to serve as a bridge between general cultural values (such as views of the self) and specific attitudes towards litigation.

Hamilton and Sanders argue that legal culture is not solely a micro process that determines the result of a particular dispute but something which constrains possible legal systems as well as specific legal outcomes. It is the interaction of macro structure and macro culture which creates a legal system. The critical question thus becomes the dynamic relationship between structure and culture. For them, 'legal culture legitimises and supports legal structural arrangements and together these macro processes constrain the alternatives available in the microlevel processing of particular disputes' (Hamilton and Sanders, 1992:198). There is thus a circular relationship between structure and culture; structural relationships affect cultural values, which in turn affect structural relationships. This mutual causality helps to create stability. Institutions and values tend to reinforce each other, though this requires constant maintenance. Japanese legal culture works to suppress a legal system that would facilitate litigation and adjudication. Despite the many differences in the two cultures, could not something similar be said about the paternalistic tendencies of Dutch legal culture (at least until very recent changes)?

The approach recommended by Hamilton and Sanders is not without its own dilemmas. Focusing on attitudes as a key to consciousness may have the unintended consequence of freezing our accounts of culture. Despite acknowledging the possibilities of change, they do tend to assume 'culturally consistent legal arrangements' which can provide a false picture even of a country like Japan (see Miyazawa, 1995). It may also be over simple to claim, as they do, that 'conceptions constrain and shape microprocesses in ways that are analogous to the constraints of macrostructural arrangements, such as the nature and availability of courts' (Hamilton and Sanders, 1992: 195.) The constraints (if this *is* the appropriate term) which flow from shared conceptions may not in fact work analogously. It seems probable that they are more likely to function at the level of taken-for-granted assumptions than as calculated responses to incentive structures. It does seem important to keep the roles of structure and culture distinct just because they are constantly interacting. Culturally patterned attitudes and behaviours may have the capacity to neutralize factors which would otherwise be expected to lead to higher litigation rates, even if eventually structural and infrastuctural variables slowly transform culture. It is by studying these processes of 'structuration', within and amongst societies (Giddens, 1976: J. Friedman, 1994), that we may best come closer to solving the puzzle of culture.

Rather than *defining* litigation rates as an indicator of legal culture, as Blankenburg does, we therefore need to think more carefully about the various ways they result from the intersection of wider cultural influences and more strictly institutional constraints. As Hamilton and Sanders rightly insist, patterns of litigation will be affected by the social relationship between the parties as well as by their wider expectations of law. But Blankenburg for his part has good reasons to argue that the outcome of disputes will also reflect more specifically the structure and infrastructure of courts and their alternatives. Some types of dispute may be inherently easier to filter out than others. But there is nothing automatic about this outcome. In particular, as Blankenburg suggests, 'repeat players', such as multinational businesses or insurance companies, as they exercise their 'strategic rationality', are more likely to be able to manipulate or neutralize the effect of local culture than 'one-shotters'. Concentrating on the behaviour of those most free from cultural influence, however, would not be the fairest way of testing for the existence of national legal cultures.

Notes

1 This is a newly revised and extended version of my paper, 'Can legal culture be measured?', presented at the Comparing Legal Cultures conference held at Macerata on 18–20 May 1994.
2 The contribution of Blankenburg in this volume combines two of the papers he presented at the Macerata workshop. A later version of the main part of this chapter was published by the *Law and Society Review*, **28**, (4), 789–809 under the title 'The Infrastructure of Legal Culture in Holland and West Germany'. As an aid to interpreting Blankenburg's argument I will also rely on another short paper (Blankenburg, 1994b) prepared for the Macerata workshop in response to my paper presented there.
3 The essay comparing German and Dutch litigation rates is reproduced as a chapter in the volume on Dutch legal culture. In that context, set alongside other ways of throwing light on Dutch legal culture, many of the criticisms set out here lose their force, but this only demonstrates how much the methodology relied on in his 'natural experiment' in fact depended on Blankenburg's tacit knowledge of Dutch culture, gained by other means, relying on what he here treats as less 'scientific' methods.
4 As Cotterrell argues in this volume, we must not beg the question whether there *is* a common cultural consciousness.
5 Blankenburg makes little reference to work in anthropology, still less does he engage with the post-modern turn in this field of writing (see, for example, Clifford and Marcus, 1986; Marcus, 1994, for an up-to-date assessment of more recent developments). Any attempt to rethink the study of legal culture in the light of these developments would take me too far from the theme of this response to Blankenburg. It would be interesting, however, to examine the relationship between Blankenburg's appeal to statistics and his reliance on other argumentative tropes in his attempt to convince us that he has first-hand knowledge of the cultures being compared.
6 Like many authors before him, Bierbrauer (1994), in his study of differences in legal culture, defines culture as 'socially transmitted norms of conduct', thus focusing on norms at least as much as behaviour.
7 In Sweden and Japan during this century, litigation rates went down as prosperity increased, largely because there was less indebtedness (Wöllschlager, 1995).
8 The same legal institution may have come historically to serve different functions in different societies, just as the same functions may be served by different legal institutions or sets of legal institutions (Renner, 1949).
9 Gibson and Caldeira (1995) do say that public opinion surveys provide some empirical support for Blankenburg's assumption. But it should be noted that these surveys relate to generalized support for what they call the values of 'liberal universalism' rather than attitudes towards litigation as such.
10 Thus Hamilton and Sanders (1992:3), following Lawrence Friedman, define legal culture as 'the attitudes values and opinion held with regard to law, the legal system and the process of holding someone accountable'. It includes attitudes about whether to take a dispute to law.
11 Blankenburg's article was placed by the Editor in a section of the journal entitled 'Legal process and civic culture: examining the link'. But in fact his paper conducts no such examination, starting as it does from the presupposition that the civic culture is so similar in Germany and Holland that it cannot serve as a sensible starting-point for seeking to solve the puzzle of the large difference in litigation rates.
12 It is this strategy which Shapiro (1981) followed in trying to show the common functions of the higher courts in cultures as different as Britain, France, China and Turkey.

13 According to Rokumoto (1995), Kawashima's ideas may have been oversimplified so as to seem more psychological and subjective and culturalist than he intended.

14 Shapiro (1980) uses the same style of argument as Blankenburg in order to establish the superiority of *institutional* over cultural explanations for Islamic legal procedure.

15 Miyazawa (1995) himself has given some signs of a move back to culturalist (or, as he calls it, neo-culturalist) accounts of Japanese legal culture, even as he continues courageously to advocate the need for change.

16 Hamilton and Sanders (1992) argue that the avoidance of courts should not be treated as the equivalent of altruism, but point out that, if all parties act altruistically, eventual settlement levels may well in any case mimic those that would have been obtained at court.

References

Baxi, U. (1979) 'People's Law, Development, Justice', *Verfassung und Recht in Ubersee*, **12**, (2), 97–114, reprinted in C. Varga (ed.), *Comparative Legal Cultures*, Aldershot: Dartmouth, 1992, pp. 465–83.

Bayley, D. (1994) 'Steinhoff's "Pursuing the Japanese Police": A Rejoinder', *Law and Society Review*, **28**, (4), 963–5.

Benda-Beckmann, Franz von (1983) 'Why Law does not Behave: Critical and Constructive Reflections on the Social Scientific Perception of the Social Significance of Law', in H. Finkler (ed.), *Papers of the Symposia on Folk Law and Legal Pluralism*, Ottowa: Commission on Folk Law and Legal Pluralism.

Bierbrauer, G. (1994) 'Toward an Understanding of Legal Culture: Variations in Individualism and Collectivism between Kurds, Lebanese and Germans', *Law and Society Review*, **28**, 243.

Black, D. (1976) *The Behavior of Law*, New York: Academic Press.

Blankenburg, E. (1994a) 'The Infrastructure of Legal Culture in Holland and West Germany', *Law and Society Review*, **28**, (4), 789–809.

Blankenburg, E. (1994b) 'Indicators for Studying Legal Cultures', unpublished paper presented at the Macerata Workshop on Comparing Legal Cultures, 18–20 May.

Blankenburg, E. and F. Bruinsma (1991; 1994) 2nd ed. *Dutch Legal Culture*, Deventer: Kluwer.

Clifford, J. and E. Marcus (eds) (1986) *Writing Culture*, Berkeley: University of California Press.

Friedman, J. (1994) *Cultural Identity and Global Process*, London: Sage.

Friedman, L. (1975) *The Legal System: A Social Science Perspective*, New York: Russell Sage Foundation.

Friedman, L. (1985) *Total Justice*, Boston: Beacon Press.

Friedman, L. (1990) *The Republic of Choice: Law, Society and Culture*, Cambridge, Mass.: Harvard University Press.

Friedman, L. (1994) 'Is There a Modern Legal Culture?', *Ratio Juris*, **7**, 117–31.

Galanter, M. (1974) 'Why the 'Haves' Come Out Ahead: Speculations on the Limits of Legal Change', *Law and Society Review*, **9**, 95–160.

Garapon, A. (1995) 'French Legal Culture and the Shock of Globalization', in D. Nelken (ed.), special issue on 'Legal Culture, Diveristy and Globalization', *Social and Legal Studies*, **4**, (4), 493–506.

Gibson, J.L. and G. Caldeira (1995) 'The Legal Cultures of Europe', unpublished paper presented at the Annual Meeting of the Midwest Political Science Association, 6–8 April, Chicago.

Giddens, A. (1976) *New Rules of Sociological Method*, London: Hutchinson.

Haley, J.O. (1978) 'The myth of the reluctant litigant and the role of the judiciary in Japan', *Journal of Japanese Studies*, **4**, 359–90.

Haley, J.O. (1991) *Authority without Power: Law and the Japanese Paradox*, Oxford: Oxford University Press.

Hamilton, V.L. and J. Sanders (1992) *Everyday Justice: Responsibility and the Individual in Japan and the United States*, New Haven, Conn.: Yale University Press.

Kawashima, T. (1963) 'Dispute resolution in contemporary Japan', in A. Von Mehren (ed.), *Law in Japan*, Cambridge, Mass.: Harvard University Press, pp. 41–72.

Lopez-Ayllòn, S. (1995) 'Notes on Mexican Legal Culture', in D. Nelken (ed.), special issue on 'Legal Culture and Globalization', *Social and Legal Studies*, **4**, (4), 478–92.

Malinowski, B. (1926/1962) *Crime and Custom in Savage Societies*, Paterson: Littlefield, Adams.

Marcus, G. (1994) 'After the Critique of Ethnography: Faith, Hope and Charity, but the Greatest of These is Charity', in R. Borofsky (ed.), *Assessing Cultural Anthropology*, New York: McGraw-Hill, pp. 40–52.

Markensinis, B. (1990) 'Litigation Mania in England, Germany and the USA: Are we so very different?', *Cambridge Law Journal*, **49**, 233–76.

Markovits, I. (1989) 'Playing the opposites game: On Mirjan Damaska's *The Faces of Justice and State Authority*', *Stanford Law Review*, **41**, 1313–41.

Marsh, N.S. (1946) 'Some aspects of the German legal system under National Socialism', *Law Quarterly Review*, **62**, 366–74, reprinted in C. Varga (ed.), *Comparative Legal Cultures*, Aldershot: Dartmouth, 1992, pp. 563–73.

Merry, S.E. (1990) *Getting Justice and Getting Even: Legal Consciousness Among Working-Class Americans*, Chicago: University of Chicago Press.

Miyazawa, S. (1992) *Policing in Japan*, Albany: SUNY Press.

Miyazawa, S. (1995) 'Taking Merry Seriously: A Neo-Culturalist Review of the Recent Scholarship and Practice in Japan', published in 'Legal Culture: Encounters and Transformations', papers from the annual meeting of RSCL/ISA, 1–4 August, Tokyo, Japan.

Munger, F. (1994) 'From the editor', *Law and Society Review*, **28,** (4), 725–8.

Nelken, D. (1994) 'Whom Can You Trust? The Future of Comparative Criminology', in D. Nelken (ed.), *The Futures of Criminology*, London: Sage, pp. 220–44.

Nelken, D. (1995) 'Disclosing/Invoking Legal Culture', in D. Nelken (ed.), special issue on 'Legal Culture, Diversity and Globalization', *Social and Legal Studies*, **4**, (4), 435–52.

Nelken, D. (1996a) 'The Judges and Corruption in Italy', in M. Levi and D. Nelken (eds), *The Corruption of Politics and the Politics of Corruption*, London: Blackwells, pp. 95–113.

Nelken, D. (1996b) 'Stopping the Judges', in M. Caciagli and D. Kertzer (eds), *Italian Politics: The Stalled Transition*, Boulder, Colorado: Westview Press, pp. 186–204.

Olgiati, V. (1985) 'Legal Systems and the Problem of Legitimacy: The Italian Case', in D. Khosla, C. Whelan and A. Podgorecki (eds), *Legal Systems and Social Systems*, Beaconsfield: Croom Helm, pp. 87–98.

Renner, K. (1949) *The Institutions of Private Law and their Social Functions*, London: RKP.

Rokumoto, K. (1995) 'Cultural Factors in Comparative Socio-Legal Analysis', paper published in 'Legal Culture: Encounters and Transformations', annual meeting of RSCL/ISA, 1–4 August, Tokyo, Japan.

Rosenne, K.S. (1971) 'The Jeito: Brazil's institutional bypass of the formal legal system and its development implications', *American Journal of Comparative Law*, **19**, 514–49.

Sarat, A. and R. Kearns (eds) (1993) *Law and Everyday Life*, Ann Arbor: University of Michigan Press.

Shapiro, A. (1976) 'Law in the Kibbutz: A Reappraisal', *Law and Society Review*, **10**, 415.

Shapiro, M. (1980) 'Islam and Appeal', *California Law Review*, **68**, 350–81.

Shapiro, M. (1981) *Courts: A Comparative and Political Analysis*, Chicago: University of Chicago Press.

Silbey, S. (1992) 'Making a place for cultural analyses of law', *Law and Social Inquiry*, **17**, 39–48.

Sperber, D. (1985) *On Anthropological Knowledge*, Cambridge: Cambridge University Press.

Steinhoff, P. (1993) 'Pursuing the Japanese Police', *Law and Society Review*, **27**, (4), 827–51.

Teubner, G. (1989) 'How the Law Thinks: Towards a Constructivist Epistemology of Law', *Law and Society Review*, **23**, (5), 727–56.

Wöllschlager, H. (1995) 'Civil litigation in Japan, Sweden and the USA since the 19th century: Japanese legal culture in the light of historical judicial statistics', paper published in 'Legal Culture: Encounters and Transformations', annual meeting of RSCL/ISA, 1–4 August, Tokyo, Japan.

Yngevesson, B. (1993) *Virtuous Citizens*, London: Routledge.

Zedner, L. (1995) 'In pursuit of the vernacular: comparing law and order discourse in Britain and Germany', in D. Nelken (ed.), special issue on 'Legal Culture, Diversity and Globalization', *Social and Legal Studies*, **4**, (4), 517–34.

5 Comparative Criminal Law for Criminologists: Comparing for What Purpose?*

Malcolm M. Feeley

Comparative analysis often means different things to those in law and in the social sciences. In law, the purpose of comparative analysis is to explore features of foreign legal systems in order to determine if there is anything worthwhile to 'borrow'. It is a normative, policy-oriented enterprise. In the social sciences, traditionally comparative analysis has explored general propositions, usually about variation in the social and legal order, in order to explain them. It is a positive enterprise. However, in the sociology of law, where law and social science intersect, these enterprises are often blurred and confused. Comparative lawyers bring their own understandings of the field when they embrace social science concerns, and social scientists do the same when they focus on law. But even within each field, even when there is *conceptual* clarity about scope, method and objective, there has been precious little scholarly, as opposed to practical, pay-off. Comparative sociolegal studies remain a problematic and ill-defined area of inquiry. This chapter will review the central aspirations of both types of comparative law inquiries, assess their contributions and potential, and offer some observations on recent and possible future developments.

*This essay was written while I was a Fellow at the Institute for Advanced Studies, Hebrew University, Jerusalem, whose support I deeply appreciate. I would also like to acknowledge helpful comments on an earlier draft from David Nelken, Lucia Zedner, Roger Cotterell at the Macerata Comparative Legal Cultures workshop, as well as Leon Sheleff at the Institute.

Comparative Law Scholarship

Typically, comparative law, including comparative criminal law and procedure, studies consist of contrasting and comparing selected legal provisions of two or more countries, in order to point out salient similarities and differences, or of describing selected features of several systems side by side. Virtually all the standard texts on comparative law enumerate the same purposes: (1) to enhance one's education and appreciation of foreign legal systems and differences from one's own for the purposes of rounding out one's education, just as foreign travel broadens one's horizons; (2) to serve as an aid to law reform and legislation (if someone else shows us how to do it better, we will consider a legal transplant); (3) to serve as a tool of construction when confronting gaps in legislation or case law in one's own system; (4) to provide, in an increasingly shrinking world, substantive knowledge of others' rules which will help in growing cross-jurisdiction practice; and (5) to facilitate unification and harmonization of the law in this shrinking world.

As can be seen, these objectives are either general and unfocused or are intensely practical. The first of them is general and suggests no particular methodology or purpose other than gaining insight into different legal systems. In contrast, the other objectives are more ambitious. In various ways, they all ask whether there are different and better ways of doing things that might profitably be adopted in or adapted to one's own setting: Here comparative analysis is a form of shopping trip.

We are of course familiar with both types of comparative analysis. For instance, the former has fostered a continuing debate about the merits of the inquisitorial and adversarial systems, the value of the jury system, and the like. The latter, more practical, set of objectives also has a long history as nations have considered legal transplants. Early American law, for instance, was a conscious adoption, adaptation and at times departure from English practices of the day. And the civil codes of modern civil law systems in place throughout Europe resulted from a conscious adoption and adaptation of Roman law. Of course, not all legal transplants have been 'borrowed'. As my old colleague Yoram Shachar once observed, 'If you want to understand why a country has a particular legal system, look at the nationality of the last foreign soldier who departed its shores.' If one considers differences between the United States and Mexico, Nigeria and Niger, and Hong Kong and China, as well as modern Japan, the wisdom in this quip is obvious. Still, there has been a great deal of voluntary borrowing and harmonization in recent years as a result of the creation of the European Community. And with the momentous changes in Eastern Europe and the former Soviet Union, as well as in Africa and other areas, jurists have sought to study other legal systems, particularly those of Western Europe and common law countries, with an eye towards rethinking their own systems.

This sort of practical activity is sure to continue and probably accelerate as Europe continues to unite, the East continues to look westward, the world shrinks and crime internationalizes still more. In Europe, for instance, a Europe-wide uniform private law is beginning to emerge, and there is no reason to think that criminal law and procedure will not follow suit. In the United States, economic interests constituted a powerful force for harmonizing many aspects of state private law in the nineteenth century, with criminal law, a much less important form of social ordering, lagging far behind. One sees similar developments in Europe.

However, the more analytic and explanatory aspects of comparative law still flounder. Scholars who systematize or seek to account for variability and similarity have never found their niche or developed a compelling framework for research that has been widely embraced. For the most part academic comparative law, including comparative criminal law and procedure scholarship, continues to consist of ad hoc 'compare and contrast' studies that show how legal provisions in one country are similar to or different from those of another country, but for no clear purpose other than general enlightenment. Or 'comparative law' consists of a series of studies of single jurisdictions (or families of law) laid out side-by-side with no sustained effort to link them together. Thus, for instance, the comparative law entries in the *Encyclopedia of Criminal Justice* consist of four separate entries which contain 'overall treatment[s] of criminal laws and enforcement in four cultures whose law has developed, to a greater or lesser degree, outside the main Western tradition': China, Islam, preliterate societies and the Soviet Union. Each entry is written by a different scholar, and three of the four are overviews of a single system with at best only passing reference to other systems. In short, they are parallel descriptions. This same format is followed in most comparative law case books, treatises and journal articles.

There are, of course, notable exceptions. One of the most well-known is Damaska's, *The Faces of Justice and State Authority* (1986), which makes an effort to reveal 'how certain ideas on the mission and shape of government justify or support particular clusters of procedural forms, thus providing means whereby recognizable patterns of procedural arrangements can be composed'. Despite this aspiration towards generality and explanation, the enterprise is only partially successful. The study never clearly links types of criminal procedure and types of state authority. Nor does it show how differences in variability in Continental and common law systems are related to, let alone spring from, different types of 'state authority' as the book's title promises, or are related to other legal, cultural, economic and political differences. The analysis also gets bogged down with unsystematic comparison of ideas with ideas (law in the books), ideas with behaviour (law in action), behaviour with behaviour, and with a host of variations within both common law and Continental systems, so that the quest for general patterns and relationships is obscured. Still, it is perhaps the best and most sustained effort at explanatory *comparative* analysis, as opposed to parallel descriptions, in recent comparative law scholarship.

Comparative Legal History

Still another type of 'comparative law' scholarship is comparative legal history. The aim of this substantial body of scholarship – which might properly be thought of as a type of history of ideas – is to trace the influences of one code or set of legal provisions on others. In its more sociological form, it serves to advance the long-standing sociological debate as to whether law is an 'expression of the larger culture' or is autonomous and hence largely shaped by legal craftspeople who can freely draw on materials from other systems (Watson, 1974).

Comparative Law Analysis in the Social Sciences

In at least the positive social sciences, comparative analysis is king. Indeed, in this tradition, all science is 'comparative' in that scientific statements are formulated as general propositions about relationships between two or more variables of the sort, 'A varies as B varies', or 'X is a function of Y'. In the natural sciences, the process of concomitant variation – that is, varying only one factor at a time while holding others constant – is often induced in laboratory or natural experiments. In the social sciences, concomitant variation is pursued through comparative analysis, a functional equivalent of experimentation. Thus a physicist who might want to understand the properties of a substance can vary temperature and pressure in the laboratory. In contrast, a sociologist who wants to understand the effect on criminal activity of, say, social stratification, education or family structure would have to select individuals who differ among themselves on these factors or otherwise statistically hold constant and vary these factors, and then compare the individuals to see if the hypothesized relationships received support. But for comparative law analysis, the unit of analysis is not likely to be an individual but a political or legal entity, the legal system. Sociologists of law are familiar with such formulations. Commonly asked questions in the field include: what accounts for different types of legal cultures, rates of litigation, levels of crime? What accounts for plea bargaining in some systems but not others? Some of these issues can be examined on an individual level (what types of people in the United States and Japan commit crimes?) but comparative legal scholars often have system-level concerns in mind, and thus focus on them.

A variation on cross-national comparative analysis is longitudinal analysis, a comparison of aspects of the same phenomena across time. For instance, one might compare the criminal or violent activity of different groups of males of ages 15, 20 and 25, or follow the criminal careers of the same cohort of males over time, periodically recording their criminal activity. Similarly, one might seek to explore and explain variations in levels of crime through an examination of rates in several countries, or within the same jurisdiction as crime varies over time.

One form of this type of longitudinal analysis is the before/after study, which seeks to examine compliance with or the impact of a new change in substantive law, procedure or administrative practices. Indeed, in American sociology of law this type of analysis, treating policy changes as 'natural' experiments', is perhaps the most common form of comparative analysis. Such studies, often framed as evaluations, are so common that we tend not to think of them as 'comparative', despite the fact that the logic of natural or quasi-experimental analysis is identical to that of comparative analysis. At times, of course, both cross-jurisdiction and longitudinal comparisons can be made for the same end. For instance, students of the death penalty have used time series analysis in single jurisdictions which have had an on again/off again experience with provisions for capital punishment, and have also compared jurisdictions with and without the death penalty. Both enterprises are geared to the same end, to determine the effects of capital punishment. Thus both historical analysis and evaluation or impact studies within a single setting can be, and often are, formulated as types of comparative analysis.

This is the logic of the comparative method in the social sciences, but what are the facts in comparative sociolegal studies? Have sociologists of law more generally produced a body of research that develops theory, tests propositions and accounts for variation using the method of concomitant variation? The answer is no. Although evaluation research, using comparative methods, has at times yielded valuable assessment of policy changes, comparative analysis aspiring to a more general and theoretically sophisticated analysis has not yet developed. Comparative law studies involving foreign jurisdictions carried out by social scientists tend to be as descriptive, substantive and as law reform-focused as studies by legal scholars. For instance, one leading volume on comparative criminal justice systems prepared by criminologists is largely descriptive and follows the format of volumes prepared by legal scholars (Cole *et al.*, 1981). Although it begins with a brief introduction entitled 'Comparative Criminal Justice', each of the book's nine main chapters is devoted to the exploration of a separate criminal justice system. There is no effort to systematically identify, let alone account for, variation among these systems.

The predominantly descriptive nature of this work should not be surprising. Like comparative political studies more generally, comparative sociolegal studies face substantial problems that frustrate efforts to follow the path of concomitant variation: there are few data points which easily permit a country, a legal system or a family of law to be the unit of analysis, especially in the absence of elegant theory. And there are few compelling theories to shape and focus comparative analysis. In addition, there is the perennial conceptual problem: what is the object of analysis – the law on the books, the law in action, some combination of the two that captures the 'spirit of the laws', or some other salient features of a society's legal system as a whole? Social science, including comparative criminal law studies, has always struggled to identify concepts and 'variables' that are general and not single culture-bound.

Let us illustrate some of these problems. Some comparative scholars have sought to account for plea bargaining – both provisions permitting it and its actual practice – and its variable presence in different legal systems in terms of variations in the level of adversarial practice within these systems. This proposition has an appeal, and evidence to support it can be marshalled: Germany, with an inquisitorial system with 'strong' judges who dominate proceedings, has had little if any plea bargaining. In contrast the United States, with a vigorous adversarial system, aggressive lawyers and a 'passive' judiciary which is deferential to lawyers, has widespread plea bargaining. England also has an adversarial system, but it is 'gentlemanly' and its judges are more aggressive (by US standards) vis-à-vis the lawyers. In terms of the prevalence of plea bargaining, it falls somewhere in between the United States and Germany. This suggests that plea bargaining may be fostered by systems which encourage partisan combat, defer to aggressive lawyers and accept passive judges.

This proposition sounds plausible, but rival plausible hypotheses and counter-examples abound. Schulhofer (1984) has shown, for instance, that there is little plea bargaining in Philadelphia, an American jurisdiction with a high crime rate and crowded courts, but also a vigorous adversarial system. And in recent years plea bargaining has been making a marked appearance in Germany, Italy and other European countries. It we are to modify the proposition, no readily available 'variables' come to mind, and the 'N' may quickly come to exceed the number of variables so as to preclude systematic examination of the relevant factors.

Furthermore, plea bargaining can be easily reconceptualized to lead to a quite different inquiry. For example, if one understands plea bargaining as a means of facilitating rapid disposition of cases in order to circumvent full-fledged criminal proceedings, then perhaps every system has its functional equivalent. In Germany, it may be the *Strafbefehl*, or penal order which permits an accused to plead guilty and pay a fine by mail, a process which accounts for from 40 to 60 per cent or more of all criminal dispositions in several northern European countries (Felstiner, 1979).

Reconceiving the issue of plea bargaining this way radically shifts the nature of the comparative analysis and leads us to look for functional equivalents and similarities in 'system' behaviour, rather than variation. In the first example, the dependent variable was plea bargaining and the object was to account for variation in its prevalence as a mode of disposition. As reformulated, the concern is with constancy: it derives from general systems theory which seeks to identify functional equivalents, and to explore the mechanisms that systems use to maintain themselves.

Variations on the Standard Comparative Paradigm

Searching for Uniformities

Although the explanation of variation is the most common objective of comparative research, there is also a tradition, anchored in general systems theory, which searches for uniformities in the face of apparent differences. Indeed, this effort is one of the more successful forms of comparative scholarship in the sociolegal studies. One well-known example, for instance, is Martin Shapiro's study, *Courts: a Comparative and Political Analysis* (1981). Shapiro puts forward the proposition that always and everywhere the central function of courts is social control consistent with regime interests. Appeal, for instance, serves this function; rather than correcting legal errors, it serves to police the decentralized lower courts to see that they remain in line with national regime interests. Regardless of time, place and type of legal system, Shapiro argues, this social control function is maintained. He uses the comparative method effectively to support his propositions. He tests his propositions against what presumably are the strongest counter-examples which would undermine them and, when he finds no evidence to support them, he concludes that his propositions must be supported. Despite the small Ns, he employs the comparative method effectively because he has developed a parsimonious theory, seeks to account for uniformity rather than variation, and tests his thesis against the strongest instances that would 'disprove' it.

Comparative Analysis as a Basis for Challenging Conventional Wisdom

One of the most obvious contributions of social science, including comparative analysis of law, has been 'negative', in the sense that it questions unwarranted generalizations. For instance, Nelken (1994) has drawn upon his cross-national research to challenge the truism that to be effective the police must be a civilian force with close ties to the community in which they work. He argues that police in Italy are probably as effective and perceived as legitimate as police elsewhere, despite the fact that they are organized nationally not locally, and are under military and not civilian control. Indeed, it can be argued that the source of their legitimacy stems in large part from the fact that they are a national military and not local civilian force. Similarly, Nader and Parnell (1986) have shown that definitions of crime vary widely and by culture, but in no easily identifiable pattern.

Beirne (1983) has pointed out that many concepts used in comparative analysis are culture-bound and thus infuse a strong bias into any comparative analysis. Thus there is the danger of unwittingly asking, 'How far do other countries differ from our own?' Such warnings are obviously well taken, but are more successful in challenging unfounded generalizations and revealing the culture-bound quality of comparative research than in establishing an agenda for comparative analysis and formulating general propositions to explore.

Legal Evolution Studies

One of the standard concerns in sociolegal studies has been evolutionary analysis of the law. Between Sir Henry Maine and Donald Black, a host of sociolegal scholars have put forward theories that attempt to account for legal 'development'. In his book, *Ancient Law* (1963), which contrasts the 'primitive' (Hindu) law of India with modern (mid-nineteenth-century) English law, Maine linked legal development with sociopolitical development and considered the then existing law in India as roughly at the same 'stage' of development as English law in the feudal period. Feudal law, he argued, was anchored in a social order based upon 'status', while modern law celebrates the individual and rests upon a social order based upon 'contract'. Indeed, his observation that the history of progressive societies has been the shift from 'status to contract' is one of the most well-known observations in the sociology of law.

Durkheim (1964) was influenced by Darwin's theory of evolution as were many other nineteenth-century social scientists. He too developed an evolutionary theory of law which argued that, as societies become more complex, the primary form of legal sanction shifts from repressive to restitutive.

Marxists also developed evolutionary theories of society, and scholars who have adapted these theories to law have developed various theories of legal development which relate the rise of individualism (contract, in Maine's terms) with the rise of capitalism.

Max Weber (1978) also contributed to this tradition. In distinguishing between forms of law, and particularly differences between substantive and formal legal rationality, he sought at times to relate the differences to factors in the economic order. Modern capitalism, he argued, required the predictability inherent in formal legal rationality and thus this factor accounted for the demise of certain legal forms and the rise of still others. Here, too, modern sociolegal scholars have taken issue with Weber by pointing to examples of formal legal rationality in pre-capitalist societies and to examples of substantive legal rationality in advanced capitalist societies.

Although still widely read today, these several evolutionary theories have been roundly challenged by a number of sociolegal scholars and anthropologists. Sheleff, for instance, has challenged notions of linear development of several 'legal development' theories, and critical legal scholars have raised significant questions about the 'determinism' inherent in some legal development theories. Some of these concerns are articulated in a book by Philippe Nonet and Philip Selznick, *Towards Responsive Law* (1978) which while positing different 'types' of law (repressive, bureaucratic and responsive) underscores their belief that, despite a tendency to move from repressive to bureaucratic to responsive, legal systems can and do in fact move from any one type to any other.

Still another example of such grand theorizing is Donald Black's attempt to account for changes in both the 'amount' and the 'form' of law. In *The Behavior of Law* (1976), he draws on ethnographies and a host of sociolegal studies to argue that the form, nature and 'amount' of law vary widely according to such factors as social stratification, status, culture and the like. As intriguing as his work is, however, it has not precipitated any substantial following, and it stands in near isolation in sociolegal scholarship.

It is beyond the scope of this chapter to explore even in a cursory manner the works of Maine, Durkheim, Weber, Black and others. Rather they are raised here to acknowledge that there is a long-standing tradition of theoretically concerned comparative analysis in sociolegal studies. But the fate of this work appears to have discouraged many others from following in their footsteps. 'Development' studies in the social sciences generally have gone out of fashion and, with respect to the work of these scholars in particular, a small subfield has emerged which seeks to challenge the empirical basis of their generalizations.

Newer Developments in Comparative Sociolegal Analysis

In recent years social scientists have reacted to these grand theories by (re)turning to more local ethnographic research. Their reasons vary. Some have rejected the determinism implied in some of the grand theories (such as Marxism). Other recognize the methodological limitations of concomitant variation inherent in the use of legal or political systems as units of analysis. And many are influenced by the anti-positivism of ethnomethodology and post-modernism, and seek a more humanistic social science. For all these and still other reasons a number of would-be comparativists have embraced a variety of new and novel forms of analysis. Some have not only rejected the logic of comparative analysis, but also the quest for generalization. Indeed, some of those who embrace ethnomethodology and the various schools of post-modern analysis proclaim the death of generalization, intersubjective reliability and science itself. Not surprisingly, comparative analysis does not fare well under such conditions. Indeed, the quest of scholarship is often understood as the identification of the ineffable uniqueness of the subject, or at times simply the reader's 'representation' of the subject. Within such a framework, comparative analysis may best be understood as 'your story', 'my story' and 'her story' and, indeed, much recent social science scholarship has proceeded along these lines, offering descriptions from various 'perspectives' (see generally Rosenau, 1992).

Still, some of those who embrace these new trends see a place for cross-national comparative analysis. Description, even 'thick' description of a single minute setting or event for the purpose of representing its distinctiveness or uniqueness, may be facilitated by comparison. To describe the distinctiveness of an event, a place or a person, it may be useful to say what it is not, to show how one particular differs from other particulars. Thus Nelken (1994) in attempting to reveal the distrust Italians have for some of their laws and governmental institutions contrasts their views with those of the English, who, he argues, have a much greater capacity for impersonal trust. His enterprise is not explanatory; it does not seek 'explanation' of differences between England and Italy. Rather it seeks to offer a convincing 'interpretation' of one feature of Italian legal culture. Nelken's comparisons with England serve in this sense as a type of background in his bas-relief designed to present as boldly as possible features of Italian law and legal culture.

In *Legalism* (1964), Judith Shklar makes a similar point in her observation about Max Weber's comparisons of Oriental and Western legal tradition: she wrote that Max Weber's attempt to expose the contrast between the Occident and the rest of the world 'was not to analyze the non-European world, but to discover, by comparing it with Europe, the unique cultural traits of the West. The question he asked was not what are they like, but why are they different from us, and therefore what makes us what we are?'

This is a form of comparative description with which we are all familiar. For instance, in an effort to describe a person, we might give a description of the salient features of that person and contrast them with those of others. We might say, 'Rivka has red hair, not as blond as Susan's and not as dark as Helen's; and she is about as tall as Miriam – shorter than Mathilda but taller than Margo.' Assuming that both the speaker and her audience know Susan, Helen, Miriam, Mathilda and Margo, this 'comparative analysis' can be a valuable aid in 'describing' Rivka. But in the process of developing a convincing description of one person by contrasting it with another, we may end up offering a convincing description of the other person as well. Thus, in his sustained effort to distinguish Italian legal culture from the English (for an English-speaking audience familiar with English legal practice) in order to describe Italian practices convincingly, Nelken also describes English practices convincingly and contrasts them with Italian, thus yielding insights into English culture as well. Similarly, in describing Rivka by means of a sustained comparison with Helen, we might not only 'see' Rivka, we might 'see' Helen as well. Thus, ironically, some of the most compelling 'comparative' studies may be useful for highlighting the 'uniqueness' or 'distinctiveness' of individual subjects, which presumably is the antithesis of 'comparative analysis'.

Conclusions

This chapter has surveyed comparative law research and found a thriving, highly practical, enterprise in legal scholarship. However, comparative analysis is much less robust once one turns to sociolegal studies. The logic of comparative analysis – concomitant variation – has rarely been exploited effectively in the field since using the legal system or legal culture as the unit of analysis limits the number of units for analysis. In addition, the field lacks compelling theoretical frameworks and analysis remains largely ad hoc and atheoretical. One result is that much of the best 'comparative' analysis, like much of social science generally, is 'negative' or 'corrective', in that it is most successful in marshalling evidence to challenge or 'disprove' the accuracy of received wisdom or generalization put forward by others. However valuable this may be, it does little to advance explanatory analysis.

More recently, some sociolegal scholars, influenced by ethnographic and post-modern methods, have employed a form of comparative analysis to contrast features of two or more legal cultures. This use of comparative description to highlight distinctive features of a single culture for interpretive purposes is a valuable enterprise, but it, too, is unlikely, as many of its proponents would be the first to admit, to lead to the promulgation of theory or explanation. Furthermore, ethnographic research has focused on a single setting. If it is to be employed in comparative analysis in a systematic manner, those who use it must develop a methodology and address the problems of comparability, functional equivalency and the like that have long stood as impediments to comparative research in anthropology.

References

Beirne, Piers (1983) 'Cultural Relativism and Comparative Criminology', *Contemporary Crisis*, **12**, 371–91.

Black, Donald (1976) *The Behavior of Law*, New York: Academic Press.

Black, Donald (1983) 'Crime as Social Control', *American Sociological Review*, **48**, 34–45.

Cole, George, Stanislaw Frankowski and Marc Gertz (eds) (1981) *Major Criminal Justice Systems*, Beverly Hills: Sage.

Damaska, Mirjan (1986) *The Faces of Justice and State Authority: A Comparative Approach to Legal Process*, New Haven, Conn.: Yale University Press.

Durkheim, Emile (1964) *The Division of Labor in Society*, New York: Free Press.

Felstiner, William L.F. (1979) 'Plea Contracts in West Germany', *Law and Society Review*, **13**, 309–26.

Maine, Henry Sumner (1963) *Ancient Law*, Boston: Beacon Press.

Nader, Laura and Parnell, Philip (1986) 'Comparative Criminal Law and Enforcement: Preliterate Societies', in Sanford Kadish (ed.), *Encyclopedia of Criminal Justice*, New York: Macmillan.

Nelken, David (1994) 'Whom Can You Trust? The Future of Comparative Criminology', in D. Nelken (ed.), *The Futures of Criminology*, London: Sage.

Nonet, Philippe and Philip Selznick (1978) *Law and Society Transition*, New York: Harper.

Rosenau, Pauline Marie (1992) *Post-modernism and the Social Sciences*, Princeton: Princeton University Press.

Schulhofer, Stephen (1984) 'Is Plea Bargaining Inevitable?, *Harvard Law Review*, **97**, 1062–1107.

Shapiro, Martin (1981) *Courts: A Comparative and Political Analysis*, Chicago: University of Chicago Press.

Shklar, Judith (1964), *Legalism*, Cambridge MA: Harvard University Press.

Watson, Alan (1974) *Legal Transplants*, Edinburgh: University of Edinburgh Press.

Weber, Max (1978) 'Economy and Law (Sociology of Law)', in Guenther Roth and Claus Wittich (eds), *Max Weber: Economy and Society Vol. 2*, Berkeley: University of California Press.

6 Sociological Uses of the Concept of Legal Culture

Carlo Pennisi

The Concepts of Culture and Legal Culture

One of the most recent attempts to summarize the meanings ascribed to the term internal legal culture,[1] putting aside those which make it coincide with the concepts of legal dogmatics or jurisprudence, distinguishes three main categories: (1) the patterns of reasoning employed by jurists to go from abstract normative premises to specific or individual legal consequences using standard techniques of formulation and justification of the decisions; (2) the specialized lexicon from which they draw their ideas, and (3) the values, ideologies, patterns of reasoning and the politics of law which contribute to the maintenance and growth of the class of the jurists as a particular professional group.

These categories which order the current uses of the concept find a use in at least three explanatory exercises. Firstly, the idea of legal culture describes a real historical phenomenon, occurring differently in every legal system: the term can refer either to the tools or the results of a process from which a well-defined social class emerges. This class is characterized by its sharing a conceptual structure able to settle its relationships with the remaining political and social structure through the attribution of specific patterns to the law, on the one hand, and to its own activities towards it, on the other. Secondly, the term refers to one of the most important consequences of this process: the normative character of legal culture as a set of meanings capable of joining abstract norms and specific decisions, legislator and legal professions. Finally, the term conjures up several functions which are accomplished both in the legal system (for example, validity, flexibility and uniformity) and in the social context (certainty, foreseeableness, efficacy, responsiveness and so on).

This conception of legal culture relates to long-established sociological uses of the concept of culture which now appear less valid. During the Enlightenment, the concept of culture was used to describe objective as opposed to personal characteristics. Later Herder and the German ethnologists considered it a distinctive feature of historical existence as contrasted to the idea of nature. Since then it has been employed to contrast human existence with animal life, or to signal differentiation amongst various forms of historical existence in time and space, and the relationships among these different forms.

Every one of these distinctions – nature/culture, culture/civilization, culture/personality, culture/society, culture/different cultures (for example, of an elite/of the mass, material/non-material culture, and so on) – has its own range of applications. The anthropological tradition also passed on to sociology its own concept which made it possible to compare different life conditions and world views.[2] The Parsonian effort to systematize the use of the concept of culture aimed to account for the normative dimension of social relationships and for the normative structure of the social system itself. But the development of Parsonian ideas tended to obscure Weber's original insights within the neo-Kantian tradition and their relation to the reflections of Windelband and Rickert. According to Weber (1975–6; 1980a; 1980b; 1980c) the difference between nature and culture does not lie either in the object or in the method, but in the explanatory intention which guides the research. Phenomena belong to *nature* if they are described and explained for the purpose of revealing general laws; they are *culture* if they are interpreted in terms of the 'relation of values' with respect to the individuality of their historical social meaning.

Weber's analysis has gained new relevance in the light of current philosophical and anthropological debates. The present study tries to explain how the problem of the comparison among legal cultures of different social systems cannot be formulated without a proper sociological definition of the legal phenomenon. The clarity of the concept depends on the criterion chosen to define what counts as 'legal', and requires a reason and a way to distinguish, amongst the wider aspects of culture, which elements pertain to the law. The concept of legal culture must be characterized so that it conforms to the sense ascribed to the term 'legal' within a sociological discourse.

Current Proposals Concerning the Definition of Legal Culture

A review of the debates about the concept of legal culture in this volume should help underline this point. In Chapter 1, Cotterrell offers several objections to the way Friedman uses the concept. He claims that his use is vague and of poor empirical utility: Friedman's use is both too broad and too narrow – too broad because it could encompass almost any phenomenon (and does not make clear how the heterogeneous levels of culture overlap with the institutions for knowledge indicated by the various legal systems) and too narrow because it does not point out any specific factor that might be useful to distinguish different types of legal phenomena. Friedman assigns to legal culture an explanatory role, considering it to be – in its 'external' dimension – what turns interests into *claims* and, in its 'internal' dimension, what selects the answers in order to avoid overloading or claims that cannot be fulfilled. But this twofold meaning is ambiguous about the relations between the two aspects of legal culture. Knowing the typical features of internal legal culture (legalism, the use of analogies, of *fictiones*, of interpretative procedures and so on) does not help us to understand their influence in different social contexts. According to Cotterrell, these difficulties with the concept of legal culture can only be overcome by replacing it with the term 'legal ideology', which is specifically connected with the professional practices of law and is detailed enough to be analysed empirically. This term does not imply any internal coherence or necessary compatibility among its components and it also usefully underlines the persistence of certain systems of beliefs while experience changes.[3]

The concept of ideology is certainly useful for explaining the meanings of law for legal professionals, but in itself is unable to help us distinguish those meanings which pertain to the law from those which belong to the general culture. It cannot therefore allow us to be certain of directing our sociological attention solely upon legal phenomena. Cotterrell first has to define legal practitioners and *afterwards* analyse their attitudes and behaviour, which pertain to the law because they are expressed by these actors. It is evident that the legal character of those meanings is pre-defined on the basis of a wider (and not fully expressed) 'empirical theory of law' that considers those actors as law profession workers. This means that we risk trying to describe or explain something (the legal phenomena) with something else that has still to be clarified (that is, the law). While this is not necessarily a problem for legal theory, it is certainly awkward for sociology because it destroys its heuristic strength, turning its claims into tautologies.

The doubts that we have about Blankenburg's proposals are roughly similar. Blankenburg (1991, 1993, 1994 and this volume) argues that the traditional use of the concept of legal culture relies upon the doctrinal definition of the nature of law, which is then attributed to ordinary people. On the other hand, an approach based on public perceptions of law would neglect the specificity of legal actions characteristic of modern sophisticated legal systems. He himself tends to rely on professional self-comprehension as the key to *internal* legal cultures. The concept of legal culture thus indicates a 'set of institutions'[4] which behave in an observable way. They are those kind of institutions that the actors of a certain culture define as 'legal'. Blankenburg offers his concept as serving to integrate four levels: (1) the level of legal consciousness of the operators and the public (ideas, attitudes, legal values and legal institutions); (2) the level of behaviour which produces legal norms and institutions, together with the behaviour which uses such norms; (3) the level of the characteristics of the legal institutions themselves; (4) the level of the norms and rules which form the corpus of law. This approach may, as Blankenburg states, overcome the traditional need to anchor law with reference to the state system so that supranational and international entities can be taken into consideration. It also offers a more complex definition than the binary logic (law/non-law) of autopoietic theorists. But the problems we have identified with Blankenburg's approach remain.

This is so, first of all, because, as with Cotterrell, the specification of the legal character of the distinctive culture of the bureaucrats and legal practitioners has to come from a pre-definition of the apparatus, and cannot be merely solved on the basis of the self-determination of the actors (the 'sociological fiat' the author refers to). Secondly, the aim of a theoretical integration of sociological knowledge about law is not satisfied by reference to the 'interrelations' indicated by the 'legal culture'. Blankenburg does not clearly differentiate between the conceptual patterns through which the public or the legally trained interpreter ascribes meaning to elements of the legal systems, the way legal institutions make use of norms and reconstruct events as justifications for courses of action, and the behaviour of 'social institutions' as such. His emphasis on the need to study the relationship between the levels of legal culture can therefore mean either (1) looking at the way meanings which exist at one level are used to interpret another; or (2) seeing whether relations among meanings give rise to more or less congruent conceptual models; or (3) examining the relations between behaviours and patterns of behaviour. As an example, let us consider the relationship between (in Blankenburg's classification) level (1) which refers to the legal consciousness of legal practitioners and the public, and level (4), the level of the norms and rules which form what is called the corpus of law. Here the relation seems to be based on meaningful connection. The same can be said of the relationship between level (4) and the level of judicial institutions (level 3). But, by contrast, the relationship between institutional behaviours (level 2) and legal consciousness (level 1) is that one is a *condition* of meaning for the other. In this sense, legal culture is a relation of meanings, but in rather a different way than before: legal culture here indicates what is understood from the behavioural level or the legal consciousness level (the latter depending on the former).

Blankenburg's idea of legal culture not only indicates heterogeneous *phenomena* but requires these to be explained using theoretical approaches which are not always compatible. In one case, the concept indicates interpretive links: that is, relations through which the interpreter reconstructs the meaning of events (for example, the data concerning the courses of action), in the light of given conceptual patterns. In another, the concept actually reconstructs meanings. In a third case it builds up relations between variables describing behaviour. The first of these is the typical link pointed to by sociological theories; the second requires a hermeneutic strategy; the third indicates a statistically predictable link and is valid independently of the others. At least we should ask for it to be made clear what these differences imply for the explanation of legal culture.

Is the Concept of Legal Culture Explanatory?

Is it possible to consider explanatory the relations that Blankenburg calls legal culture? Let us first of all consider the second and the third relationships. The second does not explain anything, but clarifies a frame of meanings, its components becoming more evident when a legal institution is historically described. The third relationship, on the other hand, can be a sociological explanation of a legal phenomenon under one condition only: that the indicators, whose relations are considered to be legal culture, are relevant with respect to legal phenomena (that is, not only must they be statistically available, but they must also be interpreted in relation to given courses of social action). In this context, 'relevant' must also mean that a relation has been reconstructed by its references to norms or to categories whose meaning is an object of elaboration also by technical–legal knowledge.

Even if this condition is satisfied, although the concept can serve in explanations of certain phenomena as part of the sense of those patterns of action, it cannot, at the same time, indicate the relationship because then either the legal culture is explained by itself or it is excluded from the meanings of those patterns of behaviour. But, were that to be the case, could they then be relevant for us? The concept of legal culture therefore does no more than point out a set of meanings through which various relationships have to be discovered and explained.

Let us now consider more carefully the first kind of relationship, one which uses patterns of meaning to interpret behaviour. Can legal culture, in this case, be considered an explanation of behaviour? Can behaviour be explained by the interpretive relation that Blankenburg defines as legal culture? Everything seems to depend on what is accepted as explanation. For this reason, Nelken (1994) rightly sets Cotterrell's and Blankenburg's proposals in terms of the connection between general and legal culture and the choice between explanation and understanding. As Nelken (1994) argues, although Blankenburg wants to give legal culture the role of an explanatory variable it remains uncertain, when he uses legal culture to describe filters and dispute alternatives, whether this is supposed to explain the existence of these structures or is merely the name we give to them.

The way out of this impasse is to recognize how our definition of legal culture must affect the choice between interpretation and explanation. For the sociologist of law, these two questions are interconnected, for two reasons: first of all, because the criterion used to distinguish legal from wider culture must be used by natives (legal practitioners and others) of the culture itself. Given that this will vary from different cultures, comparative research cannot shift the problem out of the research domain because it will re-present itself at the operational level, too. Secondly, the problem cannot be solved by taking indicators (of institutional or other legally relevant behaviour) as our starting-point, which is what Blankenburg proposes. As noted by Nelken, the interpretation of indicators is not only a technical issue: an index of criminality or a litigation index is already the result of cultural processes which require explanation.

To summarize the argument so far: the goal of sociological analysis of law is the explanation of 'legal phenomena' as social phenomena characterized by a specific reference of meaning to the law. Comparisons between different legal systems can play a part in improving these explanations (Sacco, 1992; Varga, 1992) only if legal phenomena can be clearly separated from other social phenomena in terms of what defines legal specificity in each system. Any definition of legal culture must respect the epistemological validity of what is being analysed, the heuristic capacity of explanations and the specific cognitive aim of the discipline. But the concept can only play a role when the sociologist is sure that he has a means of identifying the legal character of the social phenomena he is dealing with.

The Sociological Use of the 'Legal' Predicate

This raises two issues: what can we consider as pertaining to the law in a given cultural context and how can we compare what is defined as legal in such a context with what is considered legal in another cultural context?

As regards the first issue, to clarify what should be considered legal it is necessary to analyse the core of the underlying sociological problem, which is the use of the adjective 'legal' to indicate some particular social norms. The sociological knowledge of law is different from other forms of knowledge of law because it tries to pursue intersubjectively testable knowledge which is also empirically valid. Legal norms thus become part of a sociological problem when they can be analysed as a component of social action. For the sociologist, the law is not necessarily a *social* phenomenon (from his point of view it can be part of *nature*, of the *environment*, and so on). It can become a specific component of social phenomena only if it is inserted in a conceptualization of action where the specific meanings of that domain became relevant. To be defined as legal, social norms must be considered components of the meaning of actual courses of actions. A kind of sociology of law that deals with this cultural phenomenon is always facing a choice between different theoretical strategies: an approach which assimilates the law to other cultural domains, thus building a sociology of knowledge; an approach which studies law as a specific kind of norm that, together with other kinds, can direct action in one or the other direction; or, finally, a theoretical approach which ascribes to the law the role of a 'natural background' for action, as sometimes happens with the geographical or morphological features of a given context.

For the sociologist concerned with empirical verification, legal norms are not simply prescriptive statements. Legal norms must be considered to be the result of the attribution of meaning. This attribution is, first of all, a specific technical interpretive/applied activity. It is the *result* of the kind of institutional activity: that usually referred to as 'internal legal culture'. The legal meaning of a legal precept, a norm, is then the consequence of institutionally ruled action which is guided by the different theories of law.[5]

The legal signification which results from an institutional process may not always be sufficient to pick out 'legal phenomena' as they are meant from a sociological point of view. To consider the legal norms as components of an action process, they have to be meaningful for social actors, too – corresponding to the meaning that the interpreter/sociologist ascribes to those norms possibly wider and more complex than the one given them by involved actors. It is thus necessary for the sociologist to reconstruct the law as a joint result of an institutional social action process and of placing such social actions in a meaningful context. This is the only way to point out sociologically 'legal' phenomena.

Coming to the second issue, the question of what is defined as legal in different cultural contexts does not have to depend simply on the different definitions within legal systems. We have to reconsider this definition for each cultural context if we reconstruct the different institutional arenas where legal meanings are constituted within a given culture. We could take as an example the considerable differences that separate, in Italy, the actions of lawyers or judges in the sphere of administrative law from those of legal practitioners in criminal law. If we compare these spheres cross-culturally we may find much that is common as well as different in France or even North America.

To be sociologically meaningful, intersubjective testable knowledge about social action referring to legal norms must take into account the actor's point of view. But understanding and explanation cannot be considered alternative strategies for sociological knowledge. The understanding of the actor's meaning is a means to an end: the construction of a range of possibilities for action in reference to a given action can be explained. The attribution of effects to a given condition is not possible without adequately generalized empirical knowledge. Generalization (when it maintains the cultural meaning of the observations) is thus necessary to make a given event or action meaningful.[6] The structure of ideal-typical explanations considers the maintenance of the cultural meaning as a condition for acceptable generalizations. It ascribes to comparison the role of a test which should define the boundaries within which generalizations help to explain action and out of which, stripped of specific cultural references, they are just information.

Comparison using statistics of litigation is certainly an important activity for the understanding of those social phenomena which are culturally identified as legal phenomena. It is certainly essential to refer to limited areas of the bureaucratic apparatus, to particular kinds of legal professions and to precise areas of social action in order to build empirically testable statements.[7] But to be able to compare, that is, to control the limits of the generalizations which in given contexts make explanations possible, it is necessary to define analogous legal phenomena by similar criteria. To repeat: the law becomes an object of sociological knowledge only if legal norms are conceptualized as possible components of the meaning of social action; and legal culture pre-selects meanings for given courses of action.

Legal Culture as a Social Process Oriented Towards a Purpose

The 'purpose' that might be hypothetically chosen for the conceptualization of legal culture has already been stated. In its widest sense, that purpose is historically and culturally shared by a particular set of *institutionalized* types of action. These are those actions whose meaning is the search for an construction of an exclusive identification of law.[8] A domain of activities characterized by the practice of institutionalized competencies and professional techniques can be organized by such a purpose. It is guided by an historically consolidated and socially legitimated attitude, aiming at the construction of a peculiar exclusiveness in the identification of the set of legal norms which are (or ought to be) valid for a given situation.

This purpose points at one and the same time to those actions which directly pursue the goal of defining law (jurisprudence and administrative decisions), those which direct and control this practice, and those which might be reconstructed as explicitly and directly conditioned by that practice (politics, implementation and 'effects'). Choosing to understand legal culture in the light of this purpose means that the determination of what is considered legal will be bound to what sociological analysis can reconstruct and not to what jurists would choose. Legal culture itself becomes a sociologically qualified process of action. From this point of view, then, legal knowledge is not a tool of the research but an object of it, a component of the research project. It helps to explain why and how a given set of norms might be reconstructed as a possible meaning for defined courses of action. The legal meaning of a norm, stated by the jurists, is not the definition of the variable 'meaning of the norm' but a component of a different definition. Again, the institutional character of legal action does not come from any political or legal theory. It is the specific effect of the chosen sociological strategy of typification. This means that we must refer to the sociological concept of institution.

An institution can be characterized as being the result of the empirical observations of regularities which become rules and norms, which can be deontically meaningful for the social actors, as they are ethically and culturally justified (we may think of the theories of legal interpretations, or of a large part of what is considered philosophy of law, or of the specifically prescriptive character of the knowledge the jurists work out for their research). From the point of view of the actors, the aim is to pursue institutional goals and preserve professional monopolies. This does *not* satisfy the sociologists' search for an exclusive definition of the law, though it may distinguish the legal professional from those who deal with the law for other reasons. For the sociologist, the concern is for what defines the role of the law and of the legal system in the wider social and cultural system and in their history. It is an exclusivity which corresponds, as far as historical meanings are concerned, to what functionalistic and evolutionary theories call 'differentiation'. It points to the reasons and the historical meanings that in a given social context distinguish the legal norms from all the other ones. The religious identity of a social system and, afterwards, its political and social identity are built on these reasons and meanings.

From this point of view, the concept of institution does not mechanically point out a set of roles pre-defined with respect to the specific problem of action and the actual normative context. It rather points out those roles and those courses of action that in an actual and structured set of decisions contribute to making up the result (the effects and the outputs and the phenomena which are explained by this specific decisional structures). A typical example of institutions may be that of legal procedures, whose boundaries are differently identified by a sociological definition in comparison with a legal–technical one. The most evident differences are related to the different importance that the sociological reconstruction gives to the roles of the various participants in the procedure (a sort of contingent redefinition of the so-called 'legal apparatus'). They can be contrasted with the emptiness of some formal prescriptions, when compared with the empirical series of decisions, and with the reformulation of 'information' and 'selections' by legal procedures which shape participation, control, legitimization, outputs, and so on.[9]

The Empirical Analysis of Legal Phenomena

What does the sociologist mean by 'legal phenomena' when aiming to obtain comparable observations? There are two kinds of legal phenomena to be attended to: the courses of action for which the legal meaning is an end; and the events, the 'facts', the kinds of action indicated by this meaning. The sociologist should ask not 'Why do those norms have those effects?' but 'How is it possible to explain those behaviours if the meaning that the actors give to those norms is what we have indicated on the basis of the reconstruction of the process called legal culture?'.

This suggested characterization of the concept of internal legal culture can thus be considered as a first step towards the construction of a specific sociological thematization of the law. It is a necessary precondition for every sociological discourse about the law because it identifies legal culture as action processes which pre-select possible meanings. On the other hand, it is not a sufficient condition because it does not give any useful information about the empirical context in which the actor makes this selection meaningful, and in what sense. A big step forward has nonetheless been made. The legal norms, as meanings pre-selected by institutional actions, reconstructed on the basis of the purpose of recognizing the law, appear in the analysis as possible meanings of a probable and further process of action. This offers the possibility of specifically sociological explanations of the law.

The qualification of legality as a product of institutional types of action (the 'internal' legal culture) becomes for the sociologist an instrument to point to particular events, reinterpreting them as processes of action which, on the basis of specifically sociological hypotheses, can be considered social action. On the other hand, this should not be confused with 'normatively' foreseen consequences, allocated competencies and presupposed criteria of legitimacy, which may acquire sociological importance, but are not sociological perceptions as such.[10]

According to the approach outlined here, the aim of sociological knowledge of legal phenomena concerns the possibility of comparing foreseen consequences of events defined as legal regularities (reconstructed on the bases of the 'claim' which defines what counts as legal culture) with the expected consequences of social regularities. It then needs to formulate a hypothesis about their relationship. Explanation and comprehension have as their object the clarification of this mutuality within the expected course of each process. Comparison is an essential tool for building generalizations by which events are understood and explained, while respecting historical and cultural peculiarity without which these generalizations would become sociologically meaningless.

As we have tried to show, relevant cultural diversity in institutional social action, called 'internal legal culture' must be kept distinct from culture in a wide sense. In fact the sociologist faces the same kind of problems in conceptualizing, say, the relationship between welfare structures and deprived classes, or the forms assumed by family disputes, or administrative settlements of property. It is for this reason that the relation between lawyer and client varies less across different cultures if it concerns business lawyers than it does within the same culture, between penal and administrative domains. This results from the mutual attributions of meanings – greatly variable in each kind of relationship – between lawyers and clients. For the sociologist this is not a question of psychological considerations but of ideal-type orientations, a topic that could be studied not only as between national cultures but in a comparison of the social action domains exposed to administrativization of criminal law with those affected by the criminalization of administrative law.

Notes

1 The external/internal distinction was introduced in the work of Lawrence Friedman. For the traditional notion of 'legal culture' see Rebuffa (1993); Arnaud (1991:21–34); Ferrari (1987: 60, 127–29); Aubert (1986:28–39); Podgorecki (1991). A characteristic 'culturalistic' approach to the subject is that of Intzassiloglou (1991). Among the most recent empirical applications of the concept of legal external culture and Friedman's approach, see Hamilton and Sanders (1988); Sanders and Hamilton, (1992); Bierbrauer (1994).

2 Once it got beyond the various forms of evolutionism, anthropology emphasized the symbolic dimension of culture. Organic and natural aspects of human condition remained important, not so much in seeing man as a *social animal*, but with reference to the social character of symbolic relations. For traditional views, see Rossi (1983: 38, 105–48); Remotti (n.d.), about recent perspectives, see Hall and Neitz (1993: 1–20, 241 ff.); Swidler (1986).

3 The concept of ideology for Cotterrell is a 'form of social consciousness' reflected and expressed by legal doctrine, (Cotterrell, 1992: 114ff) which must be carefully inserted in the domain of the sociology of law as an 'empirical theory of law' (Cotterrell, 1989).

4 Blankenburg views actors as constantly surrounded by institutions which they learn to use and sometimes also try to understand. As they do so, these institutions are constantly rebuilt and transformed. Legal culture, as an institutional product, thus produces the legal system from which it is generated.

5 For further discussion, see Tarello (1968: 1974:389ff; 1980, 1–38); Scarpelli n.d.: 570–77); Routtleuthner (1983: 28ff); Wroblewski (1983); Guastini (1990:15ff); Mazzarese (1991:193–243); Pennisi (1991).

6 This standard neo-positivistic view is best understood by reading the original sources, such as Hempel (1986), von Wright (1971) and Leonardi (1986: 40–71) rather than the secondary literature.

7 We use indicators to produce regular and controlled observations according to variables' operational definitions which, in turn, redefine our theorical concepts. See Ragin (1987); Pawson (1989: 35–73); Sartori and Morlino (1991); Agodi (1992).

8 The juridical debate about the positivization of law (including its developmetns related to the welfare state) can be considered a response to the attempt to legitimize legal norms having increasingly technical characteristics.

9 For the sociological concept of 'institution', as used in the text, see March (1988); March and Olsen (1989).

10 The reason for this diversity does not lie in the dichotomy between 'is' and 'ought', but rather transcends this. The typifictions from which legal meanings derive and which law produces, although they can 'descibe facts', are oriented, built and regulated to maintain the special claims of exclusive competence of law (on pragmatic, validity and legitimation levels). Typifications of a sociological theory meanwhile are contingent cognitive tools built and regulated for accounts which claim empirical validity, instruments of and intersubjective knowledge, pursued as a value in itself. The basic divergence between pragmatic and cognitive knowledge compels sociology to construct 'its own' legal meanings by defining meanings expressed by actors of legal culture

References

Agodi, M.C. (1992) 'Dai concetti agli strumenti di rilevazione: il luogo della teoria?', paper presented at the Workshop of Methodology Section, Convegno AIS, 28–31 October 1992, Pisa.

Arnaud, A.J. (1991) *Pour une pensée juridique européenne*, Paris: PUF.

Aubert, V. (1986) 'The Rule of Law and the Promotional Function of Law in the Welfare State', in G. Teubner (ed.), *Dilemmas of Law in the Welfare State*, Berlin: de Gruyter.

Bierbrauer, G. (1994), Toward an Understanding of Legal Culture: Variations in Individualism and Collectivism between Kurds, Lebanese and Germans', *Law and Society Review*, **28**, 243–4.

Blankenburg, E. (1993) 'Culture Juridique', in A. Arnaud (ed.), *Dictionnaire Encyclopédique de Théorie et de Sociologie du Droit*, Paris: LGDJ.

Blankenburg, E. (1994) 'Indicators for studying Legal Cultures', paper presented at the Macerata Workshop on Comparing Legal Cultures, 18–20 May.

Cotterrell, R. (1989) *The Politics of Jurisprudence. A Critical Introduction to Legal Philosophy*, London: Butterworths.

Cotterrell, R. (1992) *The Sociology of Law*, 2nd edn, London: Butterworths.
Ferrari, V. (1987) *Funzioni del diritto*, Bari: Laterza.
Guastini, R. (1990) *Dalle norme alle fonti*, Turin: Giappichelli.
Hall, J.R. and M.J. Neitz (1993) *Culture: Sociological Perspectives*, Englewood Cliffs, NJ: Prentice-Hall.
Hamilton, V.L. and J. Sanders (1988) 'Punishment and the Individual in United States and Japan', *Law and Society Review*, **22** (2), 301–28.
Hempel, C.H. (1986) *Aspetti della spiegazione scientifica*, Milan: il Saggiatore.
Intzassiloglou, N. (1991) 'Système juridique et culture: une approche sociologique globale du phénomène juridique', in F. Chazel and J. Commaille (eds), *Normes juridiques et régulation sociale*, Paris: LGDJ, pp. 391–413.
Leonardi, F. (1986) *Di che parla il sociologo*, Milan: F. Angeli.
March, J.G. (ed.) (1988) *Decisions and Organizations*, Oxford: Basil Blackwell.
March, J.G. and J.P. Olsen (1989) *Rediscovering Institutions. The Organizational Basis of Politics*, New York: Free Press.
Mazzarese, T. (1991) '"Proposizione normativa". Interrogativi epistemologici e semantici', in P. Comanducci and R. Guastini (eds), *Analisi e Diritto 1991. Ricerche di giurisprudenza analitica*, Turin: Giappichelli.
Nelken, D. (1994) 'Can Legal Culture be Measured? A Theoretical Agenda', paper presented at the Macerata Workshop on Comparing Legal Cultures.
Parsons, T. (1991), *The Social System*, Glencoe, Ill.: Free Press.
Pawson, R. (1989), *A Measure for Measures. A Manifesto for Empirical Sociology*, London: Routledge.
Pennisi, C. (1991) *La costruzione sociologica del fenomeno giuridico*, Milan: Giuffrè.
Podgorecki, A. (1991) *A Sociological Theory of Law*, Milan: Giuffrè.
Ragin, Ch.C. (1987) *The Comparative Method*, Berkeley: University of California Press.
Rebuffa, G. (1993) 'Culture Juridique', in A. Arnaud (ed.), *Dictionnaire Encyclopédique de Théorie et de Sociologie du Droit*, Paris: LGDJ.
Remotti, F. (n.d.) 'Cultura, in Enciclopedia delle Scienze Sociali, Rome: IEI.
Rossi, P. (1983) *Cultura e Antropologia*, Turin: Einaudi.
Routtleuthner, H. (1983) *Teoria del diritto e sociologia del diritto*, Bologna: Il Mulino.
Sacco, R. (1992) *Introduzione al diritto comparato*, Turin: Utet.
Sanders, J. and V.L. Hamilton (1992) 'Punishment and the Individual Repertories in Japan, Russia and United States', *Law and Society Review*, **26** (1), 117.
Sartori, G. and L. Morlino (eds) (1991) *La comparazione nelle scienze sociali*, Bologna: Il Mulino.
Scarpelli, U. (n.d.) 'Norma', in *Gli Strumenti critici del sapere contemporaneo*, vol. 2, Turin: UTET, pp. 570–77.
Swidler, A. (1986) 'Culture in Action: Symbols and Strategies', in *American Sociological Review*, **51**, 273–86.
Tarello, G. (1968) 'La semantica del neustico. Osservazioni sulla parte descrittiva degli enunciati precettivi', in *Scritti in onore di W. Cesarini Sforza*, Milan: Giuffrè, pp. 761–95.

Tarello, G. (1974) *Diritto, enunciati, usi. Studi di teoria e metateoria del diritto*, Bologna: Il Mulino.

Tarello, G. (1980) *L'interpretazione della legge*, Milan: Giuffrè.

Varga, C. (ed.) (1992) *Comparative Legal Cultures*, Aldershot: Dartmouth.

Weber, M. (1975–6) 'R. Stammler's "Surmounting" of the Materialist Conception of History' I and II, *British Journal of Law and Society*, 1975, **2**, 129 ff; 1976, **3**, 17 ff.

Weber, M. (1980a) 'Il "metodo storico" di Roescher', in *Saggi sulla dottrina della scienza* Bari: De Donato, pp. 5–41; first published 1903.

Weber, M. (1980b) 'Knies e il problema dell'irrazionalità, in *Saggi sulla dottrina della scienza*, Bari: De Donato, pp. 43–100; first published 1905.

Weber, M. (1980c) 'Knies e il problema dell'irrazionalità', in *Saggi sulla dottrina della scienza*, Bari: De Donato, pp. 101–37; first published 1906.

Wright, G.H. von (1971) *Explanation and Understanding*, Ithaca, NY: Cornell University Press.

Wroblewski, J. (1983) 'Cognizione delle norme e cognizione attraverso le norme', in U. Scarpelli (ed.), *La teoria generale del diritto. Problemi e tendenze attuali*, Milan: Comunità, p. 413.

7 Comparing Legal Cultures in the Quest for Law's Identity

Michael King

1

There is no denying that comparing legal cultures can be fun. Quite apart from the opportunities it offers for international travel, for developing and using linguistic skills, for making new friends and for experiencing foreign culinary delights, the idea of making visible and accessible what up to then has remained veiled and mysterious has its unique and irresistible attractions even for academics who claim to set their sights on higher goals. For the reader of the books, reports and articles that emerge from such comparative studies, the exposure to other ways of doing and seeing things can be interesting, refreshing and even illuminating. It is no coincidence that many legal comparative researchers have been attracted to anthropologists such as Geertz (1973) and Rosen (1989), whose free-flowing narrative contrasts with the constrained and highly disciplined tradition of legal writing or the abstractions of jurisprudence. This also pleases students of law or legal systems who generally have to put up with a rather dull and repetitive diet of textbooks, statutes and cases. For them the introduction of a comparative or international flavour in their courses may often make a welcome change.

There are, of course, also those who approach comparative work with critical or ideological goals in mind. They may see in the systems of other countries better, fairer or more efficient ways of solving problems or managing people than occur within their own homeland. For them the interest lies rather in using observations of other cultures to highlight and, often, expose to critical attention the defects of their own country's laws and legal system.[1]

Neither comparative researchers nor their readers are likely to welcome the attention of autopoietic theory with its insistence that all explanations of social events should be seen as meaning productions and analysed at the level of interfaces between closed communicative systems. This kind of theorizing appears to want to subject their exercise of comparing cultures to the very kind of formalistic, disciplining and limiting categories from which they have sought to escape. Yet observations of social observers rarely leave the observed observer feeling anything other than a victim of misinterpretations and partial understandings. There is a risk, therefore, on the one hand of setting up autopoiesis as the judge, scourge or purifier of comparative research (which is not at all the intention) and, on the other hand, of provoking the defensive response that the valid evaluation of comparative research can only be that of other comparative researchers or at least a critic working within a theoretical framework which recognizes comparative research 'on its own terms', and so rendering invalid any other theoretical perspective. The comprehensive insurance cover against both these risks is the guarantee that, in the absence of accessible reality, observation is all that we have. Far from insisting that comparative research fashions itself to some purified notion of the social world consisting only of self-referential functioning systems, all that autopoiesis is doing is restating the obvious: that those who compare are no different from those who observe, in that the meanings that they bring to such comparisons are socially generated, sustained and attributable to one or other of those functionally differentiated systems that allow us to 'know' whether our communications are valid or invalid, truthful or untruthful, politically correct or politically incorrect, lawful or unlawful and so on. My experience may tell me that what you say is right (or wrong) but how have I managed to structure my experience in ways that allow me to communicate to you in what ways you are right (or wrong)?

Let us now begin to observe the way that the theory of self-referential systems makes sense of the notion of different cultures based upon politico-geographical boundaries and specifically the notion of legal cultures. A theory of autopoietic systems presupposes the existence of self-referential systems – systems that reproduce themselves from their own elements or, in terms of meaning, a network of communications which in order to give meaning to their existence always refer to other communications of the same kind. Here one encounters the first problem, for it is difficult not to agree with Niklas Luhmann when he says:

> there is no reason to describe a country as an autopoietic system. Autopoiesis is a theoretically and conceptually demanding category. You may reject it for its incapacity to see Brazil as a system, but then, my question would be now: how can you describe a country as a system without losing all preciseness of the theoretical framework? (Sciulli, 1994: 46–7)

If, in Luhmann's scheme, a country cannot be seen as a closed, self-referring system, as communications concerning, for example, Englishness or Frenchness ('the English way of life consists of …' or 'the French way of doing things is to …') are not validated by previous communications concerning Englishness or Frenchness, but by reference to political structures, laws, the arts, economic practices or even the weather, then writing about English or French *culture* is misleading in that it give the false impression that *culture* represents closure. In order for 'culture' to be treated as a system, one needs to assume that the term first has some generally accepted meaning. One could give the term its dictionary definition of 'the customs, civilization and achievements of a particular time or people' (*Oxford Concise English Dictionary*) although this does not take us very far in the search for something resembling a network of communications which always refers to communications of the same kind. On the other hand, one could adopt a more anthropological definition, a set of 'shared understandings' or 'the complex of beliefs, attitudes, cognitive ideas, values and modes of reasoning and perception which are typical of a particular society or social group'. Here, at least, one has the rudiments of a communicative system, but how does one set about identifying 'the complex of beliefs', 'attitudes' and so on for any one country and, particularly, for any one European country which today consists of people from a wide variety of ethnic groups, religious and political affiliations, to say nothing of their gastronomic, musical and literary tastes? Is a partiality for Indian food part of the British culture or does it only become so if it occurs after the pubs have closed for the evening?

2

A belief in the propriety of taking afternoon tea is today no more a feature of English culture than anti-Americanism is a characteristic of French culture. Those who set about categorizing the cultural attributes of their European neighbours invariably fall into the trap of caricature and stereotyping. Once they enter the comparative culture stakes, even those sophisticated academic researchers who in other situations are very conscious of these dangers tend to find themselves carried along by the most sweeping generalizations. This is not meant to be a criticism of individual authors, but of the very notion that the term 'culture' can ever be anything more than a shorthand which, when applied to countries, invariably requires a level of selectivity and a reductionism which is (or should be) unacceptable as an analytical tool in social science.

The obvious way to avoid such blatant stereotyping in the pursuit of cultural specificity is to compare institutions rather than shared beliefs, or typical ways of reasoning or perceiving on the (not unreasonable) basis that a country's institutions provoke, encourage, produce, influence, give rise to and raise expectations of certain beliefs and attitudes. I am now moving closer to autopoietic theory in the assumption that, if different attitudes exist, their meaningfulness must have been made possible by the prior existence of institutional structures which sustain and develop such meanings, for institutions represent the formalized and bureaucratized manifestations of communicative systems. If people, for example, understand aspects of their world in terms of the conflicting politics of government and opposition, then it is the institution of parliament which makes such meanings or interpretations available.

There is still a major problem, however, which has to do with *globalization*. For the social scientist the task is not to define the two rival teams in a competition between 'the national' and 'the supernational'. It is rather to find some way of accounting for the social fact that these terms continue to have meaning in a world where, with a few notorious exceptions, national boundaries serve neither to hold in nor to keep out. National governments are as powerless to prevent the effects of international market fluctuations upon their economies as they are to stop the influence of *Neighbours* and Madonna upon their cultural heritage. The spectacle of Iran imposing the *hijab* upon its womenfolk is only slightly less absurd than France's attempt to ban English being spoken at international conferences held on French soil.

This is not to suggest that differences between the institutional structures and practices of different countries no longer exist or are no longer able to make different meanings, and thus different attitudes and beliefs, available to people who identify with those countries. It may be becoming more difficult, as I shall show, but clearly the fascination that comparative researchers find in their work is sufficient evidence that the world is not one homogenized whole. Perhaps it is slightly worrying that some of the contributions to this volume seem to want to maintain at all costs a belief in the significance of national differences, even to the point of ignoring or denying the existence of a world society or in their depiction of globalization as 'the enemy out there'. This, however, is not an important point, not least from the perspective of the autopoietic observer.

What is important and interesting is that the concept of national characteristics continues to have meaning and to provide meaningful distinctions in a way that makes it appear valid to compare attitudes, beliefs, cultures and so on in ways which depend upon national identities, *in spite of* the obvious globalizing tendencies of modern society. For Luhmann, society, the sum of all possible meanings, is world society (Luhmann, 1982) and socially differentiated systems of communications such as law, politics, the economy, art and education exist and can only exist as part of a global network of meaning which knows no national boundaries. A family in a remote village in Botswana watching the O.J. Simpson trial on a television set understand that what they are seeing is law and that this makes it different in nature to health, religion, politics or any other kind of communicative event. This may seem obvious, but one does not need to go back very far to arrive at a time when the notion of legal as being quite distinct from other meanings would have been incomprehensible.

Religion is another example of a global way of seeing the world, in that it does not cease to have meaning once it crosses the Channel, the Atlantic or the equator. People in different parts of the globe may differ in their religious beliefs and in the emphasis that they place on religion to give meaning and structure to their lives, but the recognition that there is something called 'religion' and that it is identifiable as having a separate institutional and functional identity to, say, politics or law is a general feature of modern society.[2] It allows that society to formulate such complex notions as religious persecution and freedom of religious observance, of discrimination on the grounds of religion and anti-discriminatory measures.

3

The reason why distinctions based upon national boundaries, the notion of separate nation states, is so important despite the unprecedented interdependence of countries and continents is a matter for sociological speculation and historical interpretation. The fact is that these distinctions exist and the work of comparative researchers perpetuates and fortifies such distinctions. Any categorization and imposition of distinctions which depend upon the notion of separate nation states are clearly functional within political communications, for they allow territories to be identified as being the responsibility of particular governments and those governments to be identified as representing the interests of those territories. One should not, however, slip into the teleological trap of believing that functionality equals inevitability or desirability and that, whatever happens to the world, national cultures will continue to flourish with the same salience and utility in meaning production. The fate of national cultures when they were thrown into the melting pot of American society and emerged as sideshows in a theme park should help us to avoid such slippage. Moreover, the recent sweeping changes of boundaries and nations in what were formerly the Soviet Union and Yugoslavia and the emergence of new or renovated national identities such as that of South Africa should serve as a reminder of how fickle the notion of national cultures can be.

To attempt to build an understanding of different laws, economic systems, films, art and even politics in the modern world entirely upon such a flimsy notion as national culture may appeal to the meanings that the political system has generated, but it is a risky business simply because its selectivity has severe limitations, which need to be recognized. Global distinctions such as those based on race, gender, wealth distribution, pollution and so on may be reproduced only in terms of national variations in dealing with and regulating them as problems. Eventually, one arrives at arguments which depend for their validity on the existence of national distinctions which the observer has identified and which only have meaning within the phenomenal world which the observer and the political system have constructed. Certain factors are identified within different countries and deemed to be responsible for the different ways in which these problems are resolved. These differences in the resolution of problems themselves depend upon the identification of national characteristics (whether institutional or ideological) in resolving these kinds of problem. And so one ends up with the inevitable circularity: Luhmann's *paradox* and *tautology* (Luhmann, 1990b).

4

Autopoietic theory differs from observing systems which use national identity or national culture in their attempt to make sense of events in the world, not only through its explicit recognition of this circularity, but because it makes the recognition of circularity (in the form of paradox and tautology) a prominent feature of the theory. Social systems through paradox and redundancy inevitably reduce reality (or complexity) in such a way as to create order out of what would otherwise be (were it possible to gain access to it) chaos and disorder. Circularity lies at the very heart of the production of meaning by social systems.

This is also what is meant by 'functional'. Functionally communicative subsystems – economy, law, art, education and politics – which are functional only in the sense that, without the meanings that they produce, society not only could not function effectively, because it could not exist conceptually, but would literally have no meaning. According to Luhmann, the founding father of social autopoiesis,

> Modern society has realized a quite different pattern of system differentiation, using specific *functions* as the focus for the differentiation of subsystems. Starting from special conditions in medieval Europe with a relatively high degree of differentiation of religion, politics and economy, European society has evolved into a functionally differentiated system. This means that function, not rank, is

> the dominant principle of system building. (Luhmann, 1982: 132, emphasis in original)

To observe meaning production in society in terms of differentiated functioning subsystems is not to deny the existence of national boundaries as having meaning for people and for society. It is rather to see meanings based on these distinctions as national or cultural characteristics as depending upon a way of observing the world which is no more than a way of observing the world. Their explanatory and predictive powers are, therefore, severely limited and, in some instances, highly suspect, simply because their validation depends upon the closed communicative network which is able to reproduce complexity only on its own terms. Yet it is not merely the case that the functional subsystems provide meanings which allow the world to exist. Their distinctiveness or 'closure' also creates for them a distinctive environment which is accessible only to that subsystem. According to Luhmann,

> Modern society is differentiated into the political subsystem and its environment, the economic subsystem and its environment, the scientific system and its environment, the education system and its environment and so on. Each subsystem accepts for its own communicative process the primacy of its own function. All other subsystems belong to its environment and vice versa. (Luhmann, 1982: 132)

Religion, for example, is able to understand the world only in the terms of religion. Within this limited vision of the world other subsystems appear in religious terms, as constructions of religion. Religion is able through the processes of selection and exclusion to control explanations of events within its environment, but it cannot control its dependency upon other subsystems or the dependence of other subsystems upon religion. A crash in the stock market which wipes out a substantial part of the Church's investment may be explicable as God's will or as a just retribution for the sin of avarice, but there is no way that religion can formulate economic conditions in such a manner that the stock market will rise. Its function is confined to reacting to and interpreting events in its environment in religious terms. The loss of the church's income may result in fewer clergymen being available to undertake marriage and funeral ceremonies, with a consequent growth in secular ceremonial forms. Once again, these are matters which religion is able to 'understand' but not control.

Within modern or world society, therefore, communicative subsystems are characterized both by their closed or autopoietic nature and by their interdependence upon one another. The term 'culture' may make sense within the political, legal, religious or artistic systems of communication, but the meaning attributed to the term by each of these systems is likely to be very different. Where politics may talk of preserving and protecting French culture from the pervasive influence of the United States, law's 'understanding' is confined to outlawing the use of English terms in government documents and official communications. It could also include the banning of American films. For law, therefore, the meaning of culture is selected and confined to that which law sees itself as able to control through legal means, such as protecting (or outlawing) the rituals and practices of ethnic minorities, while for politics it may involve anything that may be constructed generally in terms of power, such as power differentials between different social groups which rely on the notion of culture for their distinctive identity. More particularly, it may concern framing of issues in terms of differences between government and opposition to that government (Luhmann, 1990a). This may include a government taking upon itself the task of upholding the 'national identity' or 'national culture' in the face of threats from 'abroad' and depicting the opposition as the party which is prepared to sacrifice these items of national heritage.

5

Several writers in this volume have analysed the difficulties concerning the use of the concept of legal culture (see Chapters 1 and 6, for example). Roger Cotterrell in particular has rightly taken Lawrence Friedman to task for the vagueness and inconsistency which characterize his attempts to compare the 'legal cultures' of different countries. Seen through the eyes of autopoietic theory, these debates are interesting if only for the assumption that the participants make about the possibility of capturing, through some conceptual formula, the essence of law what law *actually is* and, in the case of Friedman, how whatever it is varies according to different national or 'cultural' contexts.

Attempts such as these to order the world according to different institutional 'cultures', if taken to their logical conclusion, may appear to come very close to the autopoietic distinctions, based on function and coding, that I have been describing. If a legal culture can be said to exist, then why not a political culture, a scientific culture, a religious culture and so on? If all of these 'cultures' can be seen to coexist, how are their boundaries defined and what kinds of relationship may they have with one another? The reason that it is impossible to answer these questions in a satisfactory manner and why divisions of the world into different cultures cannot be taken seriously can be found in the inherent indeterminacy of the notion of 'culture'. This, unlike the autopoietic concept of 'communicative system', is simply impossible to define in a manner which would satisfy the demands of rigorous sociological observation or empirical research. All that may be grasped is *the way that people and social systems use the notion of culture*. The same is doubly true of Friedman's national legal cultures, for here the problem exists for both the term 'legal' and the term 'culture'.

As I have shown, the closest one can come to an autopoietic equivalent of legal culture is *law and its environment*. This refers to the world constructed by law using its legal/illegal coding or selectivity. It is tempting to see this idea of law creating and responding to its environment in social constructivist terms – the reality 'out there' is reconstructed by law so that it is amenable to legal operations. Unfortunately, this image is more misleading than it is helpful. Autopoiesis goes much further than the kind of relativist epistemological approach that sees society divided into different bodies of knowledge. Law, as a communicative social subsystem, has no access to reality except through its own selectivity. This selectivity is a product of law's social function of reducing complexity and providing meaning which allows society to make sense of its existence and continuity. The environment for law is a world which can only be understood in terms of (1) whether it is amenable or not to law and, if amenable (2) the legality or illegality of events. Furthermore, law itself, its identity, its self-image, exists within this legal environment, but at the same time it has to be distinguished from everything in that environment, from everything which is not law. Law's image of itself, as a social system, can be coded by law only in terms of legality/illegality. This is one of the essential aspects of law as an autopoietic system.

According to autopoietic theory, law is communication and only communication. The fact that such communication has to respond to a particular geopolitical environment does not alter the universal nature of legal communications in modern society. All it means is that at various times and in various situations law is constrained to reconstruct as law, within its own conceptual limits, events occurring in the external environment. Although there may well be local differences of procedure and tradition, the way that law sets about its task of reducing the environment to notions of lawfulness and unlawfulness does not vary in any fundamental way. These local differences may be interesting as examples of the ingenuity of law to resolve the difficult problems of its own reproduction,[3] but to extrapolate from these examples some general rules concerning the causes and effects of legal change in different settings is not the kind of task that autopoietic theory is willing or able to undertake. This does not mean that nobody should attempt it, but rather that any attempt will necessarily privilege some *a priori* notion of causality which then enters the unending competition between 'truths' and conflicting versions of the real.

In the interests of preserving some scientific integrity for sociology, autopoiesis then takes most of the fun out of comparative research. I say 'most of' because it is still possible to undertake autopoietically historical studies of law in different settings, both geographical and temporal (see, for example, Luhmann, 1982; 1985; 1988a; 1988b; 1989; 1991). These studies, it must be emphasized, do not concern themselves with identifying causes, but are confined to examining the ways in which law has responded to events in its environment and the way in which the legal system becomes 'structurally coupled' with other communicative subsystems around certain repetitive events (Luhmann, 1992).

6

While direct comparisons between legal systems may not be possible within autopoetic theory, studies of evolving communicative systems which place law alongside other such evolving systems within specific social contexts clearly do not compromise the integrity of the theoretical approach. Therefore, it one takes the subject of law's intervention in issues of child welfare, it would be quite legitimate to examine the way in which the legal system in France has developed structures and practices which are very different from those of England and Wales.

Take, for example, the unlawfulness for the French children's judge to order that a child who is not accused of any crime be locked up, even where that child is out of control and has run away from children's homes. There are no secure units in France. One might trace the evolution of this legal rule to the exposure by Alexis Danon in the late 1930s of the cruel, sadistic and repressive regimes operating in the *bagnes pour enfants* (children's penal colonies) which were opened in the 1850s as enlightened residential institutions for the education and training of problem children. Some time later the *bagnes pour enfants* scandal became a major pertubation within both politics and law, causing the French government to act to give the scandal political meaning as an event which could be brought under control through political means. This in turn produced irritations within the legal system from which emerged the image of the *juge des enfants* who appears in French legal communications at about that time as the protector of children, someone whose only concern is the welfare of the child, someone who will uses law's distinction of lawful/unlawful to protect children against the illegality of the *bagnes pour enfants* or any similar institutionalized cruelty. The French children's judge was given the responsibility not only of investigating any reports of child maltreatment, but also of inspecting annually any institution to which the court sent children.

How, then, should those seeking to compare English and French jurisdictions for the protection of children deal with these developments? Should they scan the pages of the history of the British Isles for an equivalent event to the *bagnes pour enfants* scandal and, finding no such event, conclude that this was *the factor* which determined the different directions taken by the system in France and that of England and Wales? Alternatively, do they seek to identify the complexities of French social institutions operating at the time of the scandal in an effort to explain why these institutions responded in the way they did and how these responses provoked further reactions and so on? This second way of proceeding would be much closer to an autopoietic approach than the first, but it can hardly be considered comparative research. What those intent on comparing cultures would probably attempt would be to build models of French and English societies which concentrated on the differences and similarities between them and then go on to explain the developments in the institutions of these two countries for dealing with cruelty to children as a product of the cultural differences (Cooper *et al.*, 1995). The comparative legal culturalist *à la* Friedman would approach the matter in a similar manner, except that he or she would concentrate attention on similarities and differences within the two legal systems. The development of the child protection role of the *juge des enfants* in France and their absence from Britain might, therefore, be attributed to the bureaucratic nature of the French judiciary and to the inquisitorial system which charged judges with the investigatory role in legal proceedings.

A second example, still dealing with decisions about children, is extracted from a report by Peter Ely and Chris Stanley of Kent University (Ely and Stanley, 1990). It emphasizes still further the differences between the roles of the courts in children's cases on either side of the Channel. This is how these authors describe a French children's judge in action in a case of alleged physical abuse. A 15-year-old girl had complained

> that she feared that her father was going to hit her. The police had referred the matter to the *Parquet* and the *Procureur* had arranged for the girl to be taken to a children's home pending referral to the Judge the following day.
>
> The Judge refused to end the daughter's placement and insisted that the father came to see him. A social worker who was an *éducateur de la justice* was present at this hearing, and information previously provided by him suggested that there was discord between father and mother about each of them going out separately in the evenings, and this bore on their many arguments with their daughter about her going out late. (Ely and Stanley, 1990:20)

When questioned about his view of the situation and the issue of whether there was any evidence of bruising to substantiate the daughter's claim that she had been hit before, the judge replied,

> 'Whether it is true or false is not important. No, there were no bruises. What certainly is important is that we must get father and daughter back into communication with each other. There is something keeping them apart. The important thing is not the blow, but the relationship.' (ibid.)

This, according to the authors, 'encapsulates the differences to child protection, and to children, on opposite sides of the Channel' (ibid.).

Those comparing legal cultures would most probably agree with these authors and might well go on to emphasize the differing role of the judge, differences in evidentiary requirements and the criteria for intervention, and the presence or absence of legal rights safeguarding the family against unwarranted intrusions on its privacy. Yet to compare the role of the French children's judge in such a case with that of the Family Proceedings Court in England and Wales is to assume that each of these roles can be validly ascribed to the legal system operating on either side of the Channel. For autopoietic theory, however, the legal system does not consist of the bricks, mortar or pre-stressed concrete of the courthouse or even of those people who are called judges and lawyers. Judges and lawyers may well be necessary for legal communications, but they are also quite capable as conscious beings of communicating in terms other than those of law. It is rather a system of communication which codes the environment in terms of legality/illegality or lawfulness/unlawfulness. In the situation described by Ely and Stanley, there was no such coding, so it is hardly appropriate to talk of the operation of a legal system. Indeed, under Article 375 of the French Civil Code the children's judge needs to be satisfied that there is a serious risk that the well-being of the child will be compromised. There is no indication of what constitutes a risk, what the word 'compromised' means, what evidence is admissible or inadmissible or what procedures shall be followed in making this determination. It is virtually impossible for the judge to act illegally by making a legally 'wrong' determination under this Article. Autopoietic theory therefore imposes a categorization of the event which depends not upon its formal attribution to courts, police, social service departments and so on, but upon the nature of the communication. In this case it could well be argued that the judge's communication was not 'legal' in nature, but was rather therapeutic or mediatory, applying the coding 'healthy/damaging for the child'. To compare his intervention directly with the role undertaken by English courts in child abuse cases would, therefore, seem inappropriate and misleading. It might be far more appropriate to compare the operation of all those institutions involved in the protection of children and the therapeutic promotion of child welfare in these two countries, but then, of course, one is departing from any attempt to research 'legal cultures'.

As my final example, a word about differences in the conception of time in issues of children's welfare. Here a recourse to autopoietic theory might assist comparisons but, once again, without any reference to legal cultures. Legal time refers here to the way in which law's legal/illegal coding provides a way of structuring time – a way of dividing time into past, present and future – and sees these divisions as having strictly legal implications. Law may determine from when time begins for the purpose of taking a legal action. Can an unborn child, for example, be subject to child protection proceedings? It is also likely to specify how much time is lawful and how much unlawful when, for instance, decisions are made about the division of the time a child should spend with parents who have separated or divorced. Different jurisdictions may vary in the time limits they impose or in their interpretations of lawful and unlawful time, but the actual way in which time is conceptualized and compartmentalized by the law does not differ. Legal time in France is the same as legal time in England and Wales. In child welfare cases the fundamental differences that occur in temporal conceptualizations concern divisions between law and other functional subsystems, such as health, education and child welfare science. A 12-month delay in bringing a case before the court may be perfectly lawful, but to educationalists or child psychiatrists it may have extremely damaging effects for the child.

For the French children's judge's involvement with most families, it could be argued that legal time does not even begin. The judge meets the family informally in *cabinet* and, after a discussion about 'the problem', makes no order at all. In other cases a provisional order only is made. Until recently, for children this was 'timeless', lasting until the child reached 18 years of age, and existing in many cases as the only record of the family's involvement with the judge and the courts. Legal time had a past – prior to the provisional order – and a present – the making of the order – but no structured future. The future was conceptualized by other subsystems' notions of time, in which law's time played no part.

In England, by contrast, in making any interim order (and even before) the court (judge or magistrates) operates within a time structure which is strictly regulated. Right from the start of proceedings, failure to keep to time limits is unlawful. Emergency Protection Orders 'shall have effect for a period not exceeding eight days'.[4] Child assessment orders 'shall specify the date by which the assessment is to begin and have effect for a period not exceeding 7 days beginning with that date'.[5] Whenever an application is made for a care or supervision order the court 'shall draw up a timetable with a view to disposing of the application without delay'.[6] These provisions in the Children Act are transformations by law of political concerns for protection of the civil rights of parents and children and of psychological evidence of a child's concept of time which differs from that of adults. For comparative purposes the difference between the law in England and France is that in France these transformations, for the most part, have not occurred. Civil rights have not until very recently played any major part in the child welfare work of the *juge des enfants* and the psychological concerns about the child's welfare remain very much within the psychological sphere, with no attempt to translate them into law in the form of rigid time limits or the drawing up of timetables by the judge (Cooper *et al.*, 1995). To the autopoietic theorist, these different approaches may be interpreted not as variations between legal systems or legal cultures, but as differences *in the relationship* between law and other systems.

7

If in formulating the concept of 'comparative legal cultures' one of the main objectives was to encourage legal scholars to go beyond arid and formalistic comparisons of the laws of different countries and to open up the legal system to an anthropological style of interpretation, we would certainly not wish to take the fun out of such exercises by criticizing them from the exalted theoretical high ground of rigour and methodological soundness. Problems with the idea of comparative legal cultures lie elsewhere. For a start, as has been shown, there seem to be serious problems in throwing a cordon around the activities of the courts and lawyers and calling everything that occurs within the cordon 'legal culture' and everything that occurs outside it 'general culture', 'politico-economic influences', 'noise' or what you will. Secondly, the idea that national characteristics somehow determine the shape and contents of the laws and courts of each country, and the attitudes and behaviour of those who perform the roles of judges and lawyers within those countries, needs increasingly to be questioned in the light of the global society in which we all live. There is no fundamental objection to comparative researchers working within a geopolitical framework and treating national boundaries as having a determining influence on everything that takes place within the borders that they delineate, just as long as they are aware of what they are doing and do not, as seems often to be the case, simply perpetuate in an unreflective manner the idea that the world is now, as it always has been and always will be, divided into geopolitical distinctions, which have produced, do produce and will produce the important meanings for society's self-identity. This, in the worst scenario, leads to cultural and nationalistic stereotyping and even in the hands of sensitive scholars, ignores the many effects of globalization, simply because they are not amenable to comparative analyses.

Finally, there seems to be a serious risk that comparative legal culturalists will end up with a collection of descriptions in search of a theory. There is nothing intrinsically wrong with this, if they enjoy writing travelogues and their readers enjoy reading them. It does seem, however, that this kind of work is anti-theoretical in the sense that it sees any attempt to introduce theory as an imposition of formalism and constrains something which ideally should be free to wander around and observe as it sees fit. I have tried in this chapter to introduce in autopoiesis a theoretical perspective which seeks to identify law as a communicative subsystem within a global society and to concentrate attention upon the ways in which this system reproduces its environment *in legal terms* and upon the relationships between law and other coexisting communicative systems. I would freely admit that this theoretical approach simply cannot deal with the wealth of experiences and observations that come from living and observing behaviour in different parts of the world. Nor can it offer explanations and predictions which serve to make sense of what experience tells us are important differences in the way that people in different countries behave. What it can do, however, is to stand back from these explanations and predictions so as to see them as interpretations which owe much to the ways in which meaning is organized within society. This does not solve any problems, but it does go some way towards formulating problems in a way that can give rise to new systems and new formulations, rather than endlessly repeating the same formulae in what are identified as different social contexts. I end with a quote from Niklas Luhmann which encapsulates both the ambitions and the limitations of this theoretical approach:[7]

> Systems, generally, may control selected facts or events in their own environment related to their own inputs and outputs. They cannot control interdependencies in their environment. The more we rely on systems for improbable performances, the more we shall produce new and surprising problems, which will stimulate the growth of new systems which will again interpret interdependencies, create new problems, require new systems. (Luhmann: 134)

Notes

1 Recent examples here might include the work by John Braithwaite and others on Maori shaming ceremonies (Braithwaite and Mugford, 1994) and work on crime prevention in France (King, 1988; 1989).
2 See generally Peter Beyer (1994).
3 See, for example, Luhmann (1988a); King and Schütz (1994).
4 Section 45(1) Children Act 1989.
5 Section 43(5) (a and b) Children Act 1989.
6 Section 32 (1) (a) Children Act 1989.
7 See also King and Schütz (1994).

References

Beyer, P. (1994) Religion and Globalization, London: Sage.

Braithwaite, J. and S. Mugford (1994) 'Conditions of Successful Reintegration Ceremonies', *British Journal of Criminology*, pp. 139–70

Cooper, A. *et al.* (1995) *Positive Child Protection: A View from Abroad*, Lyme Regis: Russell House.

Ely, P. and C. Stanley (1990) *The French Alternative: Delinquency Prevention and Child Protection in France*, London: NACRO.

Geertz, C. (1973) *The Interpretation of Cultures*, New York: Basic Books.

King, M. (1988) *How to Make Social Crime Prevention Work: The French Experience*, London: NACRO, NTIS.

King, M. (1989) 'Social Crime Prevention à la Thatcher', *Howard Journal of Penology*, 291.

King, M. and A. Schütz (1994) 'The Ambitious Modesty of Niklas Luhmann', *Journal of Law and Society*, 261.

Luhmann, N. (1982) 'The World Society as a Social System', *International Journal of General Systems*, 131.

Luhmann, N. (1985) *A Sociological Theory of Law* (trans. E. King and M. Albrow), London: Routledge.

Luhmann, N. (1988a) 'The Third Question: The Creative Use of Paradox in Law and Legal History', *Journal of Law and Society*, 153.

Luhmann, N. (1988b) 'The Unity of the Legal System' in G. Teubner (ed.), *Autopoietic Law: A New Approach to Law and Society*, Berlin/New York: Walter de Gruyter, p. 12.

Luhmann, N. (1989) 'Law as a Social System', *Northwestern University Law Review*, 136.

Luhmann, N. (1990a) *Political Theory in the Welfare State*, Berlin/New York: Walter de Gruyter.

Luhmann, N. (1990b) *Essays on Self Reference*, New York: Columbia University Press, ch. 7.

Luhmann, N. (1991) 'The Coding of the Legal System', in A. Febbrajo and G. Teubner (eds), *State, Law, Economy as Autopoietic Systems*, Milan: Guiffrè, 145.

Luhmann, N. (1992) 'Operational Closure and Structural Coupling: The Differentiation of the Legal System', *Cardozo Law Review*, 1419.

Rosen, L. (1989) *The Anthropology of Justice*, Cambridge: Cambridge University Press.

Sciulli, D. (1994) 'An Interview with Niklas Luhmann', *Theory, Culture and Society*, 37.

8 Gender and Nature in Comparative Legal Cultures

Hanne Petersen

> Legal culture derives from the civilization and history of each country and is crucial in determining the way of life and the condition of women – a condition which varies too widely to permit generalisation, but rather demands comparative study, which remains to be done. (Kravaritou, 1993)

> If we look at the tragedies that occur at the interfaces between the two human cultures, it is not surprising that similar tragedies occur at the interface between human societies and ecosystems leading to gross reduction or slow deterioration. (Bateson, 1987: 176)

> By legal culture we mean the ideas, values, attitudes and opinions people in some society hold, with regard to law and the legal system....
>
> Legal culture is the *source* of law – its norms create the legal norms; and it is what determines the *impact* of legal norms on society. (Friedman, 1994: 118)

Lawrence Friedman (1994) claims that studies of comparative legal culture are both in principle and in practice extremely difficult to carry out but also that data about legal culture will have to be more and more cross-cultural and to transcend boundaries in order to explore issues of sameness and difference among the various legal cultures. He underlines six traits as especially characteristic of legal systems in the 1990s. The first of these and the one I am going to refer to here is that the legal systems, like their societies, are in process of rapid change.

This chapter seeks to explore two issues of sameness among especially Western legal cultures, namely the devaluation of human gender and non-human nature. One consequence of this devaluation has been an exclusion and denigration of both women and nature in the law of so-called 'modern industrial societies'. In particular it seeks to investigate and describe some of the changes in the evaluation of these issues of sameness, especially in the legal discourse connected with the evaluation. If legal culture is ideas, values and attitudes, then changes in ideas, values and attitudes towards women and nature will change jurisprudence, law and the impact of already existing legal norms.

It is thus not my aim to compare different 'isolated' national, regional or otherwise territorially distinguished legal cultures in order to solve problems of 'compatibility' within these systems. Nor is it my aim to investigate why some Western legal cultures might allow 'nature' and women more leeway than others – this would be an interesting task for further studies. Given the relative commonality of Western legal cultures in their evaluation of gender and nature, it is from our point of view not enough to investigate and describe the situation of both in legal culture and in law; it is also necessary to contribute to a changing evaluation of both and thus to an improved situation of both also in law.

It is claimed that comparative studies of legal cultures will help us end the continual impoverishment of our sensibility (Baxi, 1991). The crisis in the relation between Western cultures (including legal cultures) on the one side and human and non-human nature on the other underlines the urgency of increased 'legal sensibility' in this respect. Increased legal sensibility aims not just at understanding or offering critiques – it aims also at 'taking suffering seriously' (Baxi, 1991: 269) and at contributing to the process of minimizing suffering and crisis, which occur not just in the social but also in the ecological field. In order to contribute to this process, 'law' must be understood in a very broad sense.

A changing and increased sensibility to the way relations between culture and nature – in this case the relation to human and non-human nature – are evaluated may later be fed back into contemporary doctrinal understanding of jurisprudence. Questions such as why the relation between 'culture' and 'nature' has been left outside 'law' will have to be addressed. It has to be considered how 'law' will have to change – and is already changing – its form and self-understanding in order to reflect a transformation of legal culture which is already taking place.

The devaluation of women in Western legal cultures has led to clashes within Western societies, and to a questioning of some of the ideas, values and attitudes held in these societies. The devaluation has also contributed to and sustained a male hegemony in modern law, and an exclusionist view of law. Within the last decades considerable quantitative changes have taken place through women's access to the legal profession, and it is to be expected that the full qualitative impact of these changes still remains to be seen.

The devaluation of nature in modern law may be one of the factors which are giving rise to the clashes and tragedies which occur at the interface between human societies and ecosystems, and of which we have been witnessing an increasing number of examples and expressions during the last decades. Also here we are probably only sensing the first waves of this impact in legal culture and law.

An identification and verification of the specific aspects of a devaluation and consequential exclusion of gender as nature and of non-human nature from Western legal cultures could perhaps be carried out through investigations and comparisons of Western legal cultures with non-Western legal cultures rather than through comparisons within Western legal culture. In such comparisons aspects of difference might perhaps arise more strongly in respect to the issues dealt with here. This is not, however, an investigation that it is possible to carry out here.

An identification of a change of the values in the legal cultures underlying the specific legal systems can perhaps be carried out through a historical comparison of Western legal cultures or a retrospective view of these cultures at specific times and periods rather than through a snapshot comparison of different Western legal cultures at the same time. The point here is that, if devaluation and exclusion of gender and nature is an issue of sameness for Western legal cultures, then exclusion may perhaps best be pinpointed and identified by making comparisons with non-Western societies, while changes in attitude – which still uphold the commonality and sameness of attitudes – may perhaps best be identified through an analysis of historical changes within Western societies.

It is my impression that the changes in the perception of both gender and nature which have been taking place over the last decades, and which are still going on in Western legal cultures, are due to changes of values and attitudes which take place with different speeds and intensities in different areas and perhaps nation states, but that they have a profound impact on almost all countries within Europe and perhaps especially in the EU.

It is also my impression that, in the process of revaluation of gender and nature, the impulse for revaluation of gender in the legal culture has come mainly from the female and feminine culture inside the Western world itself (but certainly not unlinked to a global discussion about the status of women), whereas the revaluation of nature has perhaps sought more inspiration in non-Western cultures among the legal or perhaps normative cultures. The link between women and nature has traditionally been quite strong in Western societies, and thus the revaluation of both gender and nature in these legal cultures could be (and have been) linked as well.

In this chapter I will therefore deal very briefly and superficially with the devaluation of human and non-human nature in Western legal cultures and the exclusion of both from law, and then continue to deal somewhat more fully – but still in a fragmented and superficial way – with the result of change of values and attitudes in the legal discourse about the role and status of nature.

Devaluation and Exclusion of Human Nature in Legal Culture

I have argued elsewhere that women have been excluded from modern law and that the exclusion of women has also meant an exclusion of some of the values which women have experienced in our lives, notably the non-economic values.[1] Here I want to deal especially with the aspects of this exclusion which are related to the fact that humans are also nature, that we are both natural and cultural beings.

The relation between nature and culture in human beings has long been discussed, especially in pedagogic thought. There seems to be agreement that formation of a person requires mediation between nature and culture. This process of 'socialization', which encompasses conscious and unconscious influencing of the child, is understood to lead it to become a 'person' – a cultural being. Part of this influence is formalized education; part of it is 'upbringing', 'breeding' and 'formation of attitudes' (Pahuus, 1988: 78f).

According to Alison Jaggar (1989) the separation of culture and nature in modern science had as a consequence that nature was stripped of value and reconceptualized as an inanimate mechanism of no intrinsic worth. Values were relocated in human beings, rooted in their preferences and emotional responses. Emotions, however, were portrayed as non-rational and often irrational urges that regularly swept the body, 'rather as a storm sweeps over the land' (Jaggar, 1989: 146). Bodily knowledge thus could not acquire the importance of other 'scientific' and 'cultural' knowledge.

The process of transforming 'nature' into 'culture' is one which to a large degree still takes place outside the reach of rational formal law – it takes place in the 'Lebenswelt'. According to legal doctrine, the 'life-world' has been considered as belonging to the 'private' sphere. Formal law should thus retain from intervening in and interfering with it. The rationality of formal law may see itself as threatened by nature as it sees itself also to some degree threatened by emotions. However, this does not mean that the relation between nature and culture is situated in a normative vacuum. It may be beyond the reach of modern law but not beyond normative influence. The process and the relation between the 'cultural' and 'natural' part of human nature has mainly been regulated by 'rules of conduct/etiquette' transmitted by custom, influenced by dominant values and in the present period increasingly influenced by guidelines formulated by different groups of experts on physical and mental health (see also Giddens, 1992).

The strong 'regulating powers' in this field have thus been the medical, psychological and therapeutic establishments and professions, together with religious ideas, norms and institutions, whose activities have only been vaguely influenced by 'law' in the formal sense. Feminists have long claimed the inseparability of the 'private' and the 'public' and have claimed that the private sphere and the body are a source of knowledge which must be taken into account if women's societal position is to be understood (see, for instance, Haug *et al.*, 1987; Haug, 1992).

The role of AIDS and the development of reproductive technologies are both contributing strongly to the 'deprivatization' of the relation between the 'cultural' and the 'natural' part of the human, and giving rise to increased regulation of a seemingly innovative form transcending the 'modern' understanding of law, as 'ethics' is given a more prominent place than plain substantive 'rules' (see Conradsen, 1994a). By contrast, one of the few areas where formal law has intervened in the relation between the 'cultural' and 'natural' aspects of humanity is related to sexual proclivities of a 'bestial nature', which have been outlawed as 'sodomy' (Conradsen, 1994b).

Modern legal thinking preconditions the 'cultured' person. The human being who has undergone the transformative process from 'nature' to 'culture' is the relevant legal entity. To become a legal *subject* in modern law, culturation is necessary. The identification of women as truly 'cultural' has been and still is difficult. The potential procreative powers which are an integrated part of what it (also) means to be a woman constantly remind us of the intricacies involved in distinguishing between nature and culture. For a perspective which views culture as superior to nature, as is the case in the modern view of the relationship, where nature is viewed as base and 'below', it is crucial that 'nature' be controlled, planned and mastered in order that it does not become dangerous for and threatening to 'culture' and 'civilization' – this goes for the nature of humans, as well as for nature outside humans.

For the emerging view, on the other hand, which tends to understand nature, not as dead matter, but as living organism, and as something with which to interrelate – something with which to enter into dialogue, not just something to dominate – it becomes important to be able to listen, not just to dictate. This requires a training of sensibilities and of the ability to listen to and to understand non-verbal languages and messages. This so-called 'body language' seems to be a growing field of expertise. It is, however, very seldom taken into explicit account in the legal field (perhaps with the exception of the field of evidence and alternative dispute resolution).

The inability to listen to the body in the legal field (but not only there, of course) is demonstrated by the difficulties which lawyers and legal theory have had in categorizing pregnancy and pregnancy-related conditions influencing the body. For a long time they were seen as belonging to the category of 'disease' and, when this was finally acknowledged to be an inadequate categorization, they became viewed as 'healthy', thus excluding the existence of an intermediate *sui generis* condition of the body, where it is undergoing a 'natural' transformation, and as such is in need of concrete consideration (see, among others, Finley, 1986).

The concept of 'birth law' suggested by Norwegian women's law (Hellum, 1993a) is one attempt to contribute to re-establishing the relation between the cultural and human part of nature. The attempts to view the new reproductive technologies in an ecological perspective may further link human nature to non-human nature (Hellum, 1993b). However, this link will demand serious thought and rethinking on the part of those who have been interested in feminist jurisprudence and the relation between gender and law.

For feminist critiques of modern societies and of modern law a very important focus has been criticism of the equation of women and nature, and the underlining of the social construction of gender and women (King, 1989). Modern law has been criticized by feminist lawyers for being androcentric and gender hierarchical, but not for being anthropocentric and species hierarchical (Petersen, 1993a; 1993b; 1994b). Women have sought to expand androcentrism to anthropocentrism in law but mostly without realizing or acknowledging that this would also mean an inclusion of – or greater difficulty in continuously excluding – the 'natural' part of humans as well.

Here is a great challenge to the humanistic and enlightenment part of the project of female emancipation. This project has been very uneasy about the 'biological' or 'natural' or 'essential' aspects of human life and womanhood, and has largely regarded them as chains and obstacles to emancipation. Much of this fear has been well-founded, but I believe that this is an understanding which now urgently needs to be overcome, not just in feminist thinking and feminist jurisprudence.[2]

Dominant jurisprudence views the relationship between human and nature – including human nature – as a hierarchical relationship of master and servant (subject and object). This view is increasingly becoming obsolete, and may itself be reinforcing the problems rather than contributing to their solution. This crisis may thus also be viewed and understood as a crisis for the regulatory systems and for legal scientific self-understanding, which has not yet managed to reorient and redirect itself, to include more voices and perspectives. This makes the 'post-modern' attempts to 'create' new styles and a new understanding of science more 'attractive' for humans who do not want to continue to exclude their 'natural' side, neither from personal relations nor from other relations in their living together (*con vivium*) with humans and non-humans (Griffin, 1988).

The dependence of the human body on ecological conditions, or ecological welfare as it has been expressed, is giving rise to new normative statements about the (declining) health of humans and nature and about how to bring back equilibrium in this relation. Some suggestions for affirmative change are presented as isolated descriptive adjectives in the comparative form 'slower, less, better, more beautiful', thus underlining the concrete relativity and contextuality of the suggestions for improvement of the relation (Glauber and Korczak, 1993).

Other suggestions are presented as 'recommendations' stressing the 'need to generate more public awareness', among other means through the 'promotion of research capabilities with emphasis on development of problem-solving multidisciplinary studies that are analytical and action-oriented and which will have policy implications' (Skakkabæk *et al.*, 1991). A revaluation and a change of attitudes towards human nature will thus probably lead to 'legal' norms of a different kind from the ones we are most familiar with today.

Devaluation and Exclusion of Non-human Nature: the Mechanistic World View and Jurisprudence

The way relations between human and non-human nature are understood in a particular context is part of the world view or cosmology, which dominates this context. A world view is a synthesis of a particular people's belief about the place of self within society and cosmos.[3] The world view which has been dominant in the Western world since the scientific revolution of the seventeenth century has been the mechanistic world view, which sees nature as dead and matter as passive.

> Mechanism, which superseded the organic framework, was based on the logic that knowledge of the world could be certain and consistent, and that laws of nature were imposed on creation by God. The primacy of organic process gave way to the stability of mathematical laws and identities. (Merchant, 1980: 102)

Nature became instrumentalized and viewed as a means, not as an end. Cosmos was viewed as a machine: the grand watch. The modern view of science is closed, complete and immutable. It is to be understood as a pre-programmed machine, straightforwardly and without mystery (Mortensen, 1989: 64).

This mechanistic world view permeates thinking and understanding, imagery and iconography in modern Western societies.

> A society's symbols and images of nature express its collective consciousness. They appear in mythology, cosmology, science, religion, philosophy, language and art. Scientific, philosophical and literary texts are sources of the ideas and images used by controlling elites, while rituals, festivals, songs and myths provide clues to the consciousness of ordinary people. (Merchant, 1989: 19)

Legal thinking in Western legal culture is of course not left uninfluenced by the emerging mechanistic world view. According to Carolyn Merchant, mechanical language derived from European philosophers permeated the writings of the founding fathers of the United States and their fundamental documents: the Declaration of Independence and the Constitution (Merchant, 1989: 200).

The view of order also changed from the dominant understanding within the framework of the organic world view, where order meant the function of each part within the larger whole as determined by its nature, while power was diffused from the top downwards through the social or cosmic hierarchies.

> In the mechanical world, order was redefined to mean the predictable behaviour of each part within a rationally determined system of laws, while power derived from active and immediate intervention in a secularized world. Order and power together constituted control. Rational control over nature, society and the self was achieved by redefining reality itself through the new machine metaphor. (Merchant, 1980: 192f)

The influence of the ideas and ideals of predictability, rationality and active intervention for the sake of control on modern legal thinking is hard to overlook.

The view of nature as dead matter, as a machine which can and should be controlled – and exploited – is reflected in modern legal doctrine in the distinction between legal subjects and legal objects. Only legal subjects can have rights, whereas legal objects are viewed as passive and subjugated to legal transactions as 'property', 'commodity' or otherwise. The legal subjects or legal 'persons' do not necessarily have to be 'natural' persons, but they must be 'artificial' persons, and 'nature' can be no such 'artificial' person. It is actually considered a characteristic of modern law that it is a type of order, which only relates to social – not 'natural' – relations (Luhmann, 1986). This understanding has also dominated most feminist writers. 'Jurisprudence, after all, is about human beings,' writes Robin West at the beginning of an article on 'Jurisprudence and Gender' (1988).

The view of nature which is built into modern jurisprudence emphasizes that jurisprudence is not decontextualized knowledge but is a cultural artefact. In an early article on 'Legal Culture and Social Development', Lawrence Friedman writes that the idea of 'social engineering' – a metaphor that is in itself strongly influenced by the mechanistic world view – through law itself is an important aspect of the legal culture of change-oriented modern societies. In these societies demands for change are addressed to governments, not to gods (Friedman, 1969: 38). 'It is the legal culture, that is the network of values and attitudes relating to law, which determines when and why and where people turn to law or government, or turn away' (1969: 34).

The Austrian legal philosopher, Michael W. Fischer, does not consider it inappropriate to view science as one world view among others, as it fulfils the general function of world views. Also science produces solutions, explanations and rationalizations which aim at successful action but also at emotional working up of the factual. To consider science as a world view illuminates its respective dependence on specific values. Writing in 1984, Fischer said that we live in a period where science not only *solves* problems, but above all *creates* problems (Fischer, 1984: 439). He claims that we need fundamental convictions of relevance for actions and decisions, that we need 'values'. It is becoming increasingly clear that every science has become what it is and as such also may change. 'It is not even unthinkable that it may one day totally disappear in its present form' (p. 445); '"Nature" especially "human nature" forces itself to the forefront of every scientific contemplation' (p. 445).

Thus we must evaluate the fundamental values of a science, that is its ethics. It is this view which guides the valuation which Fischer calls 're-existentialization' (1984: 463). He claims that existence is the primary value for every 'world orientation' (*Weltorientierung*), and that it has normative and constitutive function for a world view that is oriented towards humans. The scientific efforts of humans, including their successes and failures, are always also an accomplishment and fulfilment of our existence. This understanding of science carries the potential that humans understand themselves as nature and that the old epistemological controversy about the primacy of matter and mind, object and subject becomes obsolete (1984: 468). This view of science as a world view in itself, linked to the importance of the question of nature and culture, supports the view that science, including jurisprudence, is facing a severe challenge and will be obliged to scrutinize its cultural and axiological foundations.

Non-human Nature Revalued in Western Legal Culture and Legal Discourse?

A number of legal authors have embarked on the effort to illuminate not only the cultural relativity but more specifically also the cosmological preconditions of Western jurisprudence in its understanding of 'nature'. I shall present some of these views by citing selected authors. This selection does not claim to be an exhaustive presentation of the writing on this subject, but they are some of the writers which most directly address the issue.

These authors contribute to an illumination of the cosmological and cultural foundations of Western legal thinking and an awareness of the emergence of other understandings. They should perhaps be viewed as harbingers and intensifiers of transformations in progress rather than as representatives of finalized views.

To investigate why this change in legal culture is taking place would require an investigation of the actual ecological and social conditions and the changes in respect to those which have taken place within a number of Western societies over the last decades. This is beyond the scope of this chapter.

The French philosopher Luc Ferry (1992) is very critical of what he claims is an anti-humanist trend in the emerging cosmological understanding of law. He remarks that ecology does not have the same impact in France and other southern European Catholic societies as in the Anglo-Saxon and Germanic part of the world. Thus he suggests that the hypothesis about a link between religious affiliation and care for nature should be studied more closely.

The famous article by Christopher Stone from 1972, 'Should Trees have Legal Standing? Toward Legal Rights for Natural Objects' can probably be said to have raised or at least intensified the debate about the view of nature in law. The very title of the article was undoubtedly largely perceived as absurd in the Western legal world at the time of its publication. The article itself does not discuss the view of nature underlying dominant doctrine explicitly, but attempts to sensitize this doctrine towards the very idea of rights of nature. Stone does, however, preview a reversal of the relationship between humans and nature when he writes:

> the time is already upon us when we may have to consider subordinating some human claims to those of the environment per se.... I do not think it too remote that we may come to regard the Earth, as some have suggested, as one organism, of which Mankind is a functional part – the mind perhaps: different from the rest of nature, but different as a man's brain is from his lungs. (Stone, 1972: 490 and 498)

The German Klaus Bosselmann argues that a reorientation of law in an ecological direction will imply a shift of emphasis in legal ethics and an acknowledgement of the legal subjectivity of nature. To the legal ethical foundation of this shift belongs the questioning of the conventional Western ethical systems. The reduction of the independent value of nature to its servant function is a necessary consequence of anthropocentric jurisprudence, which must be overcome. Bosselmann emphasizes that in the legal cultures of what he calls 'natural peoples' (*Naturvölker*) legal subjectivity and stewardship (*Treuhandschaft*) have remained. Thus beyond every legal decision lies a value decision, in this case about the values of nature and humans (Bosselmann, 1986).

The Swiss author, Beat Sitter, argues for a reconstruction and renewed understanding of 'natural law' as also including rights for nature. He sees it as a deficiency of traditional natural law thinking that it has concentrated on *human* nature and the conditions of its societal existence as if all decisive aspects of social order were thus negotiated, and as if human existence did not in determined ways depend upon the natural environment (Sitter, 1984: 28f). If we consider the will to survive, we must today ask ourselves how norms of conduct can be derived from the ecological intertwining of humans. Humans have provided themselves with unprecedented means of power which are brought into action on a planetary scale. Such norms of conduct would, according to Sitter, be no less arbitrary than those social regulations which are considered the minimum content of natural law. He argues that, although nature does not confront humans as a person in the ethical (*sittlich*) understanding, it does confront us as at least an equal authority, which demands respect and thus compels humans who want to survive to acknowledge non-arbitrary norms in their conduct towards nature, as well as to follow and enforce such norms socially.[4] Sitter underlines the historical character of the concept of legal standing and legal subjectivity, and draws upon the often mentioned example of the legal acceptance of slavery. The possibilities that legal standing should not only be granted according to anthropocentric interest lies at hand.

The legal standing of non-human nature, according to Sitter, originates from the respect that humans owe it. Unqualified respect, which humans owe towards everything we do not create ourselves and on which we are dependent, belongs to the 'legal foundational relation' (*rechtliches Grundverhältnis*), insofar as it is extended to extra-human nature (Sitter, 1984: 38). Sitter understands the discussion about rights of nature as more than a discussion of 'efficiency' of protective and other measures, which is why he argues that prohibitions and rules of protection do not suffice. The reason for this is that these regulations do not make it clear that nature as such cannot be disposable (*verfügbar*). Because of this deficiency they do not defy the centrality of human interest, but uphold the view of nature's disposability and instrumental character for humans. Such regulations therefore renounce a possible educatory effect of law from the outset. Sitter links cosmology and jurisprudence when he writes, 'With the questioning of the leading principles of human practice legal thinking which is dependent on these principles will also have to face fundamental questioning' (1984: 33).

Another Swiss author, Jörg Leimbacher, argues in *Die Rechte der Natur* (Nature's Rights: 1988) for an acknowledgement of new legal subjects. He claims that legal standing for nature is nothing but a consequential continuation of a century-long process of expansion of the group of legal subjects (Leimbacher, 1988: 27). He argues for an 'ecological foundational duty' (*Ökologiegrundpflicht*) of humans towards nature, for instance in relation to property or commercial transactions. A relationship between humans and nature that is conceived of as one of dominance is hardly capable of putting a stop to further damaging of nature (1988: 28). Today protection of the environment (*'Umwelt'schutz*) is predominantly protection of humans and their survival. Nature as a legal object today is protected as a reflection of the need for protection of humans. In the theory of nature as a (legal) object, nature is conceived of as matter. Nature seems to be an opponent of man, which must be conquered, subjugated or destroyed as an instrument for human purposes.

Leimbacher asks whether it is necessary that the relationship between man and nature be one of master and servant or whether it would be possible to find another position beyond dominance and suppression, another relation to nature (1988: 37). In line with Sitter, he discusses nature as something fundamentally undisposable and as something which requires respect. To acknowledge the rights of nature or to grant nature rights would, compared with the current situation, create a radical separation from the idea that nature is nature for humans and nothing but that. On the basis of a holistic world view we can acknowledge rights of nature, he claims (ibid.: 47). Legal subjectivity does not necessarily have to be linked to the ability to safeguard rights personally, and Leimbacher rejects the linkage between legal subjectivity and the ability to bear duties (ibid.: 51).

> The division of human and nature, of res cogitans and res extensa (Descartes), of mind and matter, which lies at the root of the division between (rational) legal subject and (irrational) legal object, disregards that also man is part of nature, and that nature is part of man. (Leimbacher, 1988: 57)[5]

To view man and nature as equals provides the opportunity and even the compulsion to address the actually existing differences between humans and non-human nature.

Leimbacher also points to the historical and cultural conditionality of the concept of legal subjectivity (1988: 61) and to the fact that this concept has encompassed a constantly expanding group (ibid.: 65f). The arguments *against* a legal subjectivity of nature are thus not of a legal technical character, but rather ethical, political or pragmatic (ibid.: 78). He discusses the arguments for a consideration of everything, and writes that the view of humans upon which such a consideration is based has been claimed to be understandable only in the context of religious ethical concepts, as a result of which it cannot be conveyed to everybody (ibid.: 81). He sees his own work as dependent upon what he calls an 'existential orientation', which he himself prefers to the term 'religious'.

It is, however, obvious from the discussion on ecological questions, including the discussion of the normative relation between humans and nature, that it is a discussion which has involved many theologians as well as other writers concerned about the relation between mind and matter (Bateson, 1987; Cobb, 1988; Daly and Cobb, 1989; Dodson Gray, 1981; Griffin, 1988; Mortensen, 1989; Ruether, 1975; and others).

Leimbacher underlines the need for a new cosmology and a new world view when he writes:

> emancipation of humans and nature, the demand for a new relationship between humans and nature can thus be understood as the demand for a doubly new view: a new view of humans, but also a new view of nature (by humans) ....
>
> Humans as part of nature may only realize ourselves when we accept our own and also the external nature, when we acknowledge our adherence to nature (Naturhaftigkeit). Only a human who does *not* define himself through the subjugation of nature may experience himself as non-oppressor. And only a nature that is not only considered as resource, that is not only means, that rather has an innate value, can be recognized and respected by humans. And in the same way, as humans recognize and respect ourselves in the recognition and respect of the fellow being, so we recognize and respect ourselves in the recognition and respect of our inner and outer nature. Emancipation of nature is emancipation of nature from humans through humans. (Leimbacher, 1988: 84 and 85)

If nature is society, then the determination of our relation to nature is also a societal task, and this societal task is expressed through the duty to legitimate interventions in nature. Human interests will have to be subordinated to the interests of nature if speaking about nature as indisposable is to be taken seriously (1988: 113). This could consist of a decision about the permissibility of planned interventions in the rights of nature according to whether they would be tolerable from an ecological point of view (ibid.: 114).

The authors and texts quoted above are dealing with some of the consequences for contemporary legal thinking of the emergent changes in cosmology in the views of nature and human nature.

Changing Legal Cultures: New Paradigms of Order?

The relation between body and nature is one of the examples of the way in which questions of nature push themselves to the forefront of the sciences, including jurisprudence. It is not a relation which is easily understood and, as is emphasized repeatedly by legal authors, it probably requires another understanding of the word 'legal'. Again this understanding may and probably will come about as a result of a change in the general understanding of concepts such as 'nature' and 'culture'.

Biochemists such as the Dane, Jesper Hoffmeyer (1993) and the Englishman, Rupert Sheldrake (1988) have both been inspired by Charles Sanders Peirce in their reflections about whether nature develops habits by which it is governed rather than by laws. Hoffmeyer discusses the tendency of nature to repeat itself and to obtain habits. He sees in this process a mediation between the determinism expressed in the thoughts about absolute laws of nature and the indeterminism expressed through ideas of predictability which are not acquired through laws of nature, but rather through habits which are results of evolution – such habits which have themselves grown and might have developed otherwise.

Sheldrake also ponders about 'The Laws of Nature as Habits' in an article subtitled 'A Post-modern Basis for Science', and one can only speculate about the implications of an abandonment of the 'modern' notion of 'law' and 'order' as 'predictable behavior of each part within a rationally determined system of laws' (Merchant, 1980: 193). Sheldrake writes:

> The universe of classical physics, formulated near the outset of the modern age, was a vast and eternal machine, composed of indestructible particles of matter, propelled by indestructible energy, and governed by changeless mathematical laws. By contrast, the universe of the new cosmology is an evolving organism. It recalls the mythological accounts of the Cosmic Egg, from which the universal organism grew, forming within itself all that is. (Sheldrake, 1988: 79)

The old paradigm of changelessness is in conflict with the paradigm of evolutionary change, and this gives rise to questions not yet answered.

> If the universe has evolved and is still evolving, then has it done so against the background of changeless laws of nature which already existed in a virtual form before the Big Bang? Or do the laws of nature themselves come into being in time and evolve along with the universe? Is it impossible for them to evolve because they represent an eternal system of mathematical order that governs all things in the universe? Or do they depend on what has actually happened; could they be more like habits, as C.S. Peirce suggested a century ago?

> Such a change in our understanding of the 'laws of nature' would be consistent with a change of paradigm from the machine to the organism which would be a change from a modern to a post-modern basis for science. The ordering of machines comes from designs imposed on them by their creators; the ordering of organisms depends on habits and dispositions they have inherited or acquired. All organisms, and the universal organism itself, may be creatures of habit, rather than mechanisms following eternally given, changeless laws. (Sheldrake, 1988: 80)

It is interesting to contrast the language in the documents which came out of the United Nations Conference on Environment and Development in Rio de Janeiro in 1992. In the Rio Declaration on Environment and Development there is talk of 'establishing a new and equitable global partnership' among states, not among humans and the human environment. The declaration upholds the anthropocentric approach to regulation, stating in Principle 1 that 'Human beings are at the centre of concerns for sustainable development. They are entitled to a healthy and productive life in harmony with nature'. It does, however, reflect some deviation from the mechanistic paradigm and its view of nature as a predictable machine which it is possible to control in the introduction of the so-called 'precautionary approach', which is described in Principle 15 as implying that 'Where there are threats of serious or irreversible damage, lack of full scientific certainty shall not be used as a reason for postponing cost-effective measures to prevent environmental degradation'.

Both the Rio Declaration and the Convention on Biological Diversity stress the importance and the role of other types of knowledge than modern scientific knowledge in the process of managing and conserving the environment. In Principle 22 of the Rio Declaration this is expressed as follows:

> Indigenous people and their communities, and other local communities, have a vital role in environmental management and development because of their knowledge and traditional practices. States should recognize and duly support their identity, culture and interests and traditional practices. States should recognize and duly support their identity, culture and interests and enable their effective participation in the achievement of sustainable development.

In the Convention on Biological Diversity, similar considerations are contained in Article 8, which concerns In-situ Conservation, and which states:

> Each Contracting Party shall, as far as possible and as appropriate:
> (j) subject to its national legislation, respect, preserve and maintain knowledge, innovations and practices of indigenous and local communities embodying traditional lifestyles relevant for the conservation and sustainable use of biological

> diversity and promote their wider application with the approval and involvement of the holders of such knowledge, innovations and practices and encourage the equitable sharing of the benefits arising from the utilization of such knowledge, innovations and practices.

What becomes clear from this formulation is that modern scientific knowledge can no longer be considered the form of knowledge which exclusively can contribute to the maintenance of a sustainable relation between humans and the environment or to the conservation of this environment – other forms of knowledge have to be taken into account. That this is a process which is not without its inherent risks and pitfalls should not be denied (see Kuppe, 1994), but these risks do not preclude the possibility that the formulations are also a sign of the emergence of another paradigm of knowledge and order. This emerging paradigm of order is also inherent in the following quotation by Baxi:

> The astonishing jural creativity of ordinary peoples throughout the world must inspire a sense of awe and wonder. The infinite variety of the people's law should serve to some day liberate us from the preferred poverty of state law. Do not we learn immensely more than we learn from the state law, concerning the province and function of law, for example, from the Cheyenne or the Cherokee, from the great cosmologies of the aborigines of Gove Island whose notion of the Dreamtime encompasses all legal forms and processes? Or from the Barotse and Tiv? From the Eskimo's 'situational pluralism'? And from the Kabyles of Algeria concerning the ways of achieving practical coherence in the ritual practice as well as 'acts of jurisprudence'? And from the Tolai of New Guinea? Truly, the jurisprudence of humanity began millennia ago; to ignore this in the teaching and doing of law and jurisprudence, and this is what we learn above all, is to squander the common heritage of mankind. (Baxi, 1991: 276).

The quotation underlines the changing understanding of 'law' and jurisprudence as a result of a changing world and world view. In this context it illuminates the fact that there are links between the changes in legal cultures and legal thinking brought about because of social changes, decolonization and female emancipation, and because of ecological revolutions – changes in the realities and in the perceptions of realities in the relations between humans and non-humans.

In the field of jurisprudence the emerging paradigm seems to be one which is more concerned with order in chaos, and with indeterminacy and precaution than with laws of certainty.

Notes

1 Hanne Petersen (1994a). (The paper forms a chapter of *Homeknitted Law: Norms and Values in Gendered Rule-Making* (forthcoming), Aldershot: Dartmouth).
2 The philosopher Val Plumwood deals with some of these issues in her book, *Feminism and the Mastery of Nature* (London: Routledge, 1993).
3 This is Carolyn Merchant's expression in *Ecological Revolutions* (1989: 70).
4 One of the revisions of this manuscript took place less than a week after the huge hotel ferry *Estonia* sank in the Baltic Sea, on 28 September, in less than an hour, with the loss of more than 900 lives, and described by some newspapers as the biggest civil catastrophe in Europe in peacetime this century. This 'catastrophe' seems at least partly due to a neglect of nature's authority, a lack of respect for nature's power, and perhaps blind trust in mechanical devices growing ever bigger, but threatening the lives of many. Very few of the passengers survived, mainly young men.
5 All translations of quotations are my own. I have taken the liberty sometimes of translating 'Mensch' as 'human', in order to avoid the gendered association of 'man'. This is in line with Leimbacher's own reflections on questions of language at the beginning of his book.

References

Bateson, Gregory (1987) *Angels Fear*, London: Century Hutchinson.

Baxi, Upendra (1991) 'The Conflicting Conceptions of Legal Culture', in Peter Sack *et al.* (eds), *Monismus oder Pluralismus der Rechtskulturen. Anthropologische und ethnologische Grundlagen traditioneller und moderner Rechtssysteme,* Berlin: Duncker & Humblot.

Bosselmann, Klaus (1986) 'Eigene Rechte für die Natur. Ansätze einer ökologischen Rechtsauffassung', *Kritische Justiz.*

Cobb, John B. Jr (1988), 'Ecology, Science and Religion: Toward a Postmodern Worldview', in David Ray Griffin (ed.), *The Re-enchantment of Science. Postmodern Proposals*, Albany: State University of New York Press.

Conradsen, Inger Marie (1994a) 'HIV, graviditet og hvad så?' (HIV, Pregnancy and then?), *RETFÆRD*,

Conradsen, Inger Marie (1994b) 'Access and Allocation to Pregnancy Inducing Treatment in Denmark and Britain', unpublished paper, EUI, Florence.

Daly, Herman and John B. Cobb (1989) *Our Common Good. Redirecting the economy toward community, the environment and a sustainable future*, Boston: Beacon Press.

Damus, Martin (1989, 1990) 'Die Verabschiedung der Moderne. Von elitär-moderner zu affirmativ-postmoderner Kunst', *Kommune*, nos 11 & 12 (1989) and 1 (1990) (Teil I–III).

Derrida, Jacques (1992) 'Force of Law: The Mystical Foundation of Authority', in Drucilla Cornell *et al.* (eds), *Deconstruction and the Possibility of Justice*, New York: Routledge; first published 1990 (in French and English) in *Cardozo Law Review*, **11**, 919–1045.

Dodson Gray, Elizabeth (1981) *Green Paradise Lost*, Wellesley, Mass.: Roundtable Press.

Ferry, Luc (1992) *Le nouvel ordre écologique*, Paris: Editions Grasset & Fasquelle; translated into Danish 1994 as 'Den nye økologiske orden. Træet. Dyret. Mennesket', Copenhagen: Munksgaard/Rosinante.

Finley, Lucinda M. (1986) 'Transcending Equality Theory: A Way out of the Maternity and Workplace Debate', *Columbia Law Review*, **86**, 1118–82.

Fischer, Michael W. (1984) 'Wissenschaftsethik, Naturverständnis, Wissensproduktion. Plädoyer für eine "Re-existenzialisierung" unseres wissenschaftlichen Weltbildes', in *Objektivierung des Rechtsdenkens. Gedächtnisschrift fur Ilmar Tammelo*, Berlin: Duncker & Humblot.

Friedman, Lawrence (1969) 'Legal Culture and Social Development', *Law and Society*, **4** (1), 29–44.

Friedman, Lawrence (1994) 'Is There a Modern Legal Culture?', *Ratio Juris*, **7** (2), July, 117–31.

Giddens, Anthony (1992) *The Transformation of Intimacy. Sexuality, Love and Eroticism in Modern Societies*, London: Polity Press.

Glauber, Hans and Dieter Korczak (1993) 'Toblacher Thesen 1992. Gesundheit und ökologischer Wohlstand. "Langsamer, weniger, besser, schöner"', *Gaia*, **2** (1).

Griffin, David Ray (ed.) (1988) *The Re-enchantment of Science. Postmodern Proposals*, Albany: State University of New York Press.

Haug, Frigga (1992) *Beyond Female Masochism: Memory-Work and Politics*, London: Verso.

Haug, Frigga *et al.* (1987) *Female Sexualization*, London: Verso.

Hellum, Anne (ed.) (1993a) *Birth Law*, Oslo: Scandinavian University Press.

Hellum, Anne (1993b) 'New Reproductive Technology in an Ecological Perspective', in A. Hellum (ed.), *Birth Law*, Oslo: Scandinavian University Press.

Hoffmeyer, Jesper (1993) *En snegl på vejen. Betydningens natur-historie* (A Snail on the Road. The Natural History of Meaning), Copenhagen: Rosinante/ Munksgaard.

Jaggar, Alison (1989) 'Love and Knowledge: Emotion in Feminist Epistemology', in A. Jaggar and Susan Bordo (eds) in *Gender/Body/Knowledge. Feminist Reconstruction of Being and Knowing*, New Brunswick/London: Rutgers University Press.

King, Ynestra (1989) 'Healing the Wounds: Feminism, Ecology and Nature/Culture Dualism', in Alison M. Jaggar and Susan R. Bordo (eds), *Gender/Body/Knowledge. Feminist Reconstruction of Being and Knowing*, New Brunswick/London: Rutgers University Press.

Kravaritou, Yota (1993) 'Feminist Approaches to Law and Cultural Diversity', paper given at a conference at the European University Institute as an introduction to an anthology of the same title edited by Kravaritou - forthcoming.

Kuppe, René (ed.) (1994) 'Indigenous people's natural resources, environment and legal pluralism', *Yearbook of Law and Anthropology*, Vienna.

Leimbacher, Jörg (1988) *Die Rechte der Natur*, Basle/Frankfurt-am-Main: Helbing & Lichtenhain.

Luhmann, Niklas (1986) *Ökologische Kommunikation. Kann die moderne Gesellschaft sich auf ökologische Gefährdungen einstellen?*, Opladen: Westdeutscher Verlag, Braunschweig.

Merchant, Carolyn (1980) *The Death of Nature. Women, Ecology and the Scientific Revolution*, New York: Harper & Row.

Merchant, Carolyn (1989) *Ecological Revolutions*, Chapel Hill/London: University of North Carolina Press.

Mortensen, Viggo (1989) *Teologi og naturvidenskab* (Theology and Natural Science), Copenhagen: Munksgaard.

Pahuus, Mogens (1988) *Naturen & den menneskelige natur. En filosofisk og litterær analyse af mennesket i naturen og naturen i mennesket* (Nature and Human Nature), Århus: Forlaget Philosophia.

Peterson Hanne (1993a) 'Feminist and Ecological Perspectives on Legal Thinking', unpublished conference paper delivered at a keynote panel at the Vth International and Interdisciplinary Women's Congress, February, Costa Rica.

Petersen, Hanne (1993b) 'Bæredygtighed, børn og badevand. Feministiske og økologiske perspektiver på retlig tænkning' (Sustainability, Children and Bathwater. Feminist and Ecological Perspectives on Legal Thinking), *RETFÆRD*, **60**, 15–30.

Petersen, Hanne (1994) 'On Women and Legal Concepts', *Working Papers in Law*, no. 8, European University Institute, Florence.

Petersen, Hanne (1993c) 'Gendered Norms in Western Societies. Support or Obstacle for Sustainability?' in Harold Finkler (ed.), *Proceedings of the Commission on Folk Law and Legal Pluralism*, IXth International Symposium, Mexico City.

Prigogine, Ilya and Isabelle Stengers (1985) *Den nye pagt mellem mennesket og universet*, Århus: Ask. (Translation of a revised version of 'La Nouvelle Alliance: Metamorphose de la Science'; English version 'Order out of Chaos: Man's New Dialogue with Nature', New York, 1984.)

Ruether, Rosemary (1975) *New Women/New Earth. Sexist Ideologies and Human Liberation*, New York: The Seabury Press.

Sennett, Richard (1976) *The Fall of Public Man*, Cambridge University Press.

Sheldrake, Rupert (1988) 'The Laws of Nature as Habits: A Post-modern Basis for Science', in David Ray Griffin (ed.), *The Re-enchantment of Science. Postmodern Proposals*, Albany: State University of New York Press.

Sitter, Beat (1984) *Plädoyer für das Naturrechtsdenken. Zur Anerkennung von Eigenrechten der Natur. Beihefte zur Zeitschrift für Schweizerisches Recht*, Basle: Helbing & Lichtenhahn Verlag AG.

Stone, Christopher (1972) 'Should Trees Have Legal Standing? Toward Legal Rights for Natural Objects', *Southern California Law Review*, **I**.

Skakkebæk, Niels E., Andrés Negro-Vilar, Frank Michal and Mahmoud Fathalla (1991) 'Impact of the Environment on Reproductive Health. Report and Recommendations of a WHO International Workship', 30 September–4 October.

Tammelo, Ilmar (1980) 'Über die Zeitdimension der Gerechtigkeit', in H. Miehsler *et al.* (eds), *Ius Humanitatis. Festschrift zum 90. Geburtstag von Alfred Verdross*, Berlin: Duncker & Humblot.

West, Robin (1988) 'Jurisprudence and Gender', *University of Chicago Law Review.*

PART II
DISCLOSING LEGAL CULTURE: THE PRODUCTION OF DIFFERENCE

9 An Entrepreneurial Conception of the Law? The American Model through Italian Eyes

Maria Rosaria Ferrarese

Introductory Notes on Legal Systems and Their Differences

Broadly speaking, the difference between the legal systems of Continental Europe and the Anglo-American legal system is conveyed by the image of two great legal families: that of common law, and that of civil law. These two types of legal system are often conceived as two 'functional equivalents': that is, as two structures which, although they employ different instruments, methods and organizations, end up by performing substantially similar functions. The aim of this article is to show that the function of the law in common law systems, and especially in the American one, is profoundly different from its function in Continental legal systems.

The essential idea developed in these pages is that, whereas European legal doctrine, under the influence of legal positivism, has fostered the image as well as the functioning of a legal system modelled on political referents, predominant in the American case is an image and a functioning of the law inspired by economic referents. The argument developed here therefore seems to contradict Weber's celebrated thesis that Continental legal systems are best suited to satisfying the needs of a modern capitalistic economy (Weber, 1980). We will argue instead that the functional nexus between law and economic needs is much closer in the Anglo-American tradition, and especially in the American one. As Trubek has pointed out, Weber himself 'recognized that there is a potential conflict between legal nationalism of the logical formal type and a legal system's creative capacity to generate the new substantive concepts and institutions required by changing economic situations' (Trubek, 1972: 746).

In order to sustain this thesis, rather than conduct parallel analysis of the two types of legal system, we will endeavour to describe how an Italian observer sees the American legal system. Many references will be made to American legal doctrines and scholars, because scholarship has considerable influence on legal practice in the United States and this 'is perhaps the feature which most distinguishes American from English law' (Sacco, 1991: 348). Overall we will dwell on those features of the American legal system that seem most antithetical to one of its counterparts in Continental Europe. In and of themselves, these features may appear obvious to a public with an American legal background, but, observed from the perspective of a foreign observer, they yield new insights.

In order to grasp the significance of these features it is necessary to be fully aware of the difference, in both cultural and organizational terms, between Continental legal systems and common law systems. It is customary to characterize this difference as lying in the pre-eminence of legislative law in the European tradition, and of judge-made law in the Anglo-American system. In other words, a distinction is drawn between 'written' and 'unwritten' law. Yet this superficial difference conceals others that are much more significant. For example, as has been pointed out, in order to explain the paradox of an 'unwritten law', which is collected in thousands and thousands of pages of case law reports, one must make reference to that 'declaratory theory' of common law, which is 'the true doctrinal foundation of the functioning and legitimation of Anglo-American judge-made law' (Mattei, 1992:88).

It should be stressed above all that legislation in the Continental European system, like judge-made law in the Anglo-American system, has a paradigmatic value: in other words, they both permeate the entire functioning of the legal system. Thus the existence of nominally similar elements in the two systems may in fact correspond to the fulfilment of different functions and to the assertion of different principles.

Significant in this regard is the difference that marks legislation in the two contexts. In Continental Europe, the primacy of the legislator was fully part of the project for the monopolization of political power described by Weber. In the United States, statute law was born and developed as a result of forces and exigencies of the opposite kind: not in the name of so-called 'sovereignty' and of an overall government design, but as the outcome of popular pressures that were particularist, diversified and localized. As Hurst has convincingly shown, American legislation was characterized by an 'open door principle' which deliberately exposed it to the demands and pressures of the most diverse claimants (Hurst, 1982a:10). The intention was to give voice to the new needs and interests that had arisen in the social and economic spheres and which failed to find satisfaction through the traditional channels of judge-made law. Consequently, American legislation has always been 'a great target for opportunity' (Hurst, 1972:11).

More interesting, however, is the fact that, in a certain sense, legislation appropriated features from judge-made law and came to function 'in a fashion almost as passive as the courts, in effect only acting upon the issues framed before it by parties most closely involved' (Hurst, 1972:38–9). At the beginning of this century, statutes, as the fruit of the efforts and litigation of interest groups, were still forged by an 'adversary process in the legislature' which transformed legislators and political parties into 'brokers among divergent interests' (ibid.:40).

To this overstated opposition between the features of European and American legislation it can be objected that, today, matters are different. Certainly, European legislation has long since shed its features of generality and abstractness to assume the guise of 'negotiated laws' and 'by-laws' (as the Italian *leggine*, which cater to micro interests). All parliaments are now assailed by lobbies, assuming they were once immune to them.

However, it would be a mistake to presume that the legislative process has been identical in the two contexts. As, for example, the experience of regulation (which is discussed further below) shows, interests are allowed to raise their voice in opposition to the regulators: the paradigmatic value of the trial before the courts continues to influence the legal process. Not coincidentally, administrative process is based on a 'quasi-judicial' model. As Damaska has pointed out, in a liberal state the form proper to power is a judicial form, which restricts itself to arbitration among interests (Damaska, 1986).

An Entrepreneurial Conception of the Law

The general thesis of this chapter is that American law appears to be inspired by economic rather than political referents. This idea is not a new one, since it has been developed on several occasions and from various points of view in the American literature. Apparently shared by all these often extremely diverse formulations is a view of law as *legal instrument* rather than *legal command*. Indeed, the notion of the instrumentalism of the law is not extraneous to the European tradition of legal positivism: Kelsen, for instance, talks of the law as a 'social technique' which may pursue the most diverse of ends (Kelsen, 1985). However, it is principally in America that the idea of the instrumentalism of the law has been given not only explicit treatment but also, and especially, an economic slant. As Hurst has written: 'Uses of law and disputes over uses of law are so woven into economic growth in the United States that legal and economic history cannot be separated' (Hurst, 1972:9).

When discussing instrumentalism, the obligatory reference is to Summers, who has claimed that American pragmatic instrumentalism is the fourth great tradition in Western legal theory, together with analytical positivism, the doctrine of natural law and historical jurisprudence (Summers, 1982:19). The feature shared by the various instrumentalist theories is that they all consider the law to be an instrument used to achieve practical ends. It is a theory, therefore, with a protean ability to present itself in a variety of guises. Thus, since its first appearance under the aegis of legal realism and sociological jurisprudence, it has exerted its influence on more recent schools like the law and economics one.

Summers, as we have seen, labels instrumentalism 'pragmatic'. This qualification concerns the fact that the various instrumentalist theories stress the role performed by public subjects, above all by judges, in the evolution of the law. They are, in Pound's 1916 term, true 'social engineers'. Now, as Summers himself emphasizes, the excessive stress placed by the instrumentalists on the role of public subjects, and especially of the judiciary, in 'law in action' unjustifiably obscures the role of private individuals in the evolution of law. In a democracy with a market economy, 'most of the [law] takes the form of private arrangements between and among private individuals and entities' (Summers, 1982:219): contracts, property transfers, donations, wills and so on become the law's life-blood, and they cast private individuals in the role of its true source. Even Weber argued that the extension of the forms of negotiative autonomy that accompany the market economy lead to the 'decentralization of legal production' (Weber, 1980:86) to private parties.

Summers' observations on the importance of the role performed by non-public subjects in 'law in action' point out a theme that will be given especial development in this chapter. For that matter, an authentically instrumentalist theory, since Jhering, must necessarily also make reference to the everyday users of legal norms and to private law (Jhering, 1879). However, this perspective has not always been maintained; indeed, we will seek to show how the various versions of instrumentalism, by laying principal stress on the *institutional components* of the law's development, have obscured the *non-institutional components* that have also had a part to play in that development. We will analyse the ways in which American law is receptive to contributions from private individuals and groups, at the same time examining how this particular functioning of 'privately supplemented' law tends to foster attitudes in legal actors which are not merely normative – that is, directed at observance or, at most, non-observance – but are 'entrepreneurial', that is, designed to obtain a gain by means of the creative use of legal instruments. In short, this chapter will seek to say something further and partly different with respect to theories of legal instrumentalism. Its intention is to show not only that in the United States there is a greater propensity to make instrumental use of the law, but that this instrumental use is markedly economic in character. Thus, from the point of view adopted here, the propensity of Americans to use the law instrumentally will be analysed under two aspects: (1) from the standpoint of private subjects, rather than from the standpoint of public subjects engaged in social engineering; and (2) for the pursuit of ends which, in the broad sense, we may define as economic in character.

Regarding the former aspect, on the premise that the instrumentalism of American law may be on the part of private subjects just as much as of public ones, we will seek to shed light on the modalities that make this behaviour possible. This means that, whereas in the tradition of Continental Europe (legislative) law is culturally conceived and technically shaped essentially as an instrument in the hands of political authority, in the United States law (mainly judicial, but also legislative and even public law, both criminal and administrative) has gradually developed into an instrument not immune from opportunistic use by private subjects. Under the second aspect, analysis will be conducted of the 'social' attitude (in the Weberian sense) of a legal actor which uses the law to pursue 'acquisitive' ends: analysis, that is, of the influence of economic motives on the behaviour of an actor which has a referent of economic type. Here again one finds an 'entrepreneurial' conception of law; that is, one based not so much on the idea that rules should be obeyed as that they may be used creatively for opportunistic purposes.

In what sense can one talk of the entrepreneurship of a legal actor? That of 'entrepreneur' is an economic concept which is associated with two principal traits: a capacity to take the initiative in an activity geared to the production of wealth, and a capacity to assume the relative risk. Nothing therefore seems further from the realm of the law, if the latter is understood as a normative model which may either be observed or not observed. If instead the law is based on an instrumental model, it also responds to the expectations of gain entertained by subjects, which therefore turn themselves into 'entrepreneurs' endowed, as we shall see, with both the capacity to take the initiative and the propensity to take risks.

Private Uses of Law and the Philosophy of Checks and Balances

Before embarking on analysis of the features that render American law amenable to instrumental use by private subjects, it is advisable to establish our premises concerning American institutional culture. It is necessary to start from a different philosophy of the American legal system, one which assigns a prominent position to the nexus between law and interests; a nexus that is not to be found in European legal systems. The American legal system was born and developed in a climate of the overt recognition of interests which typified the theory of natural rights (Pound, 1954:25,59). However, at least three more referents are important for understanding how the American system works, and especially in terms of the argument that we wish to develop here: contractualism, utilitarianism and pragmatism.

American contractualism, inspired by Locke, ascribes the origin of political power to a 'pact' among free citizens. It posits that constantly renewed consensus on the political institutions and, within the legal sphere, the predominance of private over public law, are of central importance.

When applied to the legal system, Benthamian utilitarian philosophy assumes that the set of norms imposed and sanctioned by the state must pursue the greatest happiness – conceived in terms of free individual self-fulfilment – of the greatest number of people.

Pragmatism, a philosophy of markedly American inspiration, assesses actions in terms of their efficaciousness with respect to the ends pursued rather than in relation to value judgements; whence the close connection between pragmatism and a methodology of action predicated on trial and error. Pragmatism may be regarded as the other face of instrumentalism: as we have seen, Summers talks in this regard of 'pragmatic instrumentalism'.

Rooted in these three philosophies are concepts which shed important light on the particular pattern assumed by the American institutional system, inspired as it is by a liberal political philosophy which views individual freedom as paramount and regards all aggregations of public power with suspicion. The following contraposition may serve as a summary of the characteristics which this chapter seeks to highlight: whereas European law is prevalently law 'from above' which furnishes models of behaviour, American law is prevalently law 'from below' which in many cases lends itself to instrumental use by subjects in pursuit of their opportunistic ends.

As well as drawing on a different political philosophy, the American legal system obviously derives from a consequently different form of constitutional engineering based on a system of checks and balances which systematically seeks to disperse power, rather than organize it into powerful and monolithic institutions. The analysis of the American legal system propounded here combines the traditional conception of checks and balances among diverse articulations of public power with a specific reference to the way in which, internally to the various institutions of public power, channels are devised for the injection of private interests which serve to counter-balance 'public' ones. The American legal system has been likewise designed to reflect this specific variant of the system of 'checks and balances'. Instead of being entirely constructed from above, as the expression of commands issued by the sovereign, it reserves an important role for private subjects and sets public interests against private ones. This institutionalized mix of public and private interests is especially evident when it is organized into the form of explicit bargaining. In all cases, this is indicative that the American legal system is expressly designed to be penetrated by interests.

Obviously, a major role in this respect is performed by judge-made law which generates a significant mixing of private and public interests. In pursuing this argument, moreover, some of the intricate relationships between the American judicial system and the political system can be examined. One may regard the courts as sites of non-political decision making. There are various reasons for this view: first and foremost, the predominantly individualistic nature of matters of judicial interest; and then the fact that such cases are handled individually has a disaggregating effect and allows margins of difference in judicial decisions. This further strengthens the idea that judicial treatment is non-political in nature.

However, in conducting their activities the courts absorb a proportion of potentially political demands. In these cases, the judicial system performs a specific political function. Individualizing the issue examined lifts the obligation to respond in markedly political terms. As has been pointed out, 'individual choice and demands on public authority by invoking legal rights are closely interwoven with the making of public policy without any requisite involvement by a collectivity or any necessity for a public consciousness' (Zemans, 1983:692). Accordingly, the courts give responses which are the 'functional equivalents' of political ones, but without it being necessary to set the political machine in motion. They therefore help to keep a proportion of demands below the explicitly political threshold.

This depoliticization, however, is only one of the possible relations to be observed between the courts and the political system. As well as obscuring the political aspects of a case, the judicial treatment of an issue may also help highlight such aspects. Obviously, the political importance of cases treated judicially varies greatly, ranging from ones which have an entirely circumscribed significance to those which assume a more or less marked political content. Moreover, their political weight is not an objective datum; it is 'constructed' by the actors in question in order to give a more distinctive profile to the instances brought before the courts. Indeed, the trial may serve as an occasion to give political visibility to the case under examination, in the sense that one of the parties concerned implements a 'judicial strategy' which views the courts as the first stage in the politicization of the issue at hand. The 'judicial strategy' may be preferred to other strategies because it offers certain advantages: ease of access to the courts on an individual basis, without having to resort to more complex formal structures (Zemans, 1983); and the opportunity afforded to the interested party gradually to measure the 'politicizability' of the issue, assessing both the strength of his case and the probability of gaining consensus and attention. It is no coincidence, for that matter, that it was precisely the United States that saw the forging of an instrument like class action, which allows the audacious combination of the private logic of the trial with a more extensive area of interests coincident with those of one of the parties involved. Indeed, it is precisely the facility of the judicial instrument compared with other strategies for penetrating the area of government (the legislature, for example, or the executive) that has brought a series of issues before the American courts which are no longer of individualistic significance but are already imbued with political and collective consequence. Significant examples are provided by the civil rights movements of the 1960s, which made enormous use of the courts, or by those interest groups which have come to regard the courts as an arena in which to achieve their 'representation'.

The merging of tendencies towards depoliticization and tendencies towards politicization has given rise to the paradox whereby in the United States the courts, as the paramount sites of the representation of private interests, also serve to politicize these interests. In other words, the judicial process often functions as a parapolitical channel through which private interests gain access to the area of government. This process is well illustrated by the so-called 'public law litigation' model, in which the typically private dimension of litigation intersects issues of public policy.

The judicial treatment of issues allows the balancing of the relationship between the courts and the political system in another manner as well: by organizing the relationship between legal stability and change so that they offset each other. This counterbalancing usually takes place through a sort of division of labour between the organs of political–legislative decision making, which initiate major legal changes, and the courts, which produce those micro changes which, only cumulatively and in the long term, produce broader trends. Sometimes, however, the judicial response to individual and private issues may conflict with the existing political arrangement: as has been observed, 'On occasion litigation promotes decisions which appear to threaten the sovereignty of legislative or executive branches' (Sarat and Grossman, 1975:1215). In other words, it is possible to use the courts to pass decisions which contradict the existing political set-up. In such cases, the courts act as an area of decision making which is supplementary (sometimes alternative) to political decision making. There thus comes about, to use Lockard's term, that form of 'conflict displacement' which also characterized the relationship between the civil rights movements and the courts (Lockard, 1968:142), a typical example of which is *Brown* v. *Board of Education*, and the ruling which effectively put an end to the principle of 'separate but equal' that had regulated relations between whites and blacks since the Civil War.

It is evident, therefore, that the political function of the courts is a highly complex one, and that it involves an intricate network of relationships between private inputs and public responses stemming from the judicial treatment of issues.

The American Legal System as a System 'from Below'

We have so far sought to set out some of the cultural and institutional reasons for regarding the American legal system as a system shaped 'from below'. Using a different metaphor, one may say that a legal system which allows itself to be influenced from below is an 'open' legal system. Friedman not coincidentally describes American society as an 'open society'; that is, one 'whose organs of law, authority and government are constructed so as to expose them to some degree of public opinion or public pressure, and in which these organs in fact respond, to some degree, to such pressure' (Friedman, 1990:19–20). Thus law constructed so that it can be used instrumentally acquires a sense with respect to overall political order.

We will now seek to identify the institutional features of the American legal system which permit, facilitate or indeed necessitate its operability/actionability from below. We will examine, albeit briefly and with no claim to exhaustiveness, four essential aspects: (1) the supremacy of private–judicial law; (2) the adversarial model of the trial; (3) the predominance of procedure-based law over substantive law; and (4) the exposure of law to bargaining processes. Note that all four of these aspects tend to moderate adjudication or even to act as alternatives to adjudication.

The Supremacy of Judicial–Private Law

One of the first characteristics that one notes when examining the American legal system is the centrality of judge-made law. This centrality, moreover, can be linked to the features of an open society. In its turn, the judicial system can be termed 'open' because, barriers of cost and culture notwithstanding, 'the right to go to curt is in theory totally unlimited' (Friedman, 1990:21). A large body of literature contends that the centrality of judge-made law is symptomatic of a system based on decentralization and on spontaneity, and so justifies the analogy between common law and the market. Paradoxically, however, this emphasis stems mainly from a view which holds that adjudication is the central pillar of the American legal system, and this has obviously helped to push an equally important aspect into the background: the essentially reactive nature of the courts. In other words, judge-made law is law which is solicited by pleas advanced by private subjects, and it does not exist independently of the demands, pressures, needs and options that these express. Only by assessing the importance of the process of legal mobilization is a thorough understanding of the legal system in the United States possible. Despite the various meanings that attach to the concept of legal mobilization, implicit to it is reference to a reactive perspective: the court system, in other words, functions on the basis of the motion that subjects can and will give to the law. More generally, we may agree with Zemans that, in a 'reactive' law system, 'individual litigants actually set the agenda of the judicial branch of government' (Zemans, 1983:691).

This ability to set the law in motion is important from several points of view. First, it activates, especially through the activity of the judge, the process of constant relegitimation of norms that Weber stressed (Weber, 1968). In a similar sense, Bohannan speaks of a constant 'reinstitutionalization' which accompanies the life of the law (Bohannan, 1965:34–7). Even more important is the constant selection of norms and of meanings that takes place as a result of legal mobilization.

If one neglects these aspects, the evolution of the legal system may appear to be essentially driven by public subjects and above all by judges. This flawed vision of the internal dynamics of the legal system is paralleled by the idea that the sole function of the legal system is that of resolving conflicts. It is instead possible to consider the process of setting the legal system in motion as participation in political functions. Political functions performed by citizens extend significantly to include an active role in the implementation and enforcement of legal rules. Enforcement, in fact, however much it may be inspired by a culture of rigid and severe sanctions, in its actual functioning is driven more by private impulses and by claiming mechanisms than by an endeavour to suppress deviance as such. It risks becoming 'particularist' because 'any enforcement agenda-setting attempted by a governmental agency depends upon the affected citizenry's demands for implementation' (Zemans, 1983:696). Seen from this standpoint, the legal system performs an important function of 'power dispersion' and appears 'quintessentially democratic, although not necessarily egalitarian' (ibid.: 691).

Indeed, in a certain sense, political participation via legal mobilization is more direct and easier than the participation which works through traditional political channels: and neither does it entail commitment to collective choices. A further important aspect to emerge from Zemans' analysis concerns the interaction between interests and the legal system. The latter does not solely select from among existing interests those which warrant safeguarding; it also helps to structure the interests system. In short, there do not exist either interests as objective entities or legal rules as full-fledged models. Rather, there is constant interaction between the former and the latter which unfolds in the courts: changeable social perceptions of the problems constantly come up, challenging existing legal arrangements, and help to redefine and redirect them.

An extreme metaphor with which to convey the importance of legal mobilization likens the courts to supermarkets selling legal goods: the courts are the place to resort to because they can give the customer what he or she wants (Kurland, 1986:611). With the significant difference, one might add, that the courts do not offer pre-packaged products, but products which have been customized to meet the 'customers' requirements. 'Reactive legal mobilization' is therefore a dynamic which 'reflects an entrepreneurial model of law. The latter assumes that every citizen voluntarily and rationally pursues his or her own interests, with the greatest legal welfare of the greatest number that presumably ensues from the selfish enterprise of the atomized mass. It is the legal equivalent of the market economy' (Black, 1973:138).

The Adversarial Model of the Trial

If the adaptive character of judge-made law is to be grasped to its fullest extent, account should also be taken of the adversarial model on which both civil and criminal trials are based in the United States. The cornerstone of this model is the passive role of the judge, who acts largely as arbiter, which is counterposed by the active role of the parties, who take the initiative in both the legal definition of the facts and in the discovery and gathering of the evidence. So the trial takes essentially the form of a contest between two private parties, who are almost wholly responsible for conduct of the trial.

Damaska has rightly called attention to the link between the adversarial model of the American trial and the political culture of a 'reactive' state. It is within a state inspired by the principle of *laissez-faire* that the trial is structured as a contest between parties, although parts of this model can also be found elsewhere (Damaska, 1986). Predominant in a reactive state, therefore, is a purely functional conception of the trial as the means to resolve a dispute. The judicial decision, in acknowledgement of the pre-eminent role of the private parties, is therefore framed on functional grounds and lays no claim to truth or to absolute justice.

However, although once ubiquitous, this interpretation of the judicial decision as passive and merely functional has gradually been qualified and criticized. Ideologically, this interpretation has been attacked and in part superseded by a strand of inquiry which, by reversing the direction of the adversarial tradition, has stressed the role of adjudication in the evolution of law. The debate opened by realism in American legal culture, with its critique of the merely 'declarative' function of the judge, may be also seen as an attack on the rigidly adversarial conception of the trial. There is an obvious contrast between two views: the view that it should be the parties that freely confront each other in the court, and that from this a necessarily 'bargained' decision should ensue' and the view that the true impulse to the decision should stem from the judge, who undertakes an act of adjudication. Since the 1920s and 1930s, the advent of a new legal culture associated with the names of Cardozo, Pound and the realist school has given rise to widespread criticism of the traditional model of justice based on the strictly adversarial principle (Dondi, 1993:22).

There are then the changes that have occurred in trial procedure. Adversariness cannot go so far as outright conflict, and it must avoid at least three risks, lest the adversarial model degenerate to the point that it betrays the expectations of those who regard it as the 'expression of a global ideology of justice' (Taruffo,1978:57). The first risk is that of excessive litigiousness between the parties, since this may render resolution of the contest even more difficult. The second risk is that an inordinate asymmetry of power between the two parties may give rise to a manifestly biased outcome. The third concerns those cases in which a judicial decision entails changes in public policy. When a social issue coincides with a private contest between parties, the judge's decision has repercussions at the collective level and requires that the threshold of adversariness be surpassed.

The joint effect of these and other factors has mitigated the more extreme features of the adversarial conflict, and altered the form taken by the judge's control over the trial. The cases of 'entrepreneurial litigation' now common in America (Olson, 1992) have led to tighter judicial control over the increasingly aggressive courtroom behaviour displayed by lawyers. However, this has been only a response, and an often ineffectual one at that, to the exaggerated 'entrepreneurship' of the parties, the plaintiff especially. In various ways, the role of the judge has changed: the degree of participation by the judge in the case, his or her familiarity with it, required for the purposes of overall management, entails the abandonment of the former image of the judge as 'supervisor of the trial' to the point that the 'spectre arises of a too powerful judge, too intimate with the parties, and too emotionally interested in the outcome of the controversy' (Miller, 1984).

There are numerous facets to this contradiction between a strictly adversarial legal system and one based on adjudication. First, there is the role of law with respect to welfare: the adversarial system is indifferent to the effective inequality of the parties, whereas adjudication may be sensitive to it. There is then the problem of the bargaining power of the parties, understood as substantial rather than formal. But of paramount importance is the criterion on which a decision is taken by means of an adversarial procedure or as an act of adjudication, respectively. If one adopts the adversarial model, one assumes that the dispute will be resolved mainly by bargaining between the parties, the essential feature of which is the absence of a third party acting as decision maker. If one adopts the adjudication model, then the dispute is resolved by a decision made by a third party, who is in a position of relative independence and superiority with respect to the parties to the suit.

As has been observed elsewhere, the contrast between negotiation and adjudication relates to the distinction between interests and values: negotiation is used mainly in situations where resources are scarce; adjudication is more useful when the dispute involves values, norms or facts (Gulliver, 1979:8). Obviously, values and interests can never be distinguished absolutely (Eisenberg, 1976) and, moreover, they intermingle in every trial. Nevertheless, the fact that the American trial is founded on the bargaining system means that it is considered as essentially an arena of conflicts among interests. Nor is the distinction between adversariness and adjudication ever absolute. These are two models of conflict resolution which are necessarily limited and diluted in reality. However, on the ideological and doctrinaire level as well as that of trial procedure, the American trial is still based on adversariness.

The Predominance of Procedure-based Law over Substantive law

The American legal system is largely structured by rules which delineate courses of general and external action, and which can be given the most diverse contents: 'the tenor of state law is not to announce what citizens should do substantively; rather it is to set forth procedures which make such arrangements binding and enforceable' (Damaska,1986:76). Rules, in short, are procedural in character, and it is this that differentiates them from norms, which prescribe certain forms of behaviour and leave only narrow margins of discretion.

It is possible to provide examples of this procedural law from contexts other than the United States. To begin with, property law possessed this character and was therefore, as Luhmann has pointed out, intrinsically 'de-juridifying': that is to say, it provided a general framework which made specific prescriptions unnecessary (Luhmann,1987:52–3). These features are even more marked in contract law, which, during the long period of American *laissez-faire*, was based on a merely procedural logic which gave unlimited options to the contracting parties, with no concern for equity or substantial justice, according to the well-known doctrine of the 'privity of contract'. It could be objected that this procedural character is common to all systems of private law, and that it is therefore wrong to maintain that it is a distinctive feature of American law. For that matter, Weber spoke of the sphere of 'authorizations' as a legal sector of particular importance for the development of economic activity (Weber, 1968).

However, it seems possible to counter this objection on three grounds. Firstly, it is American law that displays the purest features of procedure-based law. Its rules are conceived more as instruments to enhance the opportunities of subjects than as instruments to regulate their behaviour. Secondly, this idea, which permeates the whole of American legal doctrine, goes well beyond private law alone to shape '*all* state law as a [hypothetical] or [model] contract. And being a surrogate for actual agreement, in principle it can be deplaced and modified by the actual [private] arrangements of individuals and groups' (Damaska, 1986:76). Thirdly, the procedural character of American law seems to have responded perfectly to an economic *ratio*, enabling subjects not only to reach agreements in accord with their own interests, but, as we shall see below, to use the rules entrepreneurially.

Procedure-based law is essentially 'yielding'; that is, it serves the free choices of private subjects coherently with their interests. In the United States the term 'facilitating law' is used to refer to law conceived as an instrument designed to facilitate private bargaining. The purpose of the rules is to render private agreements not only possible but easier and legally recognizable. The pre-eminence accorded to private negotiation moves through two channels which can be considered as two different versions of facilitating law: a version which stresses the default, as opposed to the mandatory, conception of law, and a version which apparently imposes constraints on the parties but which in fact reflects a purely 'vehicular' conception of law.

The first version occurs when the emphasis is placed on a non-mandatory conception of the law, one of contractualist inspiration, which subordinates observance of rules to the different interest of the party or parties concerned: so-called 'default rules' can give legal value to agreements between private subjects, but may also be replaced by different ones.

The second version of facilitating law arises when law consists of merely formal obligations which subjects must obey in order to achieve particular legal effects: the 'formalities' traditionally viewed as guaranteeing certainty (for citizens) and restricting arbitrary power (of the judge) are prescriptions whose non-observance entails voidness for the parties. But the prescription limits itself to respect of a form within which subjects may introduce any type of substantial agreement (Kennedy, 1973). Contract law, which in the United States is traditionally interpreted in formalistic terms, is the best example of a legal form able to 'convey' any content whatever.

As well as functioning as containers of private will, formalities sometimes also serve to structure a scale of convenience used by private subjects to guide their decisions. Rules relative to tort liability, in particular, serve this purpose. In the presence of rules regulating the interaction among subjects, if one has caused damage to the other, or if one of them is in breach of contract, it is possible to gauge whether the regulative criterion adopted by the law reflects a purely 'individualistic' or a purely 'altruistic' logic (Kennedy, 1976). In other words, tort rules can respond to the end of keeping the individual's options open, independently of problems of observance, or to the end of ensuring observance of rules, giving more forceful protection to the injured party.

Yet, in the American tradition, we find an enduring tendency to restrict tort liability which symmetrically offloaded damage on to weaker parties in exchange for an incentive to economic entrepreneurship by subjects (Horwitz, 1977). Even after this period, when tort law began to assume increasing importance in American social life at the end of the last century (Friedman,1985:299), it seemed to structure rules which, behind their outward appearance of preventing breach of contract or some form of unlawful behaviour, in actual fact did no more than structure 'the private choice between damages with compensation and non-damages' (Kennedy,1976: 1698).

There emerges here a further aspect of an authentically facilitative conception of law which is alien to punitive intent and governed by purely compensatory criteria. The adoption of purely compensatory remedies in dealing with non-observance of rules has the obvious effect of encouraging transactions. In these cases, the antithesis between prescriptive and purely facilitative aspects is taken to its extreme. The choice in favour of the purely facilitative option follows a line of thought which ranges from Holmes (1881), who saw the legal system as allowing 'a person to injure another's property, even intentionally, with impunity' (Horwitz,1992:130) to the theoreticians of the law and economics school, who view the dispositions of private law as nothing but a system of tariffs which private subjects decide to pay in exchange for non-observance (Calabresi, 1970). As has been pointed out, the reference is to a context of 'social Darwinism' where the legal system is unable to enforce altruistic duty (Kennedy,1976:1744).

There is, on the other hand, a law made up of default rules (mainly of legislative origin) which may be replaced by different choices made by the interested parties. The faculty to regulate transactions in a manner at variance with the rules available constitutes an important enclave of legal freedom which can be traced back to a contractualist matrix. Moreover, the default nature of norms is not always clearly enacted, and it may become an issue of debate which reflects the classic confrontation between regulators and deregulators: the former inclined to believe that limits should be set on the self-regulation of subjects, the latter convinced that it is instead the freedom of self-regulation which should be guaranteed.

This contradiction has recently been revived in American debate on corporate law (Bebchuk, 1989) where the regulators proclaim the essentially mandatory nature of corporate law (Coffee, 1989) and the deregulators invoke the pre-eminence of contractual freedom in corporate law and therefore the essentially enabling (or default) nature of its rules (Easterbrook and Fischel, 1991).

The challenge raised against an idea of mandatory law has been essentially based on a theorization of the corporate law as a 'nexus of contracts' (Kornhauser, 1989). When corporate law is reduced to an extension of contract law, where the freedom to opt out is always guaranteed, this means a shift 'from law to economics' (Coffee, 1989). However, suffice it to point out that, because in the United States corporate law falls under the jurisdiction of states, a company can freely choose where to be incorporated: various states 'compete' to attract resources and investors and the possibility of 'opting out' is therefore in a certain sense always available.

Procedure-based law produces an idea of procedural justice as well. In a procedural conception of justice any possible outcome tends to be safeguarded, rather than one grounded in standards of some kind. It therefore represents a pre-ordained acceptance of factuality rather than of normativity. The terms 'fairness' and 'fair play' are 'closely associated with competitive sport and gambling, which pervade idiomatic English' (Fletcher, 1993:62). Something akin to a 'sporting ethic' presides over the concept of procedural justice, ensuring that all those taking part in the game have equal chances of winning (Frank, 1950:91ff).

Examples of the procedural character of American law can be found in areas other than those of common law and of private law. Paradoxically, with the decline of the 'rule of law' and with the advent of the welfare state, proceduralism came to permeate the very concept of justice. The sporting ethic also requires that all parties wishing to compete should be allowed to do so. Thus, with a relaxing of the rules and the increased importance of standards, forms of 'procedural justice' spread through the United States: together with criteria centred on equality of bargaining power in private law, there are ideas of interests representation in administrative and commercial law, and of obligation in labour law to protect the bargaining position of the trade union (Unger, 1977:207).

The criterion of interest representation predominates even in the courts, and the idea prevails that the trial should function as an arena for the representation of social or group demands. In other words, the construction of a welfare law passes not so much through redistributive measures and prescriptive norms as through the safeguarding of areas of representation for private parties (especially groups) in the institutions.

Exposure of Law to Bargaining Processes

Closely connected with a procedural conception of law and justice is the exposure of the law-making process to various forms of bargaining. As Hurst has observed, in the United States experience, 'bargaining became a prime characteristic of legal process' (Hurst,1982b:119). The idea that legal obligations and positions are essentially negotiable has a long history and finds justification on both political and constitutional grounds. Walzer recalls that when, in 1863, compulsory military service was introduced in the United States, a clause stipulated that any man whose name was drawn by lot, and who was willing to pay 300 dollars for a substitute, could obtain exemption from the call-up. Although not entirely new, this kind of disposition 'seemed to abolish the public thing and turn military service ... into a private transaction' (Walzer, 1983:99). However, it was prevented from coming into force by popular resistance and opposition, which created a 'blocked exchange', redrawing the boundary between 'what could be sold and what could not' (Walzer, 1983).

Yet the logic of exchange frequently occurs in the American legal institutions with a meaning that goes beyond the idea that money is 'the universal pander', for at least two reasons. Firstly, because the exchange does not always involve money, it may comprise other resources. Secondly, because, alongside the negative view of bargaining as the commodification of something that should not be commodifiable, stands the reverse interpretation which views bargaining as a liberal means to assume obligations and therefore as antithetical to the illiberal method of command and prescription. In short, there is a political rationale which justifies bargaining and sometimes renders it preferable in the legal process too.

From a constitutional point of view, one may distinguish between an evaluation relative to the bargaining method itself and one relative to the results that can be achieved by means of bargaining. Bargaining is justified inasmuch as it disperses power and narrows the distance between public and private subjects, giving transparency to the interests at stake. The central importance assigned to the bargaining method reflects an aspect typical of the legal culture of the 'reactive' state, which celebrates the apotheosis of private rights, whether of the individual or of the group. There thus arises a context in which laws are widely non-mandatory and in which 'absolute prohibitions or injunctions are anomalous' (Damaska,1986:141). Indeed, as Black has observed, 'in fact the criminal justice system resembles a private-law system far more than is generally recognized' (Black, 1973:129).

Different grounds are adduced to justify the idea that bargaining produces positive outcomes. From the political point of view, the basic idea is that bargaining gives rise to decisions which, as the fruit of common accord between the parties, are non-authoritarian because they establish an acceptable (and accepted) counterbalance between the opposing interests involved. From the economic point of view, the argument is that decisions arrived at by means of bargaining are, for both parties, preferable to non-agreement, which is always an option available to them. In other words, whenever an agreement is reached, it is economically convenient to each party because it enables them to gain an advantage over their previous situation.

The contract, and the various forms of bargaining that precede and (sometimes) follow it, yield the model sustaining a manner of 'doing' law which is directly exposed to pressure by the interests in conflict. On the other hand, the progressive penetration of bargaining logic into the American political and legal arenas acts as a kind of counterpoint to the opposite penetration of the market by such typically political phenomena as command and monopoly (Hurst, 1982b:93ff). This penetration is most evident, especially to an European observer, in the area of public law. Among the many examples that could be cited, we restrict ourselves to two of especial salience: plea-bargaining procedures in the criminal trial, and bargaining procedures in the sphere of public–regulative law. (Examples of the penetration of bargaining in criminal and administrative law are now present in Italy, as well as in other European countries. But they appear as heterogeneous elements in systems where law is not inspired by a judicial model.)

As regards plea bargaining, the reason for its slow but steady ability to permeate the American judicial scenario is that it has proved to be 'quick and cheap' (Friedman,1993:272). Analogously, the behaviour of the actors involved in plea bargaining has been described as one 'emphasizing the maximization of production and the minimization of work' (Alschuler, 1979:156). Plea bargaining links with the idea of a gain, of an advantage accruing to both parties; that is, with an economic idea (Feely,1979:272). If one then extends examination to the inner workings of the bargaining process, one finds that it operates as an open-ended system, one without pre-defined outcomes and directed towards decisions (for example, whether or not to go to trial) which are incrementally defined by the parties concerned. In analysis of 'the language of negotiation' involved in plea bargaining,

Maynard observes that each of the actors follows a 'bargaining sequence' in which they expound their order of preferences and make a proposal to the opposite party (Maynard,1984:171). A decision is reached when the parties find themselves aligned on common terrain. However, there are various ways in which they may formulate attempts to reach agreement, and each of these attempts is couched in terms of an 'opportunity' that the opposite party may, or may not, take up.

With regard to regulation, in a comparative study of regulative styles in England and the United States, Vogel concludes that the American system of regulation is distinctive in its legalistic and punitive character as well as 'in the amount of information made available to the public, and in the extent of the opportunities provided for participation by nonindustry constituencies' (Vogel,1986:267). Especially important in the American regulatory style is the attitude of the courts, which invite 'losers in the legislature or the administrative agency to keep fighting, claiming a denial of due process that the judges must remedy or recasting their policy goals as judicially cognizable rights' (Kagan,1988:737).

In the United States, the penetration of regulative procedure by forms of negotiation began in the 1960s and 1970s, the intention being to provide legitimation for regulative decisions. The need to protect the interests damaged by such decisions had already been felt at the end of the New Deal; and it was a need that the 1946 Administrative Procedure Act sought to meet by creating a 'quasi-judicial model' of action for the regulative agencies. Giving a judicial form to administrative procedure entailed that it should be structured according to the logic of adversariness. This logic was taken to its extreme in the 1970s, when, as a result of further changes made to administrative procedure, bargaining became a procedure designed to guarantee the competing interests under consideration by the regulators. The entry of public-interest groups as parties to the case in administrative process, made possible in the 1970s by an extension of standing, led to the extreme consequence of a merger between regulative decisions and negotiation (Ferrarese, 1992).

Once again, the regulative law displays an 'interactive structure' which enables citizens to participate in the process of the 'authoritative distribution of values'.

Uses of Law and Entrepreneurial Attitudes

We now turn to the attitudes that legal actors tend to assume when, instead of feeling themselves subjected to laws, they regard them as means with which to pursue a profit. For the sake of clarity, it is advisable to begin with an 'ideal-typical' distinction between the normative and the entrepreneurial conception of the law.

From the normative standpoint, the law is regarded as generating a sense of 'coercion' so that, according to Kelsen, subjects must adjust to an 'ought-to-be' (Kelsen,1985). Consequently, there is a tendency to hypothesize an actor who adopts an essentially normative attitude towards the law, on the basis of what Luhmann calls a 'binary' communicative code of the legal/illegal type. He therefore assumes that the choice available to the actor is between behaviour which complies with the normative precept and behaviour which does not.

From an entrepreneurial perspective, the relationship between the law and the actor tends to be different. The legal actor regards the law as less a normative model of behaviour than a source of opportunity and tends to set up a 'game' using the law to seek an advantage. In this case, the law is regarded as a 'test of skill' rather than a 'dogma', disobedience of which is a 'heresy' (Edelman,1976:47).

Even breach of the law may become part of a game played in order to achieve a pay-off, and it may be taken into account by legal actors. It is no coincidence that some of the theorizations of the American legal system mentioned in previous pages seek to introduce economic rationality into the legal system and thus regard non-observance of norms (especially of private law, but not only these) as one of the many options available to individual economic calculations. In the vast sphere of contract law, especially, legal actors are tempted to assume economic attitudes, rather than merely normative attitudes. This is even more the case in a legal climate in which the law is not expected to impose unconditionally the fulfilment of contracts but to assign to each party the choice between fulfilment and compensation for damage.

Two further points need to be made in order to give precise definition to the difference between the entrepreneurial and normative ideal types of law. First, the behaviour of legal actors is not confined to a 'binary code'; it is legal actors themselves who invent various new possible relationships with the law, assuming that creative attitude which is typical of the entrepreneur. And it is precisely understanding of the pervasiveness of the creative components in the American legal system that gives clearer insight into the essentially evolutionary nature of that system. From this point of view, one discerns a parallel with the process of the constant 'organic transformation of industry', in the quasi-biological sense, that Schumpeter identified as the essential aspect of capitalism (Schumpeter, 1954). Likewise, one may argue, the American legal system displays an evolutionary dimension in the 'entrepreneurial' contribution of private subjects which is not paralleled in the legal system of Continental Europe. Numerous commentators, of course, have stressed this evolutionary dimension, ascribing it principally to common law and to the legal decentralization that it imposes (Hayek, 1982). Legal realism, then, with its implicit tendency to regard law as experience rather than 'as a normative structure', stressed the propensity for that law to be understood 'through the lens of anthropological and evolutionist schemes' (Tarello, 1962:38).

Secondly, it is to be noted that, in the entrepreneurial ideal type of law, the legal actor has a clear idea that his relationship is not with the law but with other subjects. In other words, it is as if the distributive potential of legal roles were more overt and perceived, and that legal actors naturally tend to bend them to their own purposes in a 'zero-sum game'. This thus evidences the character of interdependence distinctive of legal norms and rights: both of them, even when they apparently prescribe behaviour, in reality always regard a situation of interdependence with other subjects (Schmid, 1987).

The salience of the interdependence intrinsic to legal norms and rights in an entrepreneurial legal model, moreover, results from a legal system constructed, as mentioned at the outset, in close interaction with the paradigm of interests. The antithesis between the behaviour of an actor with purely normative referents and that of a legal actor who uses law to gain an advantage can be illustrated by reference to the theories of two authors – Weber and Coase – distant chronologically, geographically and academically: the great German sociologist, trained in the cultural climate of legal positivism, and the Nobel prize American economist, with his emphasis on efficiency, epitomize the distance between a normative conception and an entrepreneurial conception of law.

Weber viewed modern formal law as an instrument with which to rationalize economic activity and to give greater 'calculability' to the functioning of justice (Weber, 1968): it is in the interest of a bourgeois society to aspire to an unequivocal, clear law freed from bias and arbitrariness; a law, in short, which can function in a calculable manner and guarantee legal security. Although Weber was fully aware of the crisis of the positivist legal model and of all the pressures that threaten legal security and formalism, he believed that this model was the most consummate form of law to have been achieved in the West. He therefore did not consider the risk that the predictability of legal actors operating in the market might be disrupted by calculations of economic convenience. In his view, there was no contradiction between legal actor and economic actor because the former tended to prevail over the latter.

Coase, on the other hand, bases his notion of 'costs of market transactions' (Coase, 1960) precisely on the hypothesis that the economic actor prevails over the legal actor. By highlighting the costs involved in the assessment, functioning and execution of rights, this theory opens the black box constituted by all the cases in which rights, instead of functioning, incur a further cost which was not included in the initial calculation. Since transaction costs theory has been formulated by an economist, it is widely considered to be a theory of 'market failure'. However, from our point of view, it may equally be considered a theory which reveals a patent and endemic form of 'law failure', especially of law defined in terms of positivist doctrine. Transaction costs, in fact, shift the initial distribution of resources due to rights. In other words, transaction costs theory is a theory relative to the challenge that economics raises against law, a challenge which displays two distinct aspects.

The first aspect is the 'costliness' of rights, which do not always function automatically and may often be thwarted, especially if one of the subjects in a legal relationship adopts an entrepreneurial attitude. The second aspect is the fact that rights have become the object of bargaining; that is, they too have become negotiable. At first sight, the negotiability of rights is evidence of the penetration of law and legal actors by the market. But it is equally part of that process of dematerialization of rights which has led in the American legal system to regard property more as 'value in exchange' than as 'value in use' ever since the *Slaughterhouse* cases. Not coincidentally, the first analysis of this process was conducted by Commons, who first shed light on the notion of 'transaction' (Commons,1957: 65ff).

In the evolution of the concept of property, just as in the evolution of other parallel legal notions, it is the concept of 'opportunity' that has moved to the fore. A right is less a static notion than it is a source of 'faculties', 'opportunities' and of expectations connected with them, which amounts to saying, in terms of the argument developed above, that they provide the terrain for the exercise of legal entrepreneurship.

Hence one deduces from transaction costs theory that the legal system is exposed to a redundancy of bargaining practices which frequently do not refrain from crossing the threshold of rights. The legal system's ability to govern instrumental and entrepreneurial attitudes to the law is therefore restricted, and it is in constant danger of being resisted. More generally, transaction costs express the idea that there is a potential cleavage in actors between a normative orientation and an economic attitude: whence the danger of the chronic unpredictability of legal relations, especially as regards market practices.

References

Alschuler, A. (1979) 'Plea Bargaining and its History', *Law and Society Review*, **13**, 1979.

Bebchuk, L.A. (1989) 'The Debate on Contractual Freedom in Corporate Law', *Columbia Law Review*, **89**, (7), November.

Black, D. (1973) 'The Mobilization of Law', *Journal of Legal Studies*, **11**, January.

Bohannan, P. (1965) 'The Differing Realms of the Law', *American Anthropology*, **67**, special publication, December.

Calabresi, G. (1970) *The Costs of Accidents. A Legal and Economic Analysis*, New Haven, Conn.: Yale University Press.

Coase, R. (1960) 'The Problem of Social Cost', *Journal of Law and Economics*, **3**, October.

Coffee, J.C. (1989) 'The Mandatory/Enabling Balance in Corporate Law: An Essay on the Judicial Role', *Columbia Law Review*, **92**, (3), April.

Commons, J.R. (1957), *Legal Foundations of Capitalism*, Madison: University of Wisconsin Press: first published 1924.

Damaska, M.R. (1986) *The Faces of Justice and State Authority*, New Haven, Conn.: Yale University Press.

Dondi, A. (ed.) (1993) 'Introduction', *Avvocatura e giustizia negli Stati Uniti*, Bologna: Il Mulino.

Edelman, M. (1976) *The Symbolic Uses of Politics*, Champain: University of Illinois Press.

Easterbrook, F.H. and D.R. Fischel (1991) *The Economic Structure of Corporate Law*, Cambridge, Mass.: Harvard University Press.

Eisenberg, M.A. (1976) 'Private Ordering through Negotiation: Dispute-Settlement and Rulemaking', *Harvard Law Review*, **89**, (4), February.

Feely, M. (1979), *The Process is the Punishment*, New York: Russell Sage Foundation.

Ferrarese, M.R. (1992) *Diritto e mercato. Il caso degli Stati Uniti*, Turin: Giappichelli.

Fletcher, G.P. (1993) *Introduzione elementare alla scienza giuridica*, Padua: Cedam.

Frank, J. (1950) *Courts on Trial. Myth and Reality in American Justice*, Princeton: Princeton University Press.

Friedman, L.M. (1985) *History of American Law*, New York: Simon & Schuster.

Friedman, L.M. (1990) *The Republic of Choice*, Cambridge, Mass.: Harvard University Press.

Friedman, L.M. (1993) *Crime and Punishment in American History*, New York: Basic Books.

Gulliver, P.H. (1979) *Disputes and Negotiations*, San Diego: Academic Press.

Hayek, F.A. (1982) *Law, Legislation and Liberty*, London: Routledge & Kegan Paul.

Holmes, O.W. (1881) *The Common Law*, Boston: Little Brown.

Horwitz, M.J. (1977) *The Transformation of American Law, 1780–1860*, Cambridge, Mass.: Harvard University Press.

Horwitz, M.J. (1992) *The Transformation of American Law, 1870–1860. The Crisis of Legal Orthodoxy*, New York: Oxford University Press.

Hurst, J.W. (1972) *Law and Social Process in United States History*, New York: DaCapo Press: first published 1960.
Hurst, J.W. (1982a) *Dealing with Statutes*, New York: Columbia University Press.
Hurst, J.W. (1982b) *Law and Markets in United States History*, Madison: University of Wisconsin Press.
Jhering, R. (1879) *The Struggle for Law*, Chicago: Callaghan.
Kagan, R.A. (1988) 'What Makes Uncle Sammy Sue?', *Law and Society Review*, **21**.
Kelsen, H. (1985) *Teoria generale delle norme*, Turin: Einaudi.
Kennedy, D. (1973) 'Legal Formality', *Journal of Legal Studies*, **2**, June.
Kennedy, D. (1976) 'Form and Substance in Private Law Adjudication', *Harvard Law Review*, **89**, (8), June.
Kornhauser, L.A. (1989) 'The Nexus of Contracts Approach to Corporations: A Comment on Easterbrook and Fischel', *Columbia Law Review*, **89**, (7), November.
Kurland, K.B. (1986) 'The Rise and Fall of the "Doctrine" of Separation of Powers', *Michigan Law Review*, **85**.
Lockard, D. (1968) *Toward Equal Opportunity*, New York: Macmillan.
Luhmann, N. (1987) 'L'autoriproduzione del diritto e i suoi limiti', *Politica del diritto*, **1**.
Mattei, U. (1992) *Common Law*, Turin: UTET.
Maynard, D.W. (1984) *Inside Plea Bargaining. The Language of Negotiation*, New York: Plenum Press.
Miller, A.R. (1984) 'The Adversary System: Dinosaur or Phenix?', *Minnesota Law Review*, **69**.
Olson, W.K. (1992) *The Litigation Explosion. What Happened When America Unleashed the Lawsuit*, New York: Truman Talley Books.
Pound, R. (1916) 'The Province and Function of Law', *Harvard Law Review.*
Pound, R. (1954) *An Introduction to the Philosophy of Law*, rev. edn, New Haven, Conn.: Yale University Press.
Sacco, R. (1991) 'Legal Formants: A Dynamic Approach to Comparative Law', *American Journal of Comparative Law*, **39**, (2).
Sarat, A. and J.B. Grossman (1975) 'Courts and Conflict Resolution: Problems in the Mobilization of the Adjudication', *American Political Science Review*, **69**, December.
Schmid, A.A. (1987) *Property, Power and Public Choice. An Inquiry into Law and Economics*, New York: Praeger.
Schumpeter, J.A. (1954) *Capitalism, Socialism and Democracy*, London: George Allen & Unwin.
Summers, R.S. (1982) *Instrumentalism and American Legal Theory*, Ithaca, NY: Cornell University Press.
Tarello, G. (1962) *Il realismo giuridico americano*, Milan: Giuffrè.
Taruffo, M. (1978) *Il sistema civile 'adversary' nell'esperienza americana*, Padua: Cedam.

Trubek, M.D. (1972), 'Max Weber on Law and the Rise of Capitalism', *Wisconsin Law Review*.

Unger, R.M. (1977) 'The Disintegration of the Rule of Law in Postliberal Society', *Law in Modern Society*, New York: Free Press.

Vogel, D. (1986) *National Styles of Regulation: Environmental Policy in Great Britain and the United States*, Ithaca, NY: Cornell University Press.

Walzer, M. (1983) *Spheres of Justice*, New York: Basic Books.

Weber, M. (1980) *Economia e società*, vol. 3° (Sociologia del diritto), Milan: Comunità.

Zemans, F.K. (1983) 'Legal Mobilization: The Neglected Role of the Law in the Political System', *The American Political Science Review*, **77**, September.

10 Prosecution in Two Civil Law Countries: France and Italy

Carlo Guarnieri

The aim of this chapter is to comment on the problems deriving from analysing two judicial organizations with a rather similar historical tradition but operating in two different political and institutional environments. More specifically, the chapter tries to assess the management of public prosecution in France and Italy, with an eye to the way the related problems of prosecutorial discretion and political responsibility are dealt with. The analysis – realized in part through a reassessment of a set of interviews carried out in the two countries in the 1980s – will allow us to inquire into the role of legal culture in the process of institutional and organizational change.

The Institutional Setting: a Short Overview

Historically speaking, public prosecution in France and Italy has been organized in a rather similar way. Actually, the institutional setting of the Italian judiciary was consolidated, in the period immediately following unification (in 1865) with the French Napoleonic judiciary as a model. Therefore Italy has shared with France, among many other institutional traits, the characteristic feature of having a bureaucratic – or civil service – judiciary composed of magistrates performing both judicial and prosecutorial roles, with strong powers over the careers of all magistrates entrusted to the Ministry of Justice, in charge of directly overseeing the prosecuting function (Guarnieri, 1994a). Even though the two roles were – and are – assigned to different magistrates, in both countries judges and public prosecutors have always belonged, since Italian unification, to the same organization: *la Magistrature* or *la Magistratura*.[1] On the other hand, even criminal procedure has been organized, broadly speaking, along similar lines, with the instructing or investigating judge as one of the main actors.[2]

The two cases began to follow different institutional paths in the period after the Second World War, mainly because of the reforms introduced in Italy after the fall of Fascism. In 1946, as a reaction to past abuses – occurring, even though with different intensity, both in the liberal and the Fascist period – the guarantees of public prosecutors, as well as judges, vis-à-vis the executive branch were somewhat reinforced. But the hierarchical character of the judiciary was left, at least for a while, untouched. Deeper changes were introduced by the Constitution of 1948. This envisaged the institution of a self-governing body of the whole judiciary – the Higher Council of the Judiciary, two-thirds of whose members were magistrates elected by their colleagues and one-third law professors and lawyers elected by parliament – and also introduced special guarantees for public prosecutors. Furthermore, the principle of compulsory prosecution of criminal offences by the public prosecutor was written into the Constitution: 'The public prosecutor has the duty to institute criminal proceedings' (Art. 112).

In the following years, after much pressure from lower-ranking magistrates, the traditional hierarchy was dismantled, making promotions in the judicial career more or less dependent on seniority. Also ministerial powers have been progressively eroded: not only has the minister been deprived of his traditional powers of controlling – and being responsible for – the prosecution, but even his powers over the recruitment and careers of magistrates (that is, public prosecutors and judges) have been progressively taken over by the Higher Council, following its establishment in 1959.

In the field of public prosecution this process of change has been in large part legitimized by the principle of compulsory prosecution. This principle has been interpreted as having the effect of 'judicializing' the role of public prosecutor, since it is deemed to deny to him any discretion in deciding whether or not to start a criminal prosecution and, therefore, as requiring an extension to prosecutors of judicial guarantees of independence. Even today, the great majority of Italian jurists maintain that in every case where a suspicion arises that a crime has been committed the public prosecutor must request a decision from the judge, even if she or he is convinced of the innocence of the accused. Actually, the principle has been very often interpreted in a rather formalistic way, prescribing only that, when the prosecutor finds *some* evidence of a crime, she or he must only open a file, and perhaps wait until the statute of limitations has to be applied – a situation that tends to make the prosecution virtually unaccountable for the policy choices it inevitably has to make.

In the same period, even though some innovations have been recently introduced in France, constraining to a certain extent the traditional powers of the minister,[3] the status of public prosecutors has not been substantially altered and their institutional autonomy remains definitely lower than their Italian cousins.

Prosecution in Action: Are the Two Cases so Different?

Even a first look at the behaviour of magistrates shows that, not surprisingly, in both countries they enjoy a good deal of discretion, not only over the decision whether or not to open a file – and, subsequently, to file a charge – but, above all, over the actual way of conducting the inquiry. Paradoxically, the discretion enjoyed by Italian prosecutors seems to be somewhat larger.

Even though not constrained by the principle of compulsory prosecution and legally enjoying some discretion on the basis of the *principe d'opportunité des poursuites*, French prosecutors are inserted in a complex hierarchical chain that binds the young assistant to higher-ranking magistrates, up to the minister, with the result that every magistrate is in large part controlled by his or her superiors. The power of hierarchy, as well as the degree of the centralization of the system, must not be overemphasized (Accomando, 1994), but the managing powers of the ministry are very strong, at least in comparative terms. The French Ministry of Justice is staffed mainly by magistrates belonging to the prosecutorial branch. Inside the ministry a specific unit is in charge of overseeing nationwide the way prosecution is carried out in the local offices and even to assist them in managing specific cases. We could even say that this unit acts *in some way* as a kind of national prosecution office, even though it does not have the power to intervene directly in criminal proceedings. It is especially in politically relevant cases, the so-called *cas signalés* that control by the centre, and sometimes directly by the cabinet of the minister, can be exercised in a continuous and careful way. Therefore the discretion legally enjoyed by French prosecutors – more precisely, by the chiefs of the offices – has to be exercised inside a network of strong organizational influences.

Italian prosecutors are inserted in a much less constricting organizational environment. Today, even though the chiefs of the offices still enjoy some power, especially in assigning cases to one or another assistant, the careers of the assistants are no longer dependent on the assessment of their superiors, the careers of all magistrates being at present based only on seniority. Moreover, unlike the situation in France, the different prosecutorial offices are not organized in a nationwide hierarchical chain: every office is more or less independent of the others.[5] As shown in the recent cases of political corruption, the so-called *Tangentopoli*, this situation leads to territorially very different prosecution policies (Guarnieri, 1994b).

In this context, even though many prosecutors tend to pay at least lip service to the principle of compulsory prosecution, nearly all of them tend to recognize that many of the decisions taken cannot be considered as 'dictated' by the law. Especially in complex cases, when prosecutors (and once even investigating judges) tend to assume an activist posture, their influence on police behaviour and the whole investigative activity seems to increase.[6] The prosecutor of a large city told me: 'The way investigative data will be employed depends very much on prosecutorial inclinations', recognizing in this way the emergence of discretion. Owing to the dramatic growth in this last sort of case (terrorism, organized crime, political corruption and so on), this is increasingly likely to happen and the traditional conception, developed by the Italian academic doctrine, of the prosecutor as an impartial sort of quasi-judge performing an executory, '*bouche de la loi*', decisional role (Guarnieri, 1984) can be relegated to the law books. Therefore, broadly speaking, we could say that, thanks to the less constricting controls, Italian prosecutors seem to enjoy wider margins of discretion.

The other main institutional difference between the two cases lies in the realm of political responsibility, a matter obviously not unrelated to the exercise of prosecutorial discretion. As we have seen, in France the responsibility for criminal prosecution resides, at the end of the hierarchical chain, in the Minister of Justice who is able to exert a substantial amount of control, especially in politically sensitive cases.[7] In Italy, on the other hand, there is no formal political responsibility for criminal prosecutions: the compulsory principle is thought to make it superfluous, since it is said that the public prosecutor must 'only apply the law'. In practice, the difference lies between the – at least relative – concentration of responsibility to be found in the French setting, on the one hand, and the dispersion typical of the Italian case, on the other. Because of this concentration of responsibility, in France political pressures tend to focus on the top, on the minister and his cabinet: very rarely are the pressures applied to the chiefs of the local offices. Often, in these last cases, and especially when coming from minor politicians, they are not well received.[8] Even though this representation of the system by the magistrates could be at least in part enhanced by their desire to escape responsibility and assign it all to the political top, this picture seems to be supported by the institutional setting: at least in the politically significant cases, the political centre seems to enjoy real powers.[9] In Italy, the picture is more complicated. There are examples of pressures that try to follow an institutional way – for example the prefect approaching the chief prosecutor – but they are not the norm and do not seem very effective. More often, and with 'better' results, pressures are exercised through the Higher Council, in which representatives of all major parties usually sit. A different route is to put pressure on the police, indirectly influencing the conduct of the investigation, but even these attempts are not always successful.[10] Finally, not unheard of is the case of pressures coming out of personal relationships between the chief of the office and local politicians.

Some General Remarks on the Two Cases

The results of the analysis have to be considered with great caution since they have been influenced by the fact that not all interviews were designed to obtain data congruent with our present interests.[11] The attempted comparison falls among those called 'most similar systems', with no claim to elaborate general laws or universals, but rather with the aim to describe and better understand the workings of the two systems. On the other hand, it is true that we will put forward some generalizations, but they have to be understood only as grounded hypotheses in need of further development and confirmation.

Generally speaking, the French case seems to exhibit a higher degree of correspondence between actual behaviour and legal norms. Besides this, in Italy more variation seems to exist among the practices of different offices. The difference between the two cases could be ascribed, first, to the character of legal norms, which in turn are obviously related to the general traits of legal culture. To mention what seems to be the main element, it is obvious that the principle of compulsory prosecution, especially if defined in general, sweeping terms as in Italy, does not lend itself to an easy application and, therefore, inevitably opens the way to some divarication between law and reality. Even though it is important to take into account its symbolic effects vis-à-vis both the public and the members of the prosecutorial organization,[12] the actual meaning of the principle, as well as its consequences, cannot be taken for granted but needs always to be investigated in concrete cases, as we have tried to do.

Also the role of the organizational structure, as well as of the type of personnel, in influencing the process of law application must not be discounted. The higher territorial variation that seems to characterize the process of law application in Italy can in large part be explained by the decentralized structure of the prosecution system as well as by the weakening of the controls once exercised by the hierarchical system.

Italian and French judicial systems seem to have been characterized, at least in part, by increasingly different values in the field of the administration of criminal justice. Italian legal culture tends to stress the negative consequences of allowing discretion to be exercised by judicial authorities, as well as by other public bodies. As regards political responsibility, the focus is on its practical and theoretical shortcomings, rather than on its strong relationship with the principles of democratic rule. On the other hand, even though belonging to the same civil law tradition, French legal culture seems to be more tolerant on the theme of prosecutorial discretion,[13] and relatively more confident, at least so far, on the positive consequences of the principle of political responsibility. What emerges is the lower degree of (inter)institutional trust that characterizes the Italian case: not only lower trust *in* institutions but also lower trust *between* institutions (Nelken, 1994). Making any kind of discretion unlawful means that, in order to exercise even the smallest amount of power, you always need the (at least tacit) consent of all main concerned actors. It could be said that, in a society in which impersonal trust is lacking, the need to build direct, personal trust is somewhat 'compulsory', even at the institutional level. Paradoxically, but not too much so, the apparent effort at making authority relationships fully impersonal has fostered a growing personalization.

It is easy to relate these differences to the partly different path of institutional development of France and Italy, and especially to the late formation of the Italian state. However, a closer look at the two cases shows that Italian divergence from France has perhaps much more to do with the experience of Fascist authoritarianism and later developments. The breakdown of democratic rule in the 1920s, a consequence of the crisis of political participation,[14] contributed to further weakening the already low level of political trust.

As we have seen, the growing divergence of the two judicial systems falls within the broader post-war institutional trends of the two countries. While Fifth Republic France successfully implemented a radical change of political institutions towards a more majoritarian set-up, Italy has seen – at least so far – the practice of proportionalism steadily spreading over all its institutions. Moreover, in the post-war period the Italian political class has been marked by a higher degree of ideological dishomogeneity, since in earlier periods the *de jure* or *de facto* exclusion of Catholic and socialist politicians assured a relatively higher degree of value consensus, at least inside the political and governing class. The situation has changed all too slowly over the years and with no practical consequences for the accountability of the political class.[15]

However, cultural differences explain to a large extent the institutional agenda – that is, the institutional problems that have to be dealt with – as well as the practical solutions at hand. At the Italian Constitutional Assembly of 1946 – and later in the debate among constitutional lawyers – *the* problem was cancelling discretion in the application of the law. Actually, it is fairly easy to see that the effort to erase discretion in public organizations covered some other important need. For example, the principle of compulsory prosecution has currently been interpreted as necessarily implying the independence – external and, to a certain extent, also internal (that is, vis-à-vis higher-ranking magistrates) – of public prosecutors. Since it could be easily argued that there is no 'necessary' relationship between the two principles – as, for example, the present reality of the German case shows (Weigend, 1978) – the main reason behind the success of the former argument and the corresponding institutional development must be located elsewhere, very likely in the lower trust shown the executive: prosecutors must be independent of the executive because there is no trust in the way it would employ its powers.

On the other hand, the analysis shows, not surprisingly, that discretion is something ingrained in every complex organizational activity. The cases analysed differ only in its distribution inside the organization and in the broader consequences that a different location entails. Moreover, since in both countries, as elsewhere in democratic polities, the act of prosecuting always has deep political implications, there will inevitably be pressures to make it responsible or, better, to make those in charge of public prosecution *responsive* to the 'environment' or to some sector of it. Of course, these attempts will be more numerous in Italy where, also because of the special status of its members, the political significance of prosecution seems to be higher.

Thus different cultural dispositions tend to produce partly different responses to rather similar problems, with rather different results. As we have seen, Italian legal culture tends to frame the problem of the accountability of public prosecution in terms of the need to eradicate discretion. Unlike the case of France, the principle of political responsibility for the management of prosecution is not formally recognized. As a consequence, today the Minister of Justice has no formal – nor substantial – powers over prosecutorial offices. But this situation does not mean that there are no other ways of ensuring some sort of political responsibility: it only means that they are arranged in a different, maybe less visible, way. For example, in recent years, thanks to its strong powers over the status of magistrates, the Higher Council – a body in which all main parties as well as all main groups of magistrates are represented – has become the institution to which prosecutors tend to be responsible, at least de facto. Even though the way this kind of responsibility works is rather different from classical ministerial practice, it is, nevertheless, thanks to the mixed composition of the Higher Council of the Judiciary, a form of political responsibility. Another example is the role sometimes played by the Anti-Mafia Parliamentary Commission, a body formally not connected to prosecution but with the power of summoning prosecution chiefs and questioning them about their behaviour in the field of the fight against organized crime. Moreover, in a situation exacerbated by media involvement in the administration of justice and by deep political tensions, the decision by the minister to send twice in one year, his inspectors to an important prosecutorial office can be seen as a way of sanctioning the magistrates there for their initiatives, even though the minister has neither disciplinary nor career powers over them.[16] Therefore, as a result of the lack of traditional forms of political responsibility,[17] and together with the absence of clear hierarchical lines of authority between different prosecutorial offices, in Italy, even the structure of criminal prosecution seems to mirror the fragmented, consensual setting which has characterized, at least so far, the Italian political system (Lijphart, 1984), with obvious consequences for the way discretion is exercised.[18]

Summing up, our analysis has shown the significance of comparing political systems through their legal cultures. In this context, legal culture can be understood as a set of historically learned responses that discloses not only what is valued in a society but also how institutional problems will be framed and solutions envisaged. On the other hand, the analysis of legal culture cannot be carried out without some kind of comparative analysis. Even without discussing in full the relative merits of nomothetic and ideographic approaches (Nelken, 1994), the analysis of a legal culture cannot but be comparative, because only through comparisons can its specific properties be assessed. In other words, peculiarities can be appreciated only through comparisons, even though this does not mean going in search of general laws.

More difficult is to identify common functional requisites. Here the comparison has been made easier by the relative similarity of the cases analysed. The judicial systems we have studied operate in a political environment marked by a rather similar structure of political authority, that of constitutional democracy. In other words, both the French and Italian political systems tend to subscribe to the values of equality before the law and democratic responsibility of those in charge of political power: it is obvious that in other regimes, where the commitment to these values could be lower, the value context, and therefore also institutional priorities, should be rather different.

Finally, the analysis points out the strict relationships between legal culture and political environment. Especially when dealing with internal legal culture, it is impossible not to take into account the influence of political events in changing or, better, shaping legal culture. If, paraphrasing a much-used statement, law can be defined as the 'continuation of politics through other means', change in legal culture is often the response – even though a framed response – to change in the political system.

Notes

1 Therefore Italian and French magistrates must not be confused with English magistrates, a term actually designating lay judges.
2 In 1989, Italy reformed the code of criminal procedure, introducing a more accustorial American-style model of criminal process and, therefore, abolishing the instructing judge and entrusting the prosecutor with the task of preparing the case. Even though it is still difficult to present a satisfactory assessment of this reform, its results should not much affect our conclusions here.
3 In 1993, it was established that the minister's instructions to public prosecutors must be only in written form. Moreover, after the 1994 reform, the Higher Council of the Judiciary, composed of five prosecutors, an ordinary judge, an administrative judge, the Minister of Justice, the President of the Republic and three other 'lay' members, must give non-compulsory advice on all decisions regarding the status of a public prosecutor.
4 These are cases that the ministry thinks worthy of direct attention by the centre. Therefore they have to be 'signalled' by local offices to the ministry. Broadly speaking, *cas signalés* are all cases of potential political interest.
5 This relative autonomy could be especially appreciated in the case of conflict of jurisdiction between different prosecutorial offices. Even though the conflict should be resolved by an intervention of the Cour de Cassation, the offices increasingly tend to resort to direct informal bargaining, trying to strike an agreement which often clips in some way the jurisdiction between them: as underlined by a young prosecutor, 'jurisdiction is a matter of negotiation'. Examples of this activity, which has developed at least since the 1970s – during the fight against terrorism – could be easily found today in the *Tangentopoli* cases.
6 On this matter the French situation seems to be different: police power seems, at least from a long-term perspective, to have increased (Levy, 1993).
7 However, we have to take into account the important role played in the French criminal process by the investigating judges, who are *not* supervised by the Minister of Justice.
8 As a former head of prosecutorial offices put it: 'It is very difficult for an expert politician to exert pressure directly on the local prosecution chiefs, because it is likely to find an outright refusal .... Often the pressure comes through the ministry, while the role of parliamentarians is more limited .... Requests made in public nearly always ask prosecutors to act in some areas, but without reference to specific facts, while requests not to prosecute always have a specific reference and often are made in private.'
9 Since the political significance of a case is defined by the centre itself, it would be interesting to know whether the criteria adopted are always able to spot the 'right' cases.
10 A more sophisticated variation of this approach is to understaff the police forces working with the 'wrong' prosecutors.
11 Actually we have analysed two rather different sets of interviews: the French ones were designed to investigate the general structure of public prosecution with an eye to the role of the Ministry of Justice, while the Italian ones were intended to analyse the role of the prosecutor, and of the investigating judge, in complex criminal cases.
12 As Damaska (1981) emphasizes, 'pragmatic reasons favoring the dismissals of provable charges may encounter more counterpressure when the ideal of full prosecution is written into law' (p.127).
13 As in all matters regarding public administration. See Freddi (1982).

14 As it is well known, at that time the Italian political system was unable democratically to incorporate socialist and Catholic mass movements (Farneti, 1975).

15 In post-war Italy the structure of the party system did not allow clear-cut alternation of different parties in government. As a result, political responsibility was, more than elsewhere, an empty phrase.

16 In Italy the Minister of Justice can only decide to initiate a disciplinary proceeding, but even the instruction of the case is entrusted to the Prosecutor General at the Court of Cassation who is not subordinated to the minister. Of course, the final decision is made by the Higher Council.

17 It must be appreciated that the principle of compulsory prosecution, together with the independent status of public prosecutors, makes the government unaccountable for a wide area of criminal policies, with interesting consequences. As an experienced prosecutor reported: 'The politicians, or at least some of them, are ready to help us in the fight against organized crime by giving us the material resources we need, but, for electoral reasons, they do not want to appear to be in charge of the matter.' I think that at least part of the story of the relationships between politicians and organized crime in Italy has to be understood with this statement in mind.

18 Therefore it will be interesting to watch the impact on the judicial system of what seems to be a trend towards a more majoritarian political setting in Italian politics, with the recent changes in the parliament's electoral law and the emergence of a new right-wing majority after the elections of 1994. However, maybe because the majoritarian trend still seems rather weak, so far there have been no significant changes. On the other hand, recent developments in France – showing a growing intervention of the judiciary in political affairs – could be associated with the increasing tensions inside other institutions, especially between the President of the Republic and the Prime Minister, belonging to competing political forces.

References

Accomando, G. (1994) 'Le Ministère public et la politique pénale', paper presented at the workshop 'Justice et Politics', Institut des Hautes Etudes sur la Justice, Paris.

Damaska, M. (1981) 'The Reality of Prosecutorial Discretion: Comments on a German Monograph', *American Journal of Comparative Law*, **XXIX**, 119–38.

Farneti, P. (1975) 'La crisi della democrazia italiana e l'avvento del Fascismo', *Rivista italiana di scienza politica*, **V**, 45–82.

Freddi, G. (1982) 'Vincoli storico-strutturali sulla prestazione delle burocrazie legali razionali', *Rivista italiana di scienza politica*, **XII**, 183–212.

Guarnieri, C. (1984) *Pubblico ministero e sistema politico*, Padua: Cedam.

Guarnieri, C. (1994a), 'Justice and Politics: The Italian case in a Comparative Perspective', *Indiana International and Comparative Law Review*, **IV**, 241–57.

Guarnieri, C. (1994b) 'Geopolitica della magistratura', *Limes*, (4), 101–12.

Levy, R. (1993) 'Police and the Judiciary in France since the XIXth Century', *British Journal of Criminology*, **XXXIII**, 167–86.

Lijphart, A. (1984) *Democracies*, New Haven and London: Yale University Press.

Nelken, D. (1994) Whom Can You Trust?, in D. Nelken (ed.), *The Futures of Criminology*, London: Sage, pp.220–43.
Weigend, T. (1978) *Anklagepflicht und Ermessen*, Baden-Baden: Nomos.

11 The Enigma of Japan as a Testing Ground for Cross-Cultural Criminological Studies[1]

Setsuo Miyazawa

The purpose of this chapter is to discuss methods and hypotheses of empirical comparative research on criminal behaviour from the perspective of a Japanese criminologist. Throughout this chapter the terms 'cross-cultural' and 'cross-national' will be used interchangeably. While cultural boundaries are not necessarily the same as national boundaries, units of analysis are more likely to be nations, rather than cultures in their generic sense.

Karel van Wolferen, a Dutch journalist living in Japan, wrote a best-selling book about politics in Japan, titled *The Enigma of Japanese Power* (1989). With an apparently contradictory combination of tremendous economic development and a consistently low crime rate, lower than those in most other developed countries, Japan has been an enigma for criminologists, too. For instance, in 1990, the number of Penal Code offences per 100 000 people in Japan was only 1324, compared to 8630 notifiable offences in England and Wales, 7108 *Straftat* in Germany, and 5820 Crime Index offences in the United States (traffic-related offences are excluded for all countries: Japanese Justice Ministry Research and Training Institute, 1992:23). In one of the most sophisticated quantitative research studies in comparative criminology, Archer and Gartner (1981:90) wrote that 'Japan stands out as an anomaly'. It is fair to say that Japan will provide an ideal testing ground for any approach in comparative criminology.

The chapter is divided into three parts, each representing a different type of comparative research. First, we describe testing criminological theories with data from a culture or country which is different from those where the given theories originated. Second, we mention qualitative research focusing on only two or three countries. Third, we discuss quantitative research involving a large number of cultures or countries. Our conclusion will be that comparative criminology needs all three types of research.

Before discussing these three, however, a comment is required with regard to the claim that comparative criminology is extremely difficult, if not totally impossible, because of cultural relativism.

Methodological Purism or the Second-best Method

Beirne (1983) outlines epistemological cautions to comparative criminology from the perspective of cultural relativism. Cultural relativism refers to the differences among cultures in definitions, perceptions and reactions to crime. The problem is the possibility of a comparative criminology which produces generalizable findings while maintaining this cultural relativism.

Beirne identifies three types of comparative criminology. The first type is called the method of agreement. This type of comparative criminology tries to find commonalities among a large number of different cultures, applies ethnocentric theoretical concepts which originated only in one of them and, hence, ignores cultural relativism.

The second type is called the method of difference. This type of comparative criminology focuses on anomalous cases which cannot be explained by existing general theories. Criminologists of this mode emphasize factors unique to the given culture and try to understand the given culture from an insider's perspective. However, they still draw general conclusions, even though their empirical basis is very narrow.

The third type of comparative criminology respects cultural diversity and is called methodological relativism. This type of criminologist tries to develop concepts or measurement instruments which are less culture-bound. They are methodologically the most sophisticated, but their approach totally rearranges natural phenomena by using artificial concepts.

So, how should we design a cross-cultural study? Beirne suggests the following five rules:

(1) Crime in different cultures can be compared only if the definition and meaning of criminal behavior in these cultures are the same.
(2) An event *p* (e.g., urbanization) is not the true cause of rising crime rates if it occurs when rising crime rates do not occur.
(3) *p* is not the cause of rising crime rates if it does not occur when rising crime rates do occur.
(4) *p* is not necessarily the cause of rising crime rates if one or more other variables (A, or A, B…n) is present in the same circumstances as *p*.

(5) For the generalization '*p* causes rising crime rates' to be intelligible, it must be explained by a theory. (Beirne, 1983:34–5)

In spite of his profound argument about cultural relativism, Beirne's practical solution is conventional. Analysis will be limited to a very small number of cultures with very similar cultural heritages, while causal relationships will be identified by a primitive, intuitive process of inference. However, cultural relativism logically exists even among members of the same culture. This is what we learned from ethnomethodology and other phenomenological approaches in sociology. In the strongest version of phenomenological sociology, the search for generalizable knowledge itself would be abandoned. What we should and can do is simply to live our own experiences.

Nevertheless, even scholars who are close to such approaches rarely go that far. This is natural since phenomena which need understanding and explanation exist. Therefore various ethnographic methods of data presentation have been proposed. Good examples are the 'thick description' of Geertz (1973:6) and the 'objectification' of Cicourel (1976:ch.1), which we followed in our own observational study of Japanese police (Miyazawa, 1992). Therefore, as long as we are confident that we understand insiders' perspectives of different cultures, we need not hesitate to engage in comparative analysis.

Moreover, if we try to make causal inferences, there is no reason to tie our hands so that we will not be able to use more sophisticated statistical techniques. There are, of course, problems, such as under-reporting and the unavailability of the same indices (Archer and Gartner, 1984: ch.3) as well as cultural diversity. However, if we restrict quantitative analysis for the sake of methodological purism, the political consequences will be dangerous because governments will continue to use, misuse and manipulate criminal statistics for their own political purposes. Only independent criminologists who have been trained in statistical analysis can challenge governmental interpretations of statistics and inform citizens of the methodological limitations of official conclusions. Therefore scholars should not refrain from statistical analysis, even if the data are only second-best (Miyazawa, 1990a:135). We will return to this issue later.

Furthermore, we do not believe that the method of agreement and the method of difference are incompatible. Criminologists who are engaged in quantitative analysis involving a large number of countries are working with a large sample precisely because they want to obtain a wide range of variation. It is wrong to assume that they are interested only in commonalities among countries. The question is whether we can have a set of variables for which different countries can take extremely different values. In other words, we can treat an anomaly or an exception, such as Japan, as a case which simply takes a very different value for a universally applicable variable for which most other cases take more or less the same value. If we introduce a large number of such variables, we will be able to analyse anomalous cases in terms of general theories, rather than using ad hoc explanations (Inverarity *et al*., (1983:31). Then we need to add a deeper ethnographic understanding of the societies which are compared. These issues will be taken up later in our discussion.

Let us now turn to each of the three types of comparative criminological research.

Theory Testing with Data from a Different Culture

First, one may test theories which originated in one culture, such as the United States, with data from a different culture, such as Japan. Shelley (1981:xxi) states that 'Instead of focusing on analyses done in one country or tests of theories based on the limited experience of a single society, researchers should make comparisons across societies and historical periods'. In other words, studies with data from a single country do not qualify as comparative criminology. We believe, however, that exactly because most theories originated in one country and, hence, are ethnocentric, testing a theory with data from a different culture should be encouraged as an integral part of the overall effort of comparative criminology, as a preliminary step in the attempt to develop a theory which avoids ethnocentrism.

It is easy to take a nationalistic position that the crime and criminal justice of each culture require a distinctive set of concepts, variables and propositions in order for us to understand and explain their distinctive characters. On the other hand, there is no reason to prohibit ourselves from using the fruit of scholarly efforts which have already accumulated, since thereby we will be able to go much further.

Adopting this perspective, we have organized sessions called 'Testing Theories with Japanese Data' at recent annual meetings of the American Society of Criminology. Papers presented there tested the stable criminality hypothesis (Harada, 1991), deterrence theory (Matsumura and Takeuchi, 1992), control theory (Tanioka, 1992) and differential opportunity theory (Tsutomi, 1991: Yuma, 1992) and applied the technique of event history analysis (Harada, 1992) with data from Japan, all employing sophisticated quantitative methods. We have expanded the scope of our project to include other Asian countries and have organized a session called 'Testing Theories with Asian Data' at the 11th International Congress on Criminology in 1993 at which colleagues from Taiwan, Japan and Germany presented papers.[2]

We are not doing this because we believe that Western-made theories are superior to Asian-made theories. We are doing this because we recognize that currently available theories mostly originated in Western countries, and because we believe that they need modification in order to be applied in comparative research. Our ultimate hope is that our Asian colleagues will soon propose general theories that apply to comparative criminological research.

Ethnographic Studies of a Small Number of Cultures

The value of the quantitative analysis of data from a large number of countries will be defended in the next section because only such studies will make it possible to carry out systematic examination of the relative impact of a large number of variables. However, if such a quantitative analysis is carried out by a criminologist who does not know anything about the subject countries, such analysis may be superficial, and conclusions may be drawn which do not reflect reality in the concerned countries. Therefore, before designing large-scale quantitative studies, ethnographic studies of a small number of cultures or countries should be accumulated.

The smallest and most primitive of such comparative ethnographic studies are ones in which a researcher carries out field work in a foreign country and compares its findings with patterns in his or her own country. Good examples of such ethnographic studies of Japan are the works on Japanese police by Ames (1981) and Bayley (1976).

As Araki (1985: 1988) comments, command of the language of the subject country is crucial in such ethnographic studies. Unless the foreign researcher has an equally competent collaborator from the subject country, as in the case of the study on political police by Katzenstein and Tsujinaka (1991),[3] the researcher himself or herself must understand the language. Ames clearly had an advantage in this sense, and his study presented a more nuanced picture of Japanese police than did the study by Bayley.[4]

In this regard, the enormously influential *Crime, Shame and Reintegration* (1989) by Braithwaite deserves special attention since it is probably the first example of Japan providing inspiration for the development of a major criminological theory which can be applied in comparative criminological studies. For Braithwaite, 'shaming' means 'all social processes of experiencing disapproval which have the intention or effect of invoking remorse in the person being shamed and/or condemnation by others who become aware of the shaming'. 'Most shaming is neither associated with formal punishment nor perpetrated by the state', but rather is done 'by individuals within interdependent communities of concern' (Braithwaite, 1989:100). 'Reintegrative shaming' is 'shaming which is followed by efforts to reintegrate the offender back into the community of law-abiding or responsible citizens through words or gestures of forgiveness or ceremonies to decertify the offender as deviant' and 'is not distinguished from stigmatization by its potency, but by (a) a finite rather than open-ended duration which is terminated by forgiveness; and by (b) efforts to maintain bonds of love or respect throughout the finite period of suffering' (ibid. 1989: 100–101)

Braithwaite describes Japan as a society where shaming is applied in an optimal way, and where shaming is strong enough to prevent repeat offences but not too strong, so as to produce secondary deviance through stigmatization. Braithwaite (1989: ch. 8) discusses how his theory can be tested with various methods, including ethnographic, historical research, survey research, macrosociological studies based on official statistics and experimental research designs.[5] He argues that 'In Japan ethnographic work is thus needed which explicitly sets out to assess whether reintegrative shaming is something that Japanese families, schools, corporations and criminal justice agencies actually do'.

The need for ethnographic work about Japan is agreed. However, as a hypothesis, there is a very different interpretation about the way deviants are treated in Japan. Companies and schools are major organizations of informal social control in contemporary Japanese society, and they can be characterized by their extremely harsh treatment of members who defy the existing power structure and social arrangements. Such members are simply harassed or expelled. It is more accurate to say that Japanese people conform because they know that conformity will be highly rewarded while the consequences of non-conformity are enormously costly.

For instance, it is a cliché to say that Japanese people go to a Shinto shrine on New Year's Day, to a Christian church for weddings and to a Buddhist temple for funerals, as evidence of the religious tolerance of Japanese society. However, this argument confuses ignorance with tolerance. In Japan, being ignorant or indifferent about religion is a norm enforced by enormous social, political and even legal pressure. Those who wish to assert their religious allegiance other than Shintoism or Buddhism are severely repressed, as in the case of the Christian wife of a deceased Self-Defence Force member who tried to prevent the laying to rest of her husband in a Shinto shrine which was built to honour pre-war military leaders, or as in the case of high school students who refused to take lessons in martial arts for religious reasons and were expelled from the school.

One exception may be company executives who admit moral responsibility in ritualistic shaming, leave their job, escape legal punishments for themselves and their companies, and receive retirement bonuses or a second job. However, personally they do not feel remorse, and their companies continue business as usual.

Braithwaite (1989:61–5) cites examples of reintegrative shaming practised by the Japanese police which were reported by Bayley (1976). However, on the basis of our own research (Miyazawa, 1992), we do not believe that the police are more interested in reintegrating the suspect into society than in finding evidence to justify longer detention and heavier penalties, nor that the police actually provide assistance to the suspect to make it easier for him or her to return to normal life. Other criminal justice agencies are not very reintegrative, either. For instance, the recidivism rate of former prison inmates within three years after release from prison after fully serving their terms is reported as 57 per cent (Foote, 1992:365). Indeed, Katoh (1991:79) says that 'In Japanese prison practice there is no meaningful treatment, or real therapeutic activity. Work is forced labour and at the same time serves the security of the institution.' (Compare this with an official history of criminal justice policies in Japan in Shikita and Tsuchiya, 1990.) In 1991, only 2.8 per cent of the inmates were receiving vocational training, and only 1.2 per cent participated in educational programmes (Japanese Justice Ministry Research and Training Institute, 1992:131). Moreover, as has been discussed elsewhere (Miyazawa, 1991), the government does not operate halfway houses, and the number of privately run halfway houses has been declining because of financial difficulties. We do not believe that Japanese correctional agencies are provided with resources sufficient to provide reintegrative assistance to the extent which is implied by Braithwaite's description. Furthermore, when private halfway houses want to expand or merely renovate their facilities, they face extremely hostile local opposition. This would not happen in a country characterized by reintegrative shaming.

The same line of argument, heavily influenced by the family model of criminal justice presented by Griffith (1970), has recently been presented in an important article written by Foote (1992). Foote provides a detailed description of apparently lenient treatment of criminals by criminal justice agencies, including the release of minor offenders by the police, prosecutorial discretion to not file indictments, and judicial decisions which frequently suspend execution of sentences or else give relatively short prison terms. Foote characterizes these patterns as 'benevolent'. However, he emphasizes that such benevolent treatment is granted only as a result of official discretion, not as a result of negotiation between the authority and the accused. In this sense, he characterizes the Japanese system as 'paternalistic'.

The problem is the historical and the contemporary reality of this purported 'benevolence'. For instance, the judicial system of each country may have developed a 'market value' of sentences, depending on its resources, crime rates and other factors. Therefore, five years' imprisonment may be quite heavy in one country, while it may be quite light in another. We need to understand such differences.

As Foote (1992) himself describes in detail, early release by the police, non-prosecution by prosecutors and the frequent use of suspended and shorter sentences in Japan were all introduced as measures to alleviate the financial burdens of the government when it was still striving to establish itself under pressures from the imperial superpowers of those days. Like the failures to increase the number of professional probation officers or to establish public halfway houses, and the recent partial privatization of the prison industry (Miyazawa, 1991), those measures represent the government's failure to make a significant investment in criminal justice. However, since the crime rate has been low and stable as the result of favourable social and economic factors, crime and criminal justice have never become major political issues; the above-mentioned measures stabilized and the positivist school of criminal law provided their theoretical justifications. Moreover, while the rhetoric of rehabilitation is still used by criminal justice officials (and they may be serious in their proclamations of such a philosophy), they are not given sufficient resources to put into practice their ideals for rehabilitating criminals.

So let us return to Braithwaite. Since he uses Japan more as an illustration than as a test or proof of his theory, that shaming in Japan is not reintegrative does not necessarily refute his theory. However, since Japan clearly has provided a strong inspiration for his theory, ethnographic studies comparing Japanese reality to that in other countries may affect and perhaps undermine the persuasiveness of his theory (on this point, also see Kersten, 1993). This is not to say that an insider's interpretation is necessarily more true than an outsider's interpretation. Outsiders may be more sensitive to aspects of the given culture which insiders simply take for granted. In fact, pathbreaking studies about many aspects of Japanese society have been done by outsiders. Nonetheless, the general point is repeated that a theory to be applied in cross-cultural studies should be supported by careful ethnographic studies of key countries.

Theory Testing with Data from a Large Number of Different Cultures

The Disjunction between Single Country Analysis and Cross-national Analysis

A theory which works well in explaining individual or interregional variations within a single country might not work well in explaining cross-cultural variations. At the same time, a theory which fails to explain individual or interregional variations within a single country may still explain cross-cultural variations.

An example of the first case seems to be the routine activities theory (Cohen and Felson, 1979). This theory holds constant the motivation to commit crime and explains occurrences of crime in terms of the availability of crime targets. The theory has been more or less supported, not only in the United States, but also in Japan (Nishimura, 1986; Tanioka and Glaser, 1991). However, it does not seem possible to explain extremely wide gaps between Japan and other developed countries without adding a theory to explain differences in the prevalence of motivation to commit crime (Miyazawa, 1990a:135;1990b:45). It is difficult to believe, for instance, that Japan has a far smaller amount of consumer goods suitable for property offences or a far smaller number of people carrying money suitable for robberies compared to other developed countries.

An example of the second case is the cultural orientation to violence. Williams and Flewelling (1988) tried to explain inter-city variations in homicide rates by resource deprivation, social disintegration and culturally violent orientation, by disaggregating homicides into several different types. Their proxy for the culturally violent orientation is the ratio of officially justified killings. Their results show that while resource deprivation and social disintegration are strongly significant factors in most types of homicides, culturally violent orientation is only a weak determinant of only face-to-face homicides. Nevertheless, the degree to which violence is culturally accepted as a legitimate means to solve personal problems might be a significant factor in explaining cross-cultural differences. Take, for instance, gun ownership as a proxy of such culture. Considering the differences between Japan and the United States with regard to both crime rates and the legitimate availability of firearms, this variable appears to be worth introducing in a large-scale comparative study.

Another example of the second case might be the impact of the size of police forces on crime rates. American criminologists applied experimental research designs to examine impacts of changes in manpower, budget and the ways in which police officers patrol and are dispatched. Though there were exceptions, such as for police intervention in domestic violence (Sherman, 1992), results were generally negative (Skolnick and Bayley, 1986). For instance, increases in police size or budget no longer have an effect on crime in the United States, possibly because a certain threshold has already been passed, below which personnel and money increases might have been effective. Random motorized patrolling does not reduce crime, improve arrest certainty or reduce the fear of citizens. Regular patrols on foot, which are increasingly more popular, reduce citizens' fear, but they do not affect the crime rate. (For Japanese research on fear of crime, see Ito, 1993.)

Japanese criminologists have never carried out comparable experimental studies on the police (Miyazawa, 1990b:36–42). However, in one of the most sophisticated cross-sectional analysis of interregional differences in crime rate, Yamaura (1982), a police executive, found that the crime rate increases police size, but police size does not affect the crime rate. However, these negative results may be due to the smaller range of variation within a single country. In international comparative analysis in which countries vary widely, same variables may become significant factors. For instance, consider the number of reported crimes per police officer (Miyazawa, 1990b:32–4, 46; 1992:13–15). In 1985, excluding traffic-related offences, the estimated number of major offences per police officer was 7.4 in Japan (Penal Code offences), 18.7 in the United States (Crime Index offences) and 22.0 in West Germany (*Straftat*). The estimated number of homicides per 1000 police officers was 8.5 in Japan, 14.6 in Germany and 28.6 in the United States. In other words, Japanese society is more saturated with police than other countries, and Japanese police can spend more time and personnel on each case.[6] Therefore, while it is doubtful that many countries want to saturate themselves with a level of police personnel comparable to the Japanese, the size of police forces relative to reported crime rates might still be a theoretically significant factor in international comparisons.

Disaggregated Crime Rates and the Non-Cultural Bases of Cultural Rhetoric

The problem, then, is whether we can actually design such a quantitative comparative study. One of the studies that gives us hope for the feasibility of cross-national crime rate analysis is a study on the cross-national determinants of child homicides, by Fiala and LaFree (1988). They took the rate of female labour force participation as a proxy for economic stress that pushes women into work out of economic necessity, and their results indicate that there is a remarkably strong positive relationship between economic stress and the child homicide rate. However, there are some outliers. Among the countries which have the highest level of female workforce participation (approximately 40 per cent), the homicide rates for Japan and Austria are three times that of Finland. Moreover, the rates for other Scandinavian countries are even lower than that for Finland. The authors then added variables for the social status of women and for governmental assistance, and gained very high coefficients of determination.

In other words, Fiala and LaFree focused on a type of crime for which more reliable and valid information is available from a large number of countries and found non-cultural explanations for a phenomenon which is often explained away as something culturally unique to Japan (namely *oyako shinju* or parent–children suicide). As has already been discussed, by carefully selecting theoretically meaningful general variables, a large-scale quantitative analysis can properly handle cases which appear to be anomalies.

So, can we design a similarly productive cross-national research for other types of crime? And which variables should we include in such studies? Let me present some candidates.

The Limited Explanatory Power of Urbanization and Economic Development

Neumann and Berger (1988) reviewed 17 studies which were published between 1974 and 1986 and examined their theoretical perspectives and findings. They found that cross-national studies of crime were dominated by what they call a Durkheimian-Modernization (DM) perspective. They classified the results into six hypotheses and examined how much support each of them received. While the DM perspective emphasizes the impact of urbanization and economic development, results on violent crime did not support its hypotheses, though results for property crime gave more support to the DM perspective. They then proposed what they call the Marxian-World System perspective and the Ecological-Opportunity perspective as alternatives to the DM perspective.

Therefore urbanization and economic development should be included as far as property crimes are concerned. However, Japan has been treated as an anomaly with regard to the relationship between those variables and the crime rate. As has already been said with regard to the routine activities theory, it is necessary to include variables to explain criminal motivations if we wish to design a cross-national study which can explain the enigma of Japan with general theoretical concepts. What we are going to propose is using two basic strategies in motivational theories in sociological criminology, namely Robert Merton's anomie theory and Travis Hirschi's control theory (Miyazawa, 1990b:47–51). We will examine the applicability of anomie theory first, and then that of control theory.

Anomie and the Culture of Endurance

Merton's anomie theory explains deviant behaviour as a result of the disjuncture between shared goals and legitimate means to attain those goals. For instance, we may assume that, in capitalist industrialized countries, most people value highly the quality of life related to economic well-being. If some people were severely deprived of economic resources in such a society, they might want to obtain valued objects through other means, which might include illegal, criminal behaviour. In a macro-level analysis, therefore, we may expect a positive relationship between the crime rate and indices of economic distress. Indeed, quantitative cross-national studies often included proxies of economic distress. Even physical crimes have been found to be related to economic distress, probably because some of them are committed in the course of property crimes or because severe economic distress damages the normative integration of society and motivates some people to act deviantly in many spheres of their lives.

To cite one example, Devine *et al.* (1988) wanted to explain changes in crime rates in the United States by changes in economic distress and social control. The male unemployment rate and inflation are proxies of economic distress, and they found that the male unemployment rate is a consistently strong factor. Similar results have been obtained in Japan. Evans (1977) found as early as the 1970s that changes in the crime rate in Japan are positively correlated with economic factors, particularly unemployment. While this line of analysis has not been taken up by Japanese criminologists, another non-Japanese scholar, Merriman (1991), obtained similar results in his more sophisticated econometric analysis. Moreover, in the first econometric analysis of the deterrent effects of the death penalty in Japan, Matsumura and Takeuchi (1992) also found unemployment to have a significant influence on homicide rates, while arrest rates and death penalty rates did not show significant impacts.

An interesting comparative issue regarding anomie is the possibility that economic distress does not necessarily appear as a significant factor in cross-national studies. This possibility is suggested by anthropologists Wagatsuma and De Vos (1984) in their study of the residents of Arakawa Ward of Tokyo in the 1960s. Arakawa Ward is generally considered one of the most working-class areas in Tokyo, and its crime rate is expected to be high. However, what Wagatsuma and De Vos saw were people who were generally poor, but who still maintained positive attitudes about their lives and the existing social arrangement. Wagatsuma and De Vos called such attitudes the 'heritage of endurance'. According to them, those people were accepting their economically distressing situation and maintaining positive attitudes and manners of behaviour because of their perception that passive compliance would be rewarded in the future. They then analysed mechanisms that produce and maintain such perceptions.

Therefore, even if economic distress as measured by unemployment rates can explain variations within a country, explaining wider variations among countries might require additional variables. We may use Wagatsuma and De Vos' insight in our macro-level analysis if we assume that there is a rational basis for this culture of endurance. If even those at the bottom of the social ladder believe in the continuing improvement of their economic well-being and the decreasing inequality in the distribution of economic resources, they might not become anomic. Such could be more the case in Japan than in other developed countries. As long as the economy continues growing, giving something to everyone and narrowing the inequality of distribution, the crime rate may stabilize or even decline, to the extent that the average level of economic well-being has improved. Thus we should introduce proxies for economic growth and economic inequality.

Economic growth is usually measured in terms of the annual rate of change of GNP or GDP. Japan has had a consistently high rate of economic growth, and since the Second World War has diverted only a little to non-civil, military uses (Miyazawa, 1990a:61). Since we are interested in the benefits of economic growth in civil life, we should include proxies of both economic growth and of military expenditure. Here I am reminded of an argument James Q. Wilson (1983) made, that the United States experienced both a rapidly growing economy and declining crime rates in the nineteenth century. People invested much in their efforts to conform because conformity, literally, paid off. If his argument is right, Japan is not at all anomalous. Rather, Japan's economic conditions have simply been more favourable than those of other developed countries in recent years, like those of the United States in the nineteenth century.

Economists usually measure economic inequality with the Gini coefficient. Yamaura (1982), Hansmann and Quigley (1982), and Messner (1982) used this index and found it had a positive relationship with the crime rate. Japan has had Gini coefficients with regard to income distribution consistently lower than those of the United States. France and West Germany (Miyazawa, 1990a:61). In the light of these statistics, the culture of endurance of the Japanese people is easy to explain in economic terms. Currently, inequality in distribution of assets, rather than income, appears to be expanding in Japan. However, we will have to wait a few more years to see the impact of this.

There is still another possibility for refining anomie variables. If deprivation was concentrated in a certain group of people who were identifiable by race, and were already subjected to other forms of discrimination, they would become most anomic. If such people comprised a substantial share of the population, normative disintegration would occur. Black people in the United States are a typical example, and the black percentage of the population was found by Williams and Flewelling (1988) to be a significant factor in explaining inter-city variations in crime rates in the United States. Regarding Japan, Wagatsuma and De Vos (1984) report that delinquency arrest rates of former outcasts and Koreans in Kobe are, respectively, four and seven times the average rate. Whether or not their statistics are accurate, the minority population is small in Japan, anyway, and their rate will not much affect the overall crime rate. Illegal foreign workers who have been taking the lowest-paying jobs in Japan could become a new group of minorities, but their impact on the crime rate has not yet appeared. In any event, we should introduce in our model proxies for the relative size of socially discriminated minorities and the intensity of their discrimination.

Bonds to the Conventional World and the Structural Commitment to Conformity

Hirschi's control theory explains delinquency by loss of bond to conventional associates that controls juveniles. He identifies four types of bonds: emotional attachment to conventional associates, future-oriented commitment to conventional goals, present involvement in conventional activities and belief in the legitimacy of conventional norms and their enforcement agents. Nishimura (1979) conducted the first self-report study of delinquency in Japan to test these propositions and found positive results. A more sophisticated test (with a representative sample) carried out by Tanioka (1992) also produced generally positive results.

Control theory was originally developed as a theory of delinquency, but the same logic may apply to crime in general. We may think of conventional associates, conventional activities and conventional norms for adults as well as for juveniles. Wagatsuma and De Vos (1984) suggested how strongly people in Arakawa were committed to and involved in conventional activities and believed in the legitimacy of conventional norms. As we can see from various survey results in Japan (Japanese Economic Planning Agency, 1988), the Japanese people are so satisfied with their life that many of them must feel they have a stake in their continuing conformity with the conventional world.

For many Japanese adults, their company epitomizes the conventional order. A comparative survey of American and Japanese workers by Whitehill and Takezawa (1981) indicates that, while the most frequent answer in the United States is that they pursue common goals with their employer only during work time, almost two-thirds of Japanese residents think that the company has at least the same importance to them as their private life. Japanese labour statistics (Japanese Economic Planning Agency, 1988) indicate that they are serious in their answers. Japanese work longer than most people in the world, rarely take holidays and lose almost no workdays through strikes. Furthermore, according to a survey of young workers conducted by the Japanese government (Tsuda, 1982), they use their spare time simply to rest and recover their energy for company work, and rarely spend their time in social activities. Their stake in conformity is indeed high, and it lies in the future. If they lose or change their job, they will lose whatever they would have received for seniority and as a retirement bonus. Furthermore, since their employer is likely to be their largest creditor in housing loans and other financial arrangements, it is often impossible to change employers. Under the current economic recession, many companies have started to change their employment practices and the media constantly reports company decisions about early retirement or lay-offs. It remains to be seen, however, whether the extremely high degree of company loyalty will be lost and, if it is, whether it will affect the crime rate.

The value of conformity is first taught at school. For children, school epitomizes the conventional world. Japanese schoolchildren are among the busiest children in the world. A survey conducted by the Japanese government (Sekai no Naka no Nippon o Kangaeru Kai, 1985) indicates that they do more homework than anyone else, play for a relatively short time and sleep the least. According to one source, Japanese junior high school students spend six hours in the classroom each day and more than three hours on extracurricular activities and homework. It will be interesting to compare this with figures from other countries.

Parents expect their children to succeed in school in the conventional sense – that is, in terms of academic achievement. Children appear to be trying hard to satisfy these expectations of their most important conventional associates, namely parents. However, their apparent conformity does not necessarily mean that they are emotionally attached to their parents. Indeed, the survey just cited rather suggests that Japanese children are relatively unattached to their parents. Thus their commitment and involvement might be better understood as responses to social arrangements that make the costs of deviance very high. As Nishimura (1979) aptly put it, their commitment is 'structurally enforced'.

Compared to the economic factors appropriate for anomie theory, it may be much more difficult to find macro-level proxies for these variables appropriate for control theory. We should nonetheless try this line of analysis, too.

The Measurement of the Dependent Variable

The most thorny issue in quantitative comparative research is the measurement of the dependent variable, namely crime. Archer and Gartner (1984:52–4) argue that under-reporting and different indicators of crime are not serious obstacles, as long as we are interested in comparing trends rather than absolute levels of crime. Unfortunately, however, the most interesting issue is the explanation of differences among countries in absolute levels of crime. Therefore, unless we have reliable secondary data, as in the case of Fiala and LaFree (1988), we may wish to design our own instrument to measure it at an individual level.

Victimization surveys are one such technique. Van Dijk and his colleagues (van Dijk *et al.*, 1991) are to be admired for their effort to carry out surveys with the same instrument in different countries, and it is pleasing to know that such a survey has been conducted in Japan under the sponsorship of a private organization (Murai, 1990). This survey confirmed Japan's low crime rate, while also indicating an unexpectedly large number of thefts of motorcycles and bicycles and an unexpectedly low reporting rate. Thus results from victimization surveys could be used as measures of the absolute crime levels of the countries to be compared.

However, the number of countries for which victimization surveys are available is still too small to carry out meaningful statistical analysis. Moreover, victimization surveys do not cover all major crime categories. Hence, as far as developed countries are concerned, secondary analyses of government statistics of reported crimes might still be the only practical solution. In fact, as far as the rank ordering of countries is concerned, there is virtually no difference between the rank orders by victimization surveys and the rank orders by government statistics. While such data do not allow us to apply our most powerful statistical techniques, they are still better than intuitive, impressionistic inferences.

Conclusion

We hope that we have succeeded in arguing (1) that comparative criminological research should not be limited to large-scale quantitative studies, but that theory-testing with data from a single country and the ethnographic study of one or two countries have their own places in the development of cross-cultural criminological research; and (2) that, nevertheless, we need not be too cynical about the value of large-scale quantitative research. It is also hoped that this chapter will encourage young scholars to engage seriously in any of the three types of research we have proposed. In spite of a burgeoning of books and papers on Japan in the criminological literature, Japan still awaits serious comparative research.

Notes

1 Previously published in *Annales Internationales de Criminologie*, **32** (1994).

2 Chuen-Jim Sheu, 'The Effect of Capital Punishment on Crime Rates: An Empirical Test of General Deterrence Theory in Taiwan', Haruo Nishimura, 'Explaining Delinquency among Senior High Students: The Efficacy of Western Theories upon Japanese Deviance'; Ichiro Tanioka, 'The Test of "Web of Informal Control" Theory of Delinquency in Japan: Revisited'; Bunri Tastuno, 'Employment and Delinquency: The Case of Japa-

nese Juvenile Parolees'; Joachim Kersten, 'Crime Control in Japan: Policing and Shame Revisited'.

3 The most successful and sophisticated collaborative work in the sociology of law is Hamilton and Sanders (1992). They applied techniques of experimental social psychology to large samples from Japan and the United States in order to compare central tendencies in responses to questions about responsibility and punishment. Their Japanese collaborators included leading legal sociologists, criminologists and a statistician.

4 However, Bayley carried out a follow-up study, and his second book (Bayley, 1991) is clearly an improvement. Here he is more sensitive to human rights issues in the investigation process and pays more attention to the socioeconomic determinants of the low crime rate, although he still argues that the police and other criminal justice agencies also contribute to the low crime rate.

5 Hamilton and Sanders (1992) combined survey methods with an experimental research design. Since their topics are responsibility and punishment, which appear to be related to shaming, their research design might be of interest to Braithwaite if he intends to carry out his own research in Japan.

6 The Japanese police are also assisted by an extremely enabling legal environment which allows them, for instance, to detain the suspect under their direct control for up to 23 days for each count (Miyazawa, 1992:16–25).

References

Ames, W.L. (1981) *Police and Community in Japan*, Berkeley: University of California Press.

Araki, N. (1985) 'The Flow of Criminal Cases in the Japanese Criminal Justice System', *Crime and Delinquency*, **31**, 601–29.

Araki, N. (1988) 'The Role of Police in Japanese Society', *Law and Society Review*, **22**, 1033–6.

Archer, D. and R. Gartner (1981) 'Homicide in 110 Nations: The Development of the Comparative Crime Data File', in Shelley (ed.), *Readings*, pp. 78–99.

Archer, D. and R. Gartner (1984) *Violence and Crime in Cross-National Perspective*, New Haven, Conn.: Yale University Press.

Bayley, D.H. (1976) *Forces of Order: Police Behavior in Japan and the United States*, Berkeley: University of California Press.

Bayley, D.H. (1991) *Forces of Order: Policing Modern Japan*, Berkeley: University of California Press.

Beirne, P. (1983) 'Generalization and Its Discontents: The Comparative Study of Crime', in I.L. Barak-Glantz and E.H. Johnson (eds), *Comparative Criminology*, Beverley Hills: Sage, pp. 19–38.

Braithwaite, J. (1989) *Crime, Shame and Reintegration*, Cambridge: Cambridge University Press.

Cicourel, A.V. (1976) *The Social Organization of Juvenile Justice*, London: Heinemann.

Cohen, I.F. and M. Felson (1979) 'Social Change and Crime Rate Trends: A Routine Activities Approach', *American Sociological Review*, **44**, 588–608.

Devine, J.A., J.F. Sheley and M.D. Smith (1988) 'Macroeconomic and Social-

Control Policy Influences on Crime Rate Changes, 1948–1985', *American Sociological Review*, **53**, 407–20.

Evans, R. Jr (1977) 'Changing Labor Markets and Criminal Behavior in Japan', *Journal of Asian Studies*, **16**, 477–89.

Fiala, R. and G. LaFree (1988) 'Cross-National Determinants of Child Homicide', *American Sociological Review*, **53**, 432–45.

Foote, D.H. (1992) 'The Benevolent Paternalism of Japanese Criminal Justice', *California Law Review*, **80**, 317–90.

Geertz, C. (1973) *The Interpretation of Cultures*, New York: Basic Books.

Griffith, J. (1970) 'Ideology in Criminal Procedure or A Third "Model" of the Criminal Process', *Yale Law Journal*, **79**, 359–417.

Hamilton, V. and J. Sanders (1992) *Everyday Justice: Responsibility and the Individual in Japan and the United States*, New Haven, Conn.: Yale University Press.

Hansmann, H.B. and J.M. Quigley (1982) 'Population Heterogeneity and the Sociogenesis of Homicide', *Social Forces*, **61**, 206–24.

Harada, Y. (1991) 'Testing the "Stable Criminality" Hypothesis with Japanese Data', paper presented at the 50th Anniversary Meeting, American Society of Criminology, 20–23 November, San Francisco.

Harada, Y. (1992) 'A Study on the Impact of Social Tracking on Youthful Criminal Careers in Japan', paper presented at the 44th Annual Meeting, American Society of Criminology, 4–7 November, New Orleans.

Heiland, H.G., L.I. Shelley and H. Katon (eds) (1991) *Crime and Control in Comparative Perspectives*, Berlin: De Gruyter.

Inverarity, J.M., P. Lauderdale and B.C. Feld (1983) *Law and Society: Sociological Perspectives on Criminal Law*, Boston: Little, Brown.

Ito, K. (1993) 'Research on the Fear of Crime: Perceptions and Realities of Crime in Japan', *Crime and Delinquency*, **39**, 385–92.

Japanese Economic Planning Agency (1988) 'Kokumin Seikatsu Shihyo (Indices of Life Conditions of the Japanese), unpublished report on file with the author (in Japanese).

Japanese Justice Ministry Research and Training Institute (1992) *Hanzai Hakusho* (White Paper on Crime), Tokyo: Japanese Finance Ministry Printing Office.

Katoh, H. (1991) 'The Development of Delinquency and Criminal Justice in Japan', in Heiland, Shelley and Katoh (eds), *Crime and Control*, pp. 69–81.

Katzenstein, P.J. and Y. Tsujinaka (1991) *Defending the Japanese State: Structures, Norms and the Political Responses to Terrorism and Violent Social Protest in the 1970s and 1980s*, Ithaca, NY: East Asian Program, Cornell University.

Kersten, J. (1993) 'Street Youth, *Bosozoku*, and *Yakuza*', *Crime and Delinquency*, **39**, 277–95.

Matsumura, Y. and K. Takeuchi (1992) 'Can the Death Penalty Deter Crime? An Econometric Approach with Japanese Data', paper presented at the 44th Annual Meeting, American Society of Criminology, 4–7 November, New Orleans.

Merriman, D. (1991) 'An Economic Analysis of the Post World War II Decline in the Japanese Crime Rate', *Journal of Quantitative Criminology*, **7**, 19–39.

Messner, S.F. (1982) 'Societal Developlment, Social Equality and Homicide', *Social Forces*, **61**, 225–40.

Miyazawa, S. (1990a) 'Developments in Quantitative Comparative Criminology and Agenda for Japanese Criminologists', *Hanzai Shakaigaku Kenkyu* (Japanese Journal of Sociological Criminology), **15**, 134–47 (in Japanese).

Miyazawa, S. (1990b) 'Learning Lessons from Japanese Experience in Policing and Crime: Challenge for Japanese Criminologists', *Kobe University Law Review*, **24**, 29–61.

Miyazawa, S. (1991) 'The Private Sector and Law Enforcement in Japan', in W.T. Gormley (ed.), *Privatization and Its Alternatives*, Madison: University of Wisconsin Press, pp. 241–57.

Miyazawa, S. (1992) *Policing in Japan: A Study on Making Crime*, trans. Frank G. Bennett, Jr. with John O. Haley, Albany, NY: State University of New York Press.

Murai, T. (ed.) (1990) *In Search of the Safe Society: From the 1990 International Forum on Crime Prevention (Anzen na Shakai wo Motomete)*, Tokyo: Japan Urban Security Research Institute (in Japanese).

Neumann, W.L. and R.J. Berger (1988) 'Competing Perspectives on Cross-National Crime: An Evaluation of Theory and Evidence', *Sociological Quarterly*, **28**, 281–313.

Nishimura, H. (1979) 'The Bond to Society and Persons as a Power for Forestalling Delinquency: An Empirical Study of the Validity of Control Theory in Juvenile Delinquency', *Kagaku Keisatsu Kenkyujo Hokoku Bohan Shonen Hen* (Research Reports on Crime Prevention and Juvenile Delinquency, National Research Institute of Police Sciences), **20**, 126–41 (in Japanese).

Nishimura, H. (1986) 'Routine Activities Approach to Theft', in H. Shikata (ed.), *Hanzai Shakaigaku* (Sociological Criminology), Tokyo: Gakubundo (in Japanese).

Sekai no Naka no Nippon o Kangaeru Kai (1985) *Kokusai Hikaku Nippon o Miru* (Looking at Japan in International Comparison), Tokyo: Chuo Hoki Shuppan (in Japanese).

Shelley, L.I. (ed.) (1981) *Readings in Comparative Criminology*, Carbondale: Southern Illinois University Press.

Sherman, L.W. (1992) *Policing Domestic Violence: Experiments and Dilemmas*, New York: Free Press.

Shikita, M. and S. Tsuchiya (eds) (1990) *Crime and Criminal Policy in Japan from 1926 to 1988: Analysis and Evaluation of the Showa Era*, Tokyo: Japan Criminal Policy Society.

Skolnick, J.H. and D.H. Bayley (1986) *New Blue Line*, Berkeley: University of California Press.

Tanioka, I. (1992) 'Social Control Theory at Japanese Society', paper presented at the 44th Annual Meeting, American Society of Criminology, 4–7 November, New Orleans.

Tanioka, I. and D. Glaser (1991) 'School Uniforms, Routine Activities and the Social Control of Delinquency in Japan', *Youth and Society*, **23**, 50–75.

Tsuda, M. (ed.) (1982) *Gendai no Nihonteki Keiei* (Contemporary Japanese Management), Tokyo: Japan Institute of Labour (in Japanese).

Tsutomi, H. (1991) 'Reformulating Cloward and Ohlin's Differential Opportunity

Theory into Rational Choice Perspective: Occupational Orientation of Japanese Institutionalized Delinquents', paper presented at the 50th Anniversary Meeting, American Society of Criminology, 20–23 November, San Francisco.

van Dijk, J.J.M., P. Mayhew and M. Killias (eds) (1991) *Experiences of Crime Across the World: Key Findings from the 1989 International Crime Survey*, 2nd edn, Deventer: Kluwer.

van Wolferen, K. (1989) *The Enigma of Japanese Power: People and Politics in a Stateless Nation*, London: Macmillan.

Wagatsuma, H. and G.A. De Vos (1984) *Heritage of Endurance*, Berkeley: University of California Press.

Whitehill, A.M. and S. Takezawa (1981) *Work Ways*, Tokyo: Japan Institute of Labour.

Williams, K.R. and R.L. Flewelling (1988) 'The Social Production of Criminal Homicide', *American Sociological Review*, **53**, 421–31.

Wilson, J.Q. (1983) *Thinking About Crime*, rev. edn, New York: Basic Books.

Yamaura, K. (1982) 'A Quantitative Analysis of Efficiency in Police Activities', *Keisatsugaku Ronshu* (Journal of Police Studies), **35**, (5), 83–109 (in Japanese).

Ymua, Y. (1992) 'Revisiting Cloward and Ohlin's Strain Theory with Japanese Data: Minor Deviance of Japanese Junior High School Students', paper presented at the 44th Annual Meeting, American Society of Criminology, 4–7 November, New Orleans.

12 Patients' Rights, Citizens' Movements and Japanese Legal Culture

Eric A. Feldman

Rights Talk, Japanese and American

While most observers agree that rights assertion in the United States is more common than elsewhere, their appraisals of its impact, effectiveness and appropriateness vary greatly. Mary Ann Glendon opines about an America gorged on rights, with individuals unburdened by a conception of the common good unable or unwilling to control their assertions of rights.[1] From an empirical base, Gerald Rosenberg argues that efforts to use the Supreme Court to achieve social and political change in civil rights, women's rights, and abortion have been less successful than is generally claimed.[2] Cass Sunstein believes that a 'rights revolution' resulted from congressional and presidential initiative in the 1960s and 1970s, and has transformed our understanding of constitutional democracy.[3]

Standard accounts of rights in Japan sharply contrast with evaluations of rights in America. They portray a society with no concept of rights, where disputes are gently (or at least quietly) resolved in the context of personal, informal relations.[4] Articulating one's interests in the language of rights, according to these accounts, is inappropriate because it ignores community norms by promoting individual needs. It is ineffective because, shunned by the community, rights claims are also disdained by the courts. Inappropriate and ineffective, asserting one's rights is therefore rare. A central theme of post-war literature on legal culture and consciousness is devoted to explicating this view of rights, a view based on a belief that most Japanese do not look at the world through the prism of law or rights.[5]

When comparing assertions of rights in the United States and Japan, it is necessary to distinguish between rights, rhetoric about rights, and rights rhetoric. For something to be a right, in the most fundamental legal meaning of the term, it must be guaranteed by a code or constitution and/or protected by a court – that is, it must be legally enforceable. In both the United States and Japan, there is much jurisprudential literature on precisely what rights are and how they should best be defined. In neither country is there widespread agreement on which rights should be protected, or on the precise meaning of rights.

Rhetoric about rights refers to the relative importance attributed to rights in a particular society by popular and academic writers, as well as by laypersons. The power rights are imagined to possess, the frequency with which they are supposedly invoked, and how they are thought to define the identity of a people are the key components that fuel the creation of a rhetoric about rights. In examining litigiousness in the United States, for example, an issue closely related to rights, Carol Greenhouse asserts:

> Litigation is an important activity in its own right, but it is the concern of Americans about litigiousness that is the subject of what follows. My starting point is in the observation that many Americans are ready to believe in, almost to the point of insistence, their own allegedly litigious national character, even when evidence for this characterization is absent, ambiguous, or contradictory.[6]

Greenhouse is impressed by the gap between Americans' perceptions of litigiousness and the actual amount of litigation in the United States, a gap that also exists between the perception and reality of rights assertion in the United States. The gap in Japan, in contrast, divides the rhetoric about rights – that they are incompatible with Japanese culture and thus unasserted, misunderstood and ignored – from a more empirically based understanding of the conditions that inhibit or promote rights assertion.

Rights rhetoric refers to what Stewart Scheingold calls 'the politics of rights'. Analysing it requires an examination of how rights are used to frame, discuss and debate issues relevant to social policy; paying attention to the language of actors engaged in social movements, particularly the context and timing of rights assertion; determining the efficacy of invoking rights rhetoric for mobilizing like-minded individuals; and evaluating the success of those who use rights in pursuit of particular social ends. Rhetoric about the invisibility of rights in Japan, and the use of rights rhetoric by social movements, are the subjects of this chapter.

Japan already exhibits certain characteristics of rights talk that would agitate critics of rights in the United States. An article on subway renovations in Tokyo, for example, reports claims that 'not providing bathrooms or making males and females share the same lavatories...are violations of human rights'.[7] Engaged in a battle over the family registration system, a Korean resident of Japan contends that 'a person's name is an important matter involving human rights, so it should be registered correctly...not to be correctly called by one's name is a violation of those rights'.[8] A dispute over the decibel level of public address systems is framed as 'the rights to free speech pitched against appeals to the right to peace and quiet'.[9] Whatever their merits, the claims themselves indicate a degree of rights rhetoric not usually associated with Japan.

Rights in Japan do matter, but they exhibit differences, and matter in different ways, from rights in the United States. Living in Japan and in daily contact with Japanese, one is aware of how rarely the word *kenri* (right) is used, even when there is an overt dispute that from an American perspective seems to involve rights. When individuals are angry, or feel cheated or abused, they are likely to walk away, or to change the subject, or to act extraordinarily politely, not to claim that their rights have been aggrieved. Such behaviour is not an indication that the parties do not understand rights, but that rights are not an acceptable tool of one-to-one argument. It is a bad strategy to start talking about rights, because the other party will recoil, the relationship will be severely damaged and the possibility of a fast or advantageous solution will vanish. Thus the public, aggressive assertion of rights is reserved for particular types of conflicts, generally those in which hopes of continuing a relationship between the parties have been abandoned and possibilities for informal agreement have been exhausted.

There are other differences between rights and rights rhetoric in Japan and the United States. In Japan, asserting the primacy of individual over collective interests must be done with caution, since the rhetoric about rights makes clear the identification of such assertion with selfishness and arrogance. Most often, rights are asserted on behalf of groups, once people with similar concerns are united. In addition, while many American scholars are accustomed to thinking about rights and duties as closely linked, there are various historical conflicts in Japan that are treated by scholars as implicating duties but not rights.[10] This suggests that Western scholars raised on Hohfeld may be able to use observations about Japan to rethink their beliefs and assumptions about the relationship between rights and duties.

While concepts functionally similar to rights can be found early in Japanese history,[11] until Japanese legal experts began translating European law during the Meiji Restoration (in the late nineteenth century) there was no word that directly translated as 'rights' in Japanese.[12] The translation of the word 'rights' has therefore been important in framing the discussion of rights in contemporary Japan. In itself it is an interesting piece of intellectual history; more importantly, it exemplifies how rights were understood in

Japan, by government officials, intellectuals and social reformers. Were rights merely a foreign import lacking resonance in Japan, it is unlikely that the translation would have been so hotly contested.

The Translation of 'Rights'

Meiji intellectuals translating and incorporating European law into the Japanese legal system faced the challenge of developing a new vocabulary. As in German, words in Japanese are created through agglutination, with Chinese characters combined into new blends of sound and meaning. Most new legal words were created without notice, as they had narrow technical meanings of little general interest or import. But 'rights', central as they were to the law of each European jurisdiction studied by the Japanese reformers, became the focus of a prolonged debate between proponents of different translations. The translation of 'rights' thus came to represent the difficulties of recreating Japanese law, the foreignness of Western legal thought and the complexity of capturing the precise meaning of foreign legal concepts in the Japanese language.

Competing translations of the word for 'rights', *kenri*, had two characters, and there was little disagreement about the character for *ken*. It originally meant quantity, amount or volume, and was used to discuss the measure of quantity and spiritual measure.[13] Eventually, it came to mean authority, power and influence (*ken'i*, *kensei*), an association that has continued to the present.

While there was little debate about *ken*, two different characters were proposed for the *ri* or *kenri*. One means interest, profit, gain, benefit or advantage. The other character for *ri* means reason, justice, truth and principle. From the late 1860s, and continuing for several decades, two different translations of rights,

権利 (K1) and 権理 (K2)

both pronounced *kenri*, were being used in Japan. One, K1, emphasizing interest or profit, was used in legal codes and court papers, regulations and other official documents. The other, K2, emphasizing principle or justice, was used by prominent intellectuals and social reformers. Eventually, proponents of K1 prevailed, and their translation of rights came to be used in official government and legal documents, as well as in the writings of intellectuals, journalists and others wishing to discuss rights in Japanese.

With the derivation of *kenri* from characters meaning power and interest has grown the view that there can be no understanding of rights in Japan.[14]

Devoid as it is of any moral sense of rights, the word *kenri* itself is seen as the ultimate example of the Japanese inability or unwillingness to grasp complex Western legal concepts. The translation of *kenri*, some claim, proves that in Japan rights have been misunderstood as related to the exercise of power and narrow self-interest, rather than correctly understood as rooted in justice.

But it must be remembered that the victory of K1 (interest) over K2 (principle), given the contenders, was more a consequence of political manoeuvring than of conceptual merit. It ought not to be overemphasized. Had K2 become common usage, the Japanese word for right, *kenri*, would have combined power or authority with reason or principle, instead of combining power or authority with profit or interest.[15] That alone would be an erroneous basis on which to claim that in Japan there is an appreciation for the subtleties of rights. Moreover, while rights in the West are related to morality and justice, there is also a strong association with power, benefit and interest. The creation of *kenri* from characters meaning power and interest may not be inapt, given the political context in which rights in Japan are invoked.

Transplants, Legal Culture and Rights

Culturalist explanations of rights in Japan take the translation of *kenri* as their point of departure, arguing that rights are an import from the West, incompatible with Japanese culture, an impotent appendage of the legal system. Rights are viewed as yet another example of Japan's tradition of legal borrowing, a tradition that started with the importation of Chinese law a millennium ago, continued through the nineteenth-century reliance on European law, and was most recently carried on in the twentieth century with the imposition of aspects of the US legal system. A metaphor that captures much of the way Japanese legal rules, systems and culture are thought to change, particularly salient to the tradition of legal borrowing, is the metaphor of legal transplants.

The idea that law and legal rules are portable and autonomous, and can therefore be transplanted, was a fundamental assumption of those writing on law and development in the 1960s and 1970s.[16] They took their lead from scholarship on modernization and political culture, brilliantly discussed by Reinhard Bendix in *Nation-Building and Citizenship*. Bendix describes the economic transformation of England in the eighteenth and nineteenth centuries as a model for France, and the political revolution of France as a model for England. With both nations having undergone an economic and political 'breakthrough' by the end of the eighteenth century, they became what he calls 'pioneering countries', and every other nation was thus 'backward'.

'Ever since,' he writes, 'the world has been divided into advanced and follower societies.'[17]

Which countries are advanced and which are followers has since that time changed repeatedly. But the desire of follower societies to close the gap between themselves and the advanced societies, while trying to preserve the character of their native culture, has been a constant. In a comment that is echoed by the literature on legal transplants, Bendix writes:

> All aspects of modernity are up for adoption simultaneously, and it depends upon available resources, the balance of forces in the 'follower' society, and the relative ease of transfer which aspects will be given priority. The fact that such items as medication, printed matter, educational innovations, political practices like the franchise are more easily transferred than advanced technology requiring heavy capital investment is another aspect of the divergence of processes of modernization.[18]

Alan Watson's pioneering work carries on the idea of advanced and follower nations by viewing legal change as a process of transplanting rules from donor to recipient jurisdictions. Watson's description of the shifting and sharing of legal rules and doctrines as transplants paints a colourful picture of the intimacy of exchange, the fundamental compatibility of donor and recipient, and the way different jurisdictions are united and divided by legal formulations. It allows us to think about the world's legal systems as similar in their essentials, but at different stages of evolution. Just as organ transplants succeed between similar species (such as humans) or those in the same developmental line (like children and baboons), legal transplants provide hope to ailing members of the world community that their non-functioning (or absent) parts may be replaceable with those from a related nation. In keeping with the metaphor of transplants as an aspect of the basic similarity of different nations, Watson writes:

> A successful legal transplant – like that of a human organ – will grow in its new body, and become part of that body, just as the rule or institution would have continued to develop in its parent system. Subsequent development in the host system should not be confused with rejection.[19]

Other aspects of transplantation, equally central to their success, are frequently overlooked. Transplants in the physical body are substitutions. The patient is often in a critical state, victim of a malfunctioning organ, which is heroically seized and replaced by a new or donated body part. Donors are usually dead, and are always thought of as altruistic; recipients are grateful, and will always be to some extent impaired. Transplants include both removal and replacement, not the insertion of a previously absent organ.

Despite the fact that the metaphor of legal transplants draws on but does not explicitly imitate the medical model, the dual images of high technology medicine and the human body condition how legal transplants are viewed. Law is transplanted from the West to Africa and Asia, from victors and conquerors in Europe to less fortunate neighbours. It is given by the strong, industrialized states, by those who are healthy and robust, benevolent and self-sacrificing, evolved and advanced, to nations in need of help, with diseased or missing parts, far behind in the evolutionary order.[20] With regard to the law, Japan has been consistently viewed as recipient rather than donor. First from China, then Europe and finally from the United States, the Japanese body politic has run a solid trade deficit in the exchange of legal parts.

Other metaphors may more accurately describe the process of legal exchange, particularly in the Japanese context. Grafting, the process of fusing the lives of two different living organisms or the covering of one by the other, better captures many aspects of the exchange. The Japanese translation and enactment of Western legal codes in the late nineteenth century, for example, can be thought of as grafts rather than transplants. To be judged a successful transplant, Western law had to lodge itself firmly in Japan, be accepted and grow. But thought of as a graft, the Japanese distinction between *honne* (reality, practice) and *tatemae* (formality, pretence) is pertinent. Western law can then be understood not as a new, living and vital addition, but as a superficial coating, a decoration covering actual practice. Given the unequal treaties imposed on Japan, as Chalmers Johnson writes, there was 'a practical interest in causing Westerners to see in Japan Western-type legal codes, parliamentary bodies, and commercial practices, regardless of how Japanese actually did things'.[21]

Applied to rights, modernization's emphasis on advanced and follower nations, echoed in the transplant metaphor, suggests that, prior to the Meiji Restoration and the vocabulary of *kenri*, there was neither a word for nor a concept of rights in Japan. Japan was a backward nation with a traditional legal system. Japanese modernization required the importation of Western law, thought to be a necessary element of modernity. In turn, rights were understood to be a critical feature of Western law. Given this logic, it is not surprising that a foundational issue of legal sociology in Japan has been the extent to which Japanese law has modernized, measured by its importation and operationalization of Western legal doctrines, norms and practices, including rights. A corollary of this approach is that only occasionally is Japan examined on its own terms. Whether rights-like ideas and practices existed before Western influence, and have continued, is a question overshadowed by assumptions that rights were absent. Only recently has the alleged lack of rights claims and rights consciousness in the shadow of economic success been challenged.

The New Rights

Since the 1960s, in part as a reaction to the literature on Japan's harmonious, consensual legal culture, considerable attention has been devoted to the study of conflict, including conflict over 'new rights' (*atarashii kenri*). 'New' refers only in part to the emergence of particular rights in recent decades. More importantly, 'new' describes the process through which the rights have developed. Rights that have been advanced – such as those related to the environment (*kankyo ken*), sunlight (*nissho ken*), taxpayers (*nozeisha ken*), personal integrity (*jinkaku ken*) and others – are connected by the fact that they were advanced by social movements organized around a common interest and asserted despite potential economic, political, legal, moral and social obstacles.[22] Also shared by new rights is their having been pursued through litigation.

Despite the use of the courts and the filing of lawsuits, however, members of many of the movements do not expect to win positive judgements. Though a clear win is desirable, other objectives include the desire to attract publicity, garner new supporters, increase public awareness of an alleged injustice and pressure defendants to reach a more acceptable informal solution than would otherwise be possible. Hasegawa Koichi identifies several shared characteristics of new rights-related litigation. According to Hasegawa, the lawsuits over new rights (1) are group-based, relying on the joining of many separate suits since class action is not feasible; (2) seek a variety of individually allocated compensatory damages, since obtaining an injunction is difficult; and (3) utilize both administrative appeal procedures and courts.[23]

Some of the research generated by the advent of new rights is technical, devoted to constructing models of the type of right being asserted. Yamada Takao classifies them by the subject of the right (human, animal, ecosystem and so on), the individuals with the rights (criminals, consumers, patients etc.), the 'merit' of the right (a right to do something, a right to access to some service) and the authority supporting the right (constitutional, legal, extralegal).[24] Yonosuke Inamoto categorizes new rights as those established by agreement (*shohinteki kenri*), fundamental rights that are asserted by social movements and accepted by a majority of citizens (*kihonteki kenri*) and rights that are privileged by law (*tokukenteki kenri*).[25] Konishi Minori distinguishes between rights that are not yet recognized by established law, already recognized rights, expansions of previously recognized rights and rights that are based on new grounds, like sunlight and the environment.[26] Awaji Takehisa groups new rights movements as non-legal, legal and superlegal.[27]

These models are aimed at placing new rights into categories based in established law. There is also research on new rights that focuses on their institutional and sociological significance. These have primarily taken the form of mobilization studies, examining particular rights and the movements that promoted them. Some studies use the existence of new rights movements to suggest that Japan is becoming a pluralist society, unleashing the democratic forces, indigenous or imported, that will make it more like its Western democratic counterparts. Citizens' movements and the rights they advocate, it is claimed, are evidence of 'a change in, or a transformation of, our rights consciousness, or way of thinking about rights'.[28]

The 'big four' environmental cases, the most studied of the new rights litigation, have inspired bold pronouncements. One expert writes:

> These four pathbreaking cases…demonstrated that the judicial system could be used to protect ordinary citizens against abuses by powerful institutions, and thus to break down the well-known reluctance among Japanese to use the courts…. Thus these cases have greatly affected Japanese legal culture in addition to legitimizing litigation as a tool of citizen participation.[29]

The same author, using the environmental arena to indicate the significance of citizens' movements in general, states:

> Their [citizens' movements] message is home-grown, not imported, indicating that Japanese political culture had an indigenous potential for democratic 'evolution'. To the Japanese who have become active in citizens' movements, the idea they have something called 'rights' which have been 'unjustly' trampled upon, that the system itself owes them some recourse, that democratic procedures are actually devices that exist precisely for the situation in which they find themselves, is attractive and satisfying.[30]

Optimism about new rights faded as enthusiasm about an increase in citizen participation, pluralism and rights assertion in Japan collided with bureaucratic control and authority. The glacial and ambiguous pace of social transformation was explored by scholars, including Frank Upham, who studied social, political and legal conflict, and emphasized the way that the state marginalizes protesters and contains conflict by manipulating legal rules, avoiding generalizable decisions and retaining power and control over the pace of social change.[31] Other explanations for the mixed success of new rights movements emphasized the hierarchical and conservative judiciary in Japan, the small number of attorneys, the power of the bureaucracy and the dynamics of citizens' movements themselves.[32]

New rights movements also faced significant barriers to bringing about change when seeking to influence politicians for legislative reform, or to pressure the bureaucracy to bring about change through administrative action.[33] Politicians are uninterested in issues without clear electoral consequences, infrequently initiate legislation and are institutionally subordinate to the bureaucracy. At the same time, the bureaucracy is not directly accountable politically and is thus relatively impervious to outside pressure.

Patients' Rights

In retrospect, it is clear that the significance of citizens' new rights movements was initially overstated – in part a reflection of the gap between the stated aspirations and realistic goals of the movements. Some did achieve limited success, in the form of bureaucratic largesse, mediated solutions and even legal judgements. But, for the most part, grand claims of imminent change in the Japanese social, political and legal systems went unrealized. 'Rights inflation' (*kenri no infure*) in the sense of a widespread affirmation by courts of new rights proved hyperbolic; predictions of a transformation in legal consciousness were little more than wishful thinking; litigation as a vehicle to social evolution was stymied by a powerful and entrenched bureaucracy, the institutional incapacity of courts and conflicts among the reformers.

Still, the forces that pressed for the institutionalization of new rights have had a certain long-term impact. At the very least, they laid bare the reality of rights in Japan – that rights are not remote, alien, misunderstood entities of a foreign legal system; that 'the Japanese' are not unable to articulate rights claims; that the culture of Japan is not so harmonious, consensual or hierarchical that all conflicts are solved through informal channels to the satisfaction of all parties. New rights movements also provided a model for groups with grievances that needed both a process and a framework for pursuing them. While organizing a movement, seeking publicity, going to court and applying pressure on politicians and the bureaucracy were no guarantee of success, they were the best, and perhaps the only, feasible strategies. The procedures followed by many of the 1970s movements have therefore been emulated by subsequent groups.

One current movement has clustered around the theme of patients' rights.[34] Patients' rights describes a variety of prerogatives and liberties that may be asserted by individuals in their interactions with physicians or the medical system generally. Access to treatment and medication, privacy, confidentiality, viewing one's medical records and many other things are potentially patients' rights, depending upon the legal and ethical framework of a nation's health care system. Most patients in Japan are well served by the relatively equitable system of medical care, with regard to access and cost. What is thought to be lacking is the involvement of patients in treatment decisions. Foremost among the rights demanded by Japanese patients, therefore, is the right to receive information related to diagnosis and treatment, and to participate in medical decision making. Advocates of patients' rights have grouped these claims under the term 'informed consent' (*infomado konsento*, *setsume to doi*).

The doctrine of informed consent, first enunciated at the Nuremberg trials, was bolstered in the 1970s by patients' rights declarations in the United States and Europe, and received the imprimatur of the World Health Organization in the Lisbon Declaration of 1981. Extensively litigated in the United States, its requirements have been found to include that consent be voluntary; that patients be competent; that physicians describe, in addition to other factors, treatment risks, probabilities of success and failure, potential problems with recovery, and the chance of death; and that patients understand the physician's explanation and sign a prescribed form. Weak versions of informed consent simply order doctors to verbalize information and warnings, but, taken seriously, the doctrine of informed consent requires a reallocation of information in the medical setting. In Japan, where physicians traditionally have operated with almost unbridled discretion, affirming the doctrine of informed consent requires a change in the medical power structure. Given the strength and prestige of the Japan Medical Association and other organizations of medical professionals, the history of medical paternalism and expectations that patients be deferential to medical authority, the doctrine of informed consent clearly faces substantial resistance.

Moreover, there are numerous institutional barriers obstructing the implementation of informed consent. Current reimbursement practices, for example, lead physicians to treat up to one hundred patients per day, each for only several minutes. When obtaining informed consent is necessary, appointments are simply too short for any meaningful discussion between doctors and patients.

Japan's legal system is also a barrier to the creation of a doctrine of informed consent. Without contingency fees, a sufficient number of attorneys, activist courts, class action, willing plaintiffs and defensible causes of action, informed consent (and patients' rights more broadly) would not have developed in the United States. Japan, however, in comparison to the United States, is characterized by an infrequency of litigation, protracted court proceedings, few attorneys and hierarchically organized, conservative courts. Consequently, a relatively limited number of cases related to patients' rights end up in court and judicial decisions have not inspired others to litigate.

As a result, patients in Japan have no right to examine their medical records. Their right to information about diagnosis and treatment is contingent on physician discretion, which in practice means that many patients are ill-informed. Patients do not have a right to decide which course of treatment to pursue. And in what may be the nation with the world's highest rate of prescribed and ingested medication, patients lack the right to be told about the intended and unintended effects of what they are consuming.

Echoing the literature on rights in other contexts, some claim that informed consent and the idea of patients' rights is unsettling in Japan. A Japanese medical ethicist has written:

> [Right] is originally an alien notion for the Japanese, and hence not only the notion of 'patients' rights', but also the notion of 'sharing information' and 'shared decision-making' between patients and physicians is still quite radical for many Japanese patients and particularly for many paternalistic Japanese physicians.[34]

Likewise, a radical physician who runs an advice centre for patients in the Tokyo states:

> Japanese society is still not based on contracts but rather on human emotions. So we have to discuss what kind of informed consent system can fit Japanese society because imported concepts from overseas don't work here.[36]

However, others like Bai Koichi, founder of the Japanese Association of Law and Medicine, have spent decades writing about the relationship between rights and health care, and advocating fundamental changes in the provision of medicine.[37] For Bai, the greatest challenge to bringing about legal reform supporting informed consent in Japan is the entrenched political and legal interests and power relations, not the conceptual fit of patients rights.

The movement for patients' rights in Japan was launched in the early 1970s, although academic discussion of informed consent had begun some years earlier.[38] Hirasawa Masao describes the formation of several of the first patients' rights citizens' groups.[39] One, the Saito Hospital Victims' Group, was made up of patients living in proximity to the hospital where they each claimed to have been victims of medical malpractice. Because they lived in the same area, and had suffered from similar mistreatment, their interests and actions were congruent. That was not the case with other groups, which consisted primarily of individuals who were not themselves complaining about poor medical treatment. The Kitakyushu Citizens Medical Conference, for example, was brought together by the more generic mission of fighting for citizens' rights. It consisted of members with a variety of professional and personal commitments who shared an interest in progressive politics. Calling patients involved in treatment disputes 'victims' (*higaisha*), they represented the interests of weak individuals whom they believed were unfairly treated by the powerful.

Patient associations were derided by the medical establishment; the president of the Japan Medical Association, Takemi Taro, called them 'truly despicable' (*iyashimu beki shudan*).[40] Yet they persisted, organizing plaintiffs who identified themselves as victims of malpractice and taking physicians and hospitals to court. They emphasized that their goal was not money *per se*, but rather payment that was compensation for the medical suffering they had been caused.

Current efforts to enact a patients' rights law began in 1984. A group dominated by attorneys and led by Suzuki Toshihiro formed the National Reformation Committee for a Declaration of Patients' Rights (*kanja no kenri sengen zenkoku kaikaku iinkai*).[41] The Declaration is organized into six sections: individual dignity, right to equality in receiving medical treatment, right to receive the best possible medical treatment, right to know, right to self-determination and right to privacy. These rights are claimed to be grounded in three articles of the constitution – Articles 13, 14 and 25:[42]

> Article 13: All people shall be respected as individuals. Their rights to life, liberty and the pursuit of happiness shall, to the extent that it does not interfere with the public welfare, be the supreme consideration in legislation and in other governmental affairs.
>
> Article 14: All of the people are equal under the law and there shall be no discrimination in political, economic or social relations because of race, creed, sex, social status, or family origin….
>
> Article 25: All people shall have the right to maintain the minimum standards of wholesome and cultured living. (2) In all spheres of life, the State shall use its endeavours for the promotion and extension of social welfare and security, and of public health.

The 1980 Japan Federation of Bar Associations' Declaration of a Right to Health (*kenko ken sengen*) offered additional support to the rights cited by the Committee.

In the latter half of the 1980s, several groups that previously had expressed little interest in the rights of patients began to support, at least formally, the idea of patients' rights. The Union of National Health Insurance Medical Groups (*zenkoku hoken idantai rengo kai*) issued a Declaration on Private Practice Physicians (*kaigyoi sengen*), in which it addressed issues of patients' rights. A publication of the Japan Medical Association's Life Ethics Study Group, 'A Report on "Explanation and Consent"' (*setsume to doi ni tsuite no hokoku*), explained in detail how physicians could obtain consent, and offered a model consent form.[43] The Japanese Life Cooperative Union (*Nihon seikatsu kyodo kumiai rengo kai*) issued a Code of Patients'

Rights, (*kanja no kenri shoten*). More recently, the Japan Hospital Association decided to implement rules regarding patients' rights, specifically informed consent, access to medical records and self-determination.[44]

In 1991, two new groups pressing for patients' rights were formed. One, the Medical Malpractice Plaintiffs' Organization, in Nagano Prefecture, consists of alleged victims of medical malpractice and their families. Founded by a father whose son has been bedridden for more than a decade because of an anaesthesia-related accident, the Organization raises money to aid malpractice plaintiffs and to study malpractice victims nationwide.[45]

The other group, the Organization to Establish a Patients' Rights Law (*kanja no kenriho o tsukuru kai*), consists of medical professionals, attorneys, alleged malpractice victims and their families. It was founded in 1991 with the explicit goal of enacting patients' rights legislation, as well as implementing a system to review malpractice cases. In March 1993, the group submitted a patients' rights bill to the Minister of Health and Welfare. The minister is reported to have affirmed the importance of informed consent and declared that the ministry would convene a study group to discuss the implementation of informed consent at medical institutions.[46]

The bill submitted by the Organization demands a right to self-determination (*jiki ketei ken*), a right to receive explanations and reports (*setsume oyobi hokoku o ukeru kenri*), a right to an informed consent process (*informed consent no hoshiki, tesuzuki*), a right to the protection of personal information (*kojin jyoho o hogosareru kenri*) and a right to inspect and copy medical records (*iryo kiroku no etsuran tosha seiko ken*), among more general rights such as access to medical care, not being forced to leave the hospital and not being subject to mistreatment.[47] It also specifies a procedure for notifying the public about patients' rights and suggests that a committee for the protection of patients' rights be formed. To promote its objectives, the Organization publishes a regular newsletter, *Rights Law News* (*kenriho nyuzu*), holds periodic meetings and editorializes in national newspapers.

Of the patient care-related issues that make it to court in Japan, the treatment of cancer patients is one of the most controversial. Japanese physicians have for many years withheld information about cancer diagnoses, claiming that the loss of hope experienced by patients would expedite death. Even patients at the National Cancer Centre, and the late Emperor Showa, have remained uninformed. A decision of the Nagoya District Court, upheld by the Nagoya High Court, held that 'how much information should be given [to cancer patients] is in the discretion of the doctor to the extent that the patient's right to self-determination is not infringed'.[48] The fact that the court explicitly recognized a right to self-determination may encourage patients' rights advocates, but, in practice, the court supported the wide degree of discretion allocated to physicians.[49] As interpreted by one expert on law and medicine in Japan,

> Japanese courts are willing to recognize the inviolability of the patient's body but this willingness does not extend to the patient's right to self-determination or autonomy with respect to the selection of treatment courses.[50]

Medical malpractice litigation in Japan, therefore, has not changed the common practice of informing families, but not patients, about medical diagnoses and prognoses. Some courts have affirmed a doctrine of informed consent, but it contains language that permits physicians to retain wide discretion about which risks they must disclose, whether a diagnosis should be revealed and what treatment options to pursue.[51]

While there has been a lack of overt success at securing patients' rights through the courts, litigation has other functions. It has to some extent been a factor in attracting attention and members to patients' rights groups, influencing professional associations to formally recognize patients' rights and persuading the Ministry of Health and Welfare and the Diet that paying attention to patients' rights is good politics. The connection between court decisions about patients' rights and more general concerns about their recognition is made explicit by an activist attorney in a recent book on patients' rights:

> In the West, medical malpractice litigation was an important element in the unfolding of the patients' rights movement. In Japan, however, patients' rights and informed consent have been only minimally acknowledged as legal rights by the courts. I have insisted that Japanese courts recognize that patient consent to medical deeds is critical, but medical experts seem to think that the explanation on which such consent is premised should be as limited as possible. However, courts have little by little accepted legal arguments about patients' rights. We will use this way of thinking as the basis for creating a legal structure for patients' rights.[52]

None of the foregoing should be interpreted as suggesting that the content or meaning of patients' rights in Japan could mirror that in the United States. A doctrine of informed consent in Japan, for example, is likely to preserve a greater role for family decision making than for the individual, in contrast to the emphasis on patient autonomy in the United States. This is in keeping with traditions of family responsibility in Japan and consonant with a perspective that plays down self-determination. Still, the assertion of patients' rights signals a weakening of the sovereignty of the medical profession, an increase in the power of patients and an important example of the use of rights rhetoric in contemporary Japan.

Conclusion

Several current health care-related controversies evidence the continuation, and expansion, of the assertion of rights in the Japanese medical arena. The debate over the definition of death and organ transplantation, for example, has provoked claims about the rights of the dying, the rights of families to control the treatment of other family members, the rights of the handicapped, the rights of potential organ recipients and others.[53] In the area of AIDS, tension between individuals and the state is an aspect of AIDS policy worldwide, though how it is voiced and resolved varies greatly. In contrast to the emphasis upon the primacy of public health over the protection of individual rights in nineteenth-century America, for example, AIDS exemplifies the shift toward rights in twentieth-century public health policy. 'Rights-based concern has limited what American governments may do under the banner of promoting public health,' write David L. Kirp and Ronald Bayer, arguing that 'reliance on the idea of civil rights [with regard to AIDS] has been an American exceptionalism'.[54]

In Japan, the balance between the personal and the social, respect for individual rights versus protection of public health, has been explicitly debated in the process of formulating AIDS policy. To some extent, the centrality of rights in the AIDS debate is directly inherited from the debate over patients' rights. As law professor Ebashi Takashi has written:

> In the 1970s in the U.S., there was a basic tendency to think about human rights issues in medicine, and patients' rights increased. In Japan, at first, we tried to ignore such problems, but...such discussion slowly entered Japan. It was on the groundwork of patients' rights in Japan that AIDS appeared.... If there had been no such foundation, and the AIDS problem had appeared earlier...we could have had a policy of isolating AIDS patients, and a policy that most definitely would have infringed on rights.[55]

Still, there were many who pressed for coercive public health measures in Japan, either with or without concern for the potential infringement of rights. Rikkyo University's health law expert Hatakeyama Takemichi acknowledges that '[A] feature of the AIDS Prevention Law is that, in order to protect public health, there are restrictions on the rights of HIV patients.'[56] In a more extreme vein, Ohama Hoei, spokesperson for the Liberal Democratic Party's (LDP) AIDS Committee, made the following statement at a press conference to discuss proposed AIDS legislation:

> It is more important to prevent the spread of AIDS than to protect the privacy of high-risk groups. If we respect the human rights of one person, we are depriving ninety-nine others of their right to live.[57]

To Ohama, traditional coercive public health measures were the most desirable way to control AIDS. But others, particularly groups that fear they will be subject to coercive measures, argued differently. An advocate for the haemophiliac community retorts:

> The problem with the AIDS Prevention Law is the protection of privacy. Mr. Ohama of the Liberal Democratic Party said, 'The lives of ninety-nine people are more important than one person's privacy.' If AIDS were not a sexually transmitted disease, but people could be infected through casual contact, and ninety-nine people could unknowingly become infected, then that would have to be a consideration. But the facts are different.[58]

More important than the power of these arguments themselves is what they suggest about the landscape of AIDS-based conflicts in Japan. They cannot be explained by stereotypes of a nation repelled by controversy, unfamiliar with law or culturally cloistered from rights. Instead, the political, legal and social conflicts concerning AIDS in Japan suggest that demands that individual rights be acknowledged and protected, both legally and extralegally, are forcefully asserted and defended. Debate over the privacy of HIV-positive persons, the anonymity of those wishing to obtain HIV tests, the compensation of haemophiliacs infected through blood transfusions and the array of discriminatory behaviour against those who are HIV-positive reveals an unwillingness by affected parties to accept what they believe is unfair treatment, and the use of a variety of tactics to assert their rights. In comparison to the situation in the United States, they have had only a limited impact on the state's exercise of power to protect public health. But that is a conclusion about the impact of rights assertion in the context of AIDS, not about its presence or primacy in the debate itself.

The definition of death, and AIDS, are but two examples of issues that are in part framed by, discussed in and resolved through rights and rights assertion. At the same time, the controversy over these issues will affect the rhetoric about rights, which will in turn have an impact on how future issues are conceptualized, fought over and concluded. It is through this process that Japanese legal culture is created, recreated and transformed.

Notes

1 Mary Ann Glendon, *Rights Talk: The Impoverishment of Political Discourse*, New York: The Free Press, 1991.

2 Gerald Rosenberg, *The Hollow Hope: Can Courts Bring About Social Change?*, Chicago: University of Chicago Press, 1991.

3 Cass Sunstein, *After the Rights Revolution: Reconceiving the Regulatory State*, Cambridge, Mass.: Harvard University Press, 1990.

4 Tanaka Shigeaki, *Gendai Nihon Ho no Kozu*, Tokyo: Kotokusha Chikuma Shobo, 1987: 10–14, provides a good account of this view of Japanese legal development.

5 For three consecutive years the annual journal of the Japanese Association of Sociology of Law was devoted to an examination of legal consciousness in Japan. See Nihon Ho Shakaigaku Kaihen, 'Shimpojiamu: Ho Ishiki o Meguru Shomondai' (Symposium: Various Problems Regarding Legal Consciousness), *Ho Shakaigaku* 1984–86, 36–38. Some Japanese literature on legal consciousness is reviewed in Miyazawa Setsuo, 'Taking Kawashima Seriously: A Review of Japanese Research on Japanese Legal Consciousness', *Law and Society Review,* **21** (2), 1987. An overview of the field of legal sociology in Japan can be found in Rokumoto Kahei, *Ho Shakaigaku*, Tokyo: Yuhikaku, 1986, 141–61, and Rokumoto Kahei, '"Nihonjin no Ho Ishiki" Kenkyu Gaikan—Ho Kannen o Chushin Toshite', *Ho Shakaigaku* **35**, 1983, 14–33, which contains an eight-page supplement of sources on legal consciousness. The classic work in the field is Kawashima Takeyoshi, *Nihonjin no Ho Ishiki*, Tokyo: Iwanami, 1967.

6 Carol J. Greenhouse, 'Interpreting American Litigiousness', in June Starr and Jane F. Collier (eds), *History and Power in the Study of Law*, Ithaca: Cornell University Press, 1989, 252.

7 'Subway Stations Provide Little Relief', *Asahi Evening News*, 20 April 1991, 5.

8 'Korean urges "Furigana" on Registry', *Japan Times*, 25 September 1992, 2.

9 Nagoya Satoru, 'Left Wing Rips Bid to Curb Loudspeakers', *Japan Times*, 26 May 1992, 3.

10 John Haley argues that, prior to the influence of Western law in China, Korea and Japan, 'there were no rights, only duties': *Authority Without Power*, New York: Oxford University Press, 1991, 11. Although I do not agree with his assessment that there was no concept of rights in Japan until the adaptation of Western law, I do agree that the link between rights and duties is not an essential characteristic of Japanese law.

11 The complex relationship between peasants and proprietors with regard to land use, occupancy and profit in the eleventh and twelfth centuries, for example, was based on an interlocking group of privileges and obligations that would be called rights in a Western context. The same is true, during the same period, of interest in land that entitled the bearers (non-peasants of various social positions) to income. These were negotiated, disputed and litigated through the highly developed Kamakura legal system. Even peasants had definable, legitimate expectations, which proprietors had an obligation to grant.

12 Maeda Masaharu, 'Kenri to Kenri Kakusho' (A Note on the Legal Terms 'Kenri' and 'Kenri'), *Ho to Seiji*, **25**, 1975, 347–86, Yanabu Akira, *Honyakugo Seiritsu Jijyo* (Circumstances of the Formulation of Translated Words), Tokyo: Iwanami Shoten, 1982.

13 For a more detailed discussion of the etymology discussed in the following paragraphs, see Noda Yoshiyuki, 'Kenri to yu Kotoba no Imi ni Tsuite' (About the Word 'Right'), *Gakushuin Daigaku Hogakubu Kenkyubu Kenkyu Nempo*, **14**, 1979, 23–4.

14 Some scholars seem to assume the lack of understanding of rights in Japan, and focus their work exclusively on exploring rights in Western texts. Ota Tomoyuki, for example, in 'Kenri to yu Kotoba no Imi ni Tsuite' (On the Meaning of the Word 'Right'), *Shiso*, **5**, 1964, 25–35, seeks to better understand the meaning of rights but makes no reference to the Japanese experience.

15 Suzuki Shuji, *Nihon Kango to Chugoku* (Japanese 'Chinese Words' and China), Tokyo: Chukoshinso, 1981, 626; Chapter 1, '"Sanken Bunritsu" ni Matsuwaru Yogo:

"Kenri" to "Gimu"' (Terms Used in Separation of Powers: Rights and Duties), 3–60, compares the unfortunate identification of rights, power and interest in traditional China with the Japanese understanding of these concepts.

16 See, for example, David Trubek, '"Law and Development": What We Know and What We Do Not Know', paper prepared for a conference of Chinese and American legal scholars, East–West Center, Hawaii, 19 May–2 June 1989.

17 Reinhard Bendix, *Nation-Building and Citizenship*, Berkeley, Calif.: University of California Press, 1964, 413.

18 Bendix, *Nation-Building*, 415.

19 Alan Watson, *Legal Transplants: An Approach to Comparative Law*, Charlottesville: University Press of Virginia, 1974, 27; for a defence and elaboration of the idea of legal transplants, see Alan Watson, 'Legal Change, Sources of Law and Legal Culture', *University of Pennsylvania Law Review*, **131** (5), April 1983, 1121–57.

20 See Trubek, '"Law and Development"'.

21 Chalmers Johnson (1995), *Japan: Who Governs? The Rise of the Developmental State*, New York: W.W. Norton & Co., 109.

22 Proceeding from a Symposium of the National Study Group on the Constitution, in which a number of these rights were discussed in depth, can be found in 'Atarashii Jinken', *Juristo*, **606**, 15 February 1976, 49–69; citizens' movements, and the judicial development of the new rights of sunshine and the environment, are discussed in Julian Gresser, Koichiro Fujikura and Akio Morishima, *Environmental Law in Japan*, Cambridge, Mass.: MIT Press, 1981.

23. Hasegawa Koichi, 'Gendaigata Sosho no Shakai Undoronteki Kosatsu', *Horitsu Jiho*, **61**, (12), October 1989, 65–71.

24 Yamada Takao, 'Kenri no Katalogu Zukuri ni mukete', *Ho Shakaigakku*, **39**, 1987, 2–10.

25 Yonosuke Inamoto, '"Atarashii Kenri" no Kategori to Sogo Sakuyo', *Ho Shakaigaku*, 1988, **40**, 2–8.

26 Konishi Minori, 'Kenri Gainen o Meguru Ikkosatsu', in Inoue Shigeru, *Gendai no Ho Tetsugaku*, Tokyo: Yuhikaku, 1981, 266–84.

27 Awaji Takehisa, 'Minji Ho no Ryoiki', *Ho Shakaigaku*, **38**, 1986, 8–18.

28. Ibid., 8.

29 Margaret A. McKean, *Environmental Protest and Citizen Politics in Japan*, Berkeley, Calif.: University of California Press, 1981, 78; Patricia Boling makes a similar point in 'Private Interest and the Public Good in Japan', *The Pacific Review*, **3**, (2), 1990, 143.

30 McKean, *Environmental Protest*, 267.

31 Frank Upham, *Law and Social Change in Postwar Japan*, Cambridge, Mass.: Harvard University Press, 1987.

32 Miyazawa Setsuo, 'Kenri Keisei/Tenkai no Shakai Undo Moderu o Mezashite', *Ho Shakaigaku*, **40**, 1988, 33–46; a similar argument is presented in Miyazawa Setsuo, 'Social Movements and Contemporary Rights in Japan: Relative Success Factors in the Field of Environmental Law', *Kobe University Law Review*, **22**, 1988, 63; Abe Yasutaka, 'Kenri no Keisei to Hatten', *Ho Shakaigaku*, **39**, 1987, 17–27.

33 Tanase Takao, 'Kenri Seisei no Shisutemuteki Kosatsu', *Ho Shakaigaku*, **39**, 1987, 1116.

34 An authoritative article on the subject of informed consent in Japanese health care is Robert B. Leflar, 'Informed Consent and Patients' Rights in Japan', *Houston Law Review*, **3** (1), 1996, 1–112.

35 Kimura Rihito, 'Bioethics as Preseciption for Civic Action: The Japanese Interpretation', *The Journal of Medicine and Philosophy*, **12**, 1987, 267–277, 271.
36 Quoted in Shibazaki Tomoko, 'Medical Secretiveness is Under Attack', *Japan Times*, 4 July 1991, 4.
37 One of Bai Koichi's most recent efforts in this regard is his *Iryo to Jinken*, Tokyo: Chuo Hoki Chupan, 1985.
38 For example, Bai Koichi, *Iji Hogaku e no Ayumi*, Tokyo: Iwanami, 1970 (originally published 1965).
39 Hirasawa Masao, 'Iryo Henkaku to Shimin Undo', *Juristo*, Tokushu: *Iryo to Jinken*, **548**, 25 November 1973, 273–7.
40 *Ibid.*
41 The Declaration, its background and other attempts to catalyse patients' rights legislation are discussed in Ikenaga Mitsuru, '"Kanja no Kenri Ho" Seitei Undo no Igi to Gen Dankai', *Iji Hogaku*, **7**, June 1992, 72–8.
42 Suzuki Toshihiro, 'Kanja no Kenri Sengen', *Juristo*, **826**, 1 December 1984, 48–51.
43 Nihon Ishikai Seimei Rinri Kondan Kai, '"Setsume to Doi" ni tsuite no Hokoku', *Juristo*, **950**, 15 February 1990, 149–57; discussion of the report can be found in Ogasa, '"Setsume to Doi" ni tsuite no Hokoku', *Iji Hogaku*, 6 June 1991, 164–8.
44 'Kanja ni "Kenri Shoten" – "Setsume to Doi" nado Meiki', *Asahi Shinbun*, 6 July 1993, 10.
45 'Malpractice Plaintiffs Form Group', *Japan Times*, 21 October 1991, 2.
46 'Group Lodges Demands for Patients' Rights', *Japan Times*, 2 March 1993, 2.
47 Kanja no Kenri Ho o Tsukuru Kai, *Kanja no Kenri Ho o Tsukuru*, Tokyo: Meiseki, 1992, 237–57.
48 *Makino* v. *Red Cross*, Nagoya District Court Judgement, 29 May 1989, 1325, *Hanji*, 103, 107, translated by Higuchi Norio. A review of this and other cases can be found in Higuchi Norio, 'The Patient's Right to Know of a Cancer Diagnosis: A Comparison of Japanese Paternalism and American Self-Determination', *Washburn Law Journal*, **31**, (3), 1992, 455–73.
49 Norma Field airs a slightly different interpretation of this case when interviewing Mayor Motoshima of Hiroshima: 'I've been thinking about the still-common Japanese practice of not telling cancer patients the nature of their illness. Do you remember the court case in Nagoya earlier this year, where the bereaved daughter and husband of a woman who had not pursued any treatment because she hadn't been told of her cancer brought suit against the physicians and the hospital, and the court held that it was the physician's prerogative to withhold such information? Not to mention Emperor Showa's cancer. I've begun to think that this practice is another form of the Emperor system, so to speak. The reason everybody gives is that Japanese are too fainthearted to be told such distressing news, that patients would die needlessly of shock. I don't believe that anymore. I think it makes it easier for doctors to manage cancer patients if they don't have to tell them. They don't have to address their fears and anxieties. Cancer patients tend to suspect their condition anyway, and it's common enough for people who don't have cancer to worry that they do. Current Japanese practice precludes, forbids, the airing of these feelings even between the dying and their families' (Norma Field, *In the Realm of a Dying Emperor: A Portrait of Japan at Century's End*, New York: Pantheon, 1991, 243).
50 Maruyama Eiji, 'Japanese Law of Informed Consent', *Kobe University Law Review*, 1991, **25**, 39–43.
51 Ibid. For a review of the case law on informed consent, see Maruyama Eiji, 'Informed

Consent: Ishi no Setsume to Kanja no Shodaku', *Hogaku Kyoiku*, **120**, September 1990, 6–7.

52 Suzuki Toshihiro, 'Atarashi Shimin Undo o Minna no Chikara de', in Kanja no Kenri Ho o Tsukuru Kai, *Kanja no Kenri o Tsukuru*, Tokyo: Meiseki Shoten, 1992, 19–22.

53 Eric A. Feldman, 'Legal Transplants, Organ Transplants: The Japanese Experience', *Social and Legal Studies*, Vol. 3, London: Sage, 1994, 71–91.

54 David L. Kirp and Ronald Bayer (eds), *AIDS in the Industrialized Democracies: Passions, Politics and Policies*, New Brunswick, NJ: Rutgers University Press, 1992, 371–2.

55 Ebashi Takashi, 'Kansenbyo Taisaku to Jinken', in Yamada Takuo, Oi Gen, Negishi Masayoshi (eds), *AIDS ni Manabu*, Tokyo: Nihon Hyoronsha, 1991, 151.

56 Hatakeyama Takemichi, 'AIDS Hoan o Meguru Sho Mondai', *Juristo*, **888**, 15 June 1987, 84.

57 Jocelyn Ford, 'Innocent Victims of AIDS Worry that Government Ignores their Rights', *Daily Yomiuri*, 1 March 1987, 5.

58 Osaka Tomo no Kai, 'Osaka Tomo no Kai Nyusu', May 1987, Newsletter No. 65.

13 Remembering and Forgetting: The Birth of Modern Copyright Law

Brad Sherman

Introduction

Much of what is written about comparative law is concerned with the rights and wrongs of such research, with the problems that the comparativist is likely to experience in attempting to understand foreign legal cultures and how difficulties encountered in the field are best avoided. In short, they are concerned with the task of *doing* comparative research. While the lessons to be drawn from these studies are often important, in this chapter I wish to pursue a different set of questions. Instead of developing the means by which we can improve the way comparative law is carried out, or asking how truthful or accurate particular claims made about legal cultures may be, this chapter examines the *impact* of such work on law. In particular, it takes the images of different legal systems, which are at the basis of comparative work, as yet another practice that shapes legal culture. Rather than asking, for example, what are the differences between French and British company law, it asks how the image of French company law used in the United Kingdom shapes British law. In short, rather than engaging in comparative research, the interaction of different legal systems is taken as the object of study.

Within this general framework the specific focus of attention is upon the impact that the interaction of different legal cultures has had upon copyright law in the United Kingdom. More specifically, this chapter concentrates upon the bilateral copyright treaties negotiated between Britain and other European countries in the 1840s and 1850s and the impact that these have had upon domestic law in the United Kingdom. After outlining the reasons for the introduction of these treaties, the first part of the chapter examines the ramifications that the bilateral copyright agreements had for municipal law. Drawing upon the idea that the formation of identity is usually a product of denial, a product of the claims that are made to difference, it will be argued that the bilateral agreements that were negotiated in the 1840s and 1850s played an important role in the formation of British copyright law. That is, it will be argued that the process of comparing and contrasting British law with the law in Prussia, Saxony and France played an important part in the formation of domestic copyright law in the United Kingdom. In the final part of the chapter it will be argued that the images of copyright that developed during this period continue to play an important role in shaping contemporary law. In particular, the ideas of difference and opposition that developed during the nineteenth century, which were so important in the formation of national copyright systems, are having an important impact upon the recent attempts to harmonize copyright laws in Europe.

Towards a Copyright Law

The early nineteenth century was a critical period in the development of the British law which granted property rights in mental labour. As well as witnessing the beginnings of the administrative and legal reform of patent law, the establishment of the first modern system of registration for intangible property,[1] and the move from subject-specific laws to more abstract categories, it also saw the birth, or perhaps more accurately, the crystallization of a discrete branch of jurisprudence known as copyright law.

While prior to this frequent use was made of the term 'copyright', it is incorrect to assume that the term was used in a consistent, meaningful way or that it referred to a distinct area of law: there was at the time no copyright law and certainly no law of intellectual property. One of the most notable features of the law during the eighteenth and early nineteenth centuries was the lack of consensus as to how it should be organized: no one model or image had yet come to dominate as *the* accurate representation of the law. The fluid and uncertain nature of the law in this area was captured in Godson's lament in 1823 that 'the cases of Copyright have never … been formed into a distinct and independent Treatise'.[2] Godson was objecting here not only to the absence of copyright treatises and textbooks, but more specifically to the fact that the law which provided property or property-style rights in mental labour was not organized in a consistent or coherent manner.[3] Indeed, there were various competing suggestions proposed at the time as to how this field should be organized, all which were taken seriously. One mode of organization utilized, for example, argued for the creation of a category of law which would protect the fine arts as well as 'all forms of industrial art';[4] that is, it adopted a unity of art approach.[5] Thomas Turner's idea of a law of form, which focused on the external appearance and shape of objects (and as such encompassed subject matter now incorporated in patents, design and copyright, but expressly excluded literary property), was an interesting variation on this theme. Another option suggested at the time was to do away with a copyright–patents–designs style of approach and to divide productions of the mind into 'two great classifications – works (whatever their intention) addressed to the tastes, passions, and existing circumstances of the age, and those adapted to all the fluctuations of society'.[6] Yet another approach distinguished forms of property in thought depending on whether it was expressed by visual or vocal signs.[7] While there were occasional references to what we would now take to be the copyright approach,[8] it was certainly not given priority over any of the other alternatives. At best all that could be said about the disparate series of statutes and decisions which had developed in piecemeal response to specific problems was that they protected particular forms of creation from copying.

If we move away from the way in which the law was organized to focus upon the language used we see a similar lack of consensus. The fluid and uncertain nature of the language was reflected in the fact that commentators, both legal and non-legal, expert and non-expert, frequently spoke of 'copyright in inventions', 'patents for art' and occasionally even of 'patents for copyright'. At best 'copy-right' referred to the form or style of right protected and, as such, meant something very different from what it does today.[9] Moreover, the term 'copyright' was not limited to works now seen as part of copyright law (such as literary and dramatic works) but was extended to include inventions and ornamental as well as non-ornamental designs.[10]

Despite the fluidity and openness that existed during the eighteenth and early nineteenth centuries, by the 1850s there was a much clearer idea of what copyright law was and how it differed from the other areas of law which provided protection for mental labour. That is, there had been a transition from copy-right as the right to copy applicable to many types of creations, to a law of copyright as a distinct and discrete area of law.[11] More specifically, the copyright law which took shape at this time was not only a separate area of law, but also an abstract, forward-looking law which was able to expand to accommodate new forms of subject matter: a law which offered protection for literature and the fine arts but not for designs. This is not to suggest that prior to this there had not been images of the law which dealt with mental labour and that in the 1850s, or thereabouts, one suddenly appeared. Rather, it is to argue that over this period there was a gradual change in the grammar and logic of the law; an important shift in the way the law was represented and imagined. In spite of what many modern commentators would have us believe, the formation of a law of copyright and the related division of mental labour into patent, design and copyright law was neither natural nor inevitable, nor was it an example of the law coming to occupy its 'proper philosophical position'. Rather, the process was one in which one view of organizing mental labour became *the* way of organizing mental labour.

While a variety of factors such as the development of the legal textbook[12] and the growing desire for a more rational and organized legal system helped to facilitate and mould the copyright law that took shape in the early stages of the nineteenth century, this chapter focuses on the role that the bilateral agreements entered into between Britain and other European countries in the 1840s and 1850s played in this process. More specifically, it looks at the 1838 and 1844 International Copyright Acts and the impact that these had upon domestic law. While they were frequently dismissed as mere forerunners of more important multilateral conventions that followed (namely the 1886 Berne International Copyright Convention and the 1883 Paris Convention for the Protection of Industrial Property),[13] it will be argued that the bilateral treaties and the negotiations surrounding them played a crucial role in shaping the law of copyright that we have inherited.

International Copyright

As with many of the changes that occurred in this area of law in the eighteenth and nineteenth centuries, the idea for international copyright protection was initially suggested by the French.[14] The belief that 'intellectual property should pass frontiers and sheets of water and still be property' was quickly adopted by British writers and publishers.[15] While there was occasional concern about the impact of pirated works upon the quality of literature[16] and widespread acceptance that the free exchange of literary information that the treaties would promote was desirable, the primary motivation behind the calls for international copyright in the United Kingdom was the protection of British interests (which extended not only to the United Kingdom but also to its colonies and dominions).[17] More specifically, the requests for international protection stemmed from the fact that, despite the growing interest in British literature overseas, British works were not protected in foreign jurisdictions. This was because in most countries at the time literary property protection only arose for works of nationals published in that country.[18] This meant that, while a British author could get copyright protection in the United Kingdom, no equivalent protection existed to prevent piracy of their works in, say, Prussia or in America. In short, a growing sense of loss brought about by the fact that British works could be pirated with impunity outside the United Kingdom precipitated the move towards finding some way of protecting British works in other countries.

The means favoured to achieve this was for Britain to enter into arrangements with other interested countries for the mutual protection of literary property. More specifically, these treaties were to be 'based on the principle of extending the works of foreign authors the amount of protection afforded in each country respectively to the works of the native Authors'.[19] Initially the mechanism suggested that would ensure reciprocity of protection was the establishment of a multilateral treaty.[20] After some interest in this approach, however, it was rejected. As was said at the time, this was because of the belief that it would not be possible 'to pass one general law, based upon the principle of our own law of copyright, because the law of copyright varied so much in different countries'.[21] More specifically, the reason why the option of a multilateral treaty was rejected as the means of establishing international copyright protection can be traced to the belief that copyright laws reflected the national character of the country in which they operated. As such it was considered too difficult to develop a treaty which could singularly transcend and unite all the variants that existed between the proposed member states. As a consequence of these envisaged difficulties, the plans for a multilateral treaty were rejected in favour of more flexible bilateral agreements which the Crown would be able to pass in specific circumstances. To this end, in 1838, *An Act for securing to authors in certain cases the benefit of international copyright* (1 & 2 Vict. c 59) (hereinafter the 1838 International Copyright Act) was passed. This provided Her Majesty with the power to direct that authors of books published in foreign countries have the sole liberty of printing such books within the British dominions. In so doing, it opened the way for the establishment of bilateral copyright agreements.

Without exception, all the negotiations entered into on the basis of the 1838 Act failed.[22] The simple explanation for this was that the protection offered by the 1838 International Copyright Act was much narrower than the equivalent provisions available in the countries with which Britain hoped to develop reciprocal protection. The consequence of this was, as the French said in response to the proposed Anglo-French treaty mooted in the early 1840s, 'that the effect of these articles would be to benefit English interests exclusively'.[23]

By 1843 the arrogance that underlay the early British negotiations was replaced by a renewed desire to protect British interests. This led in 1844 to the passage of the *Act to Amend the Law Relating to International Copy-*

right (7 & 8 Vict c. 12) which repealed and replaced the 1838 Act. This new Act empowered Her Majesty, by Order in Council, to give protection to the authors of books and works of art first published in a foreign country. No order was to be made, however, unless reciprocal protection had been granted by the relevant foreign power. The 1844 International Copyright Act conferred copyright protection on the authors of works of literature and art, which comprised the publications of books, dramatic works, musical compositions, drawings, paintings, sculptures, engravings, lithography and any other works whatsoever of literature and of the fine arts. The 1844 Act differed from the 1838 Act both in terms of the subject matter protected (the earlier Act focused exclusively on literary property) and in terms of the mechanisms available to police and enforce the rights.[24] It also differed from the 1838 Act in that it was successfully used by the British government to enter into copyright conventions with a number of countries. In particular, the 1844 International Copyright Act served as the basis for treaties with Prussia (1846 and 1855), Saxony (1846), Brunswick (1847), the Thuringian Union (1847), Hanover (1847), Oldenburg (1847), France (1851), Anhalt-Dessau-Coethen (1853), Hamburg (1853 and 1855), Belgium (1854 and 1855), Spain (1857), Sardinia (1860) and Hesse Darmstadt (1861).

Although the International Copyright Acts of 1838 and 1844 played a central role in establishing a regime of international copyright protection and are important in their own right, the focus of this chapter is on the impact that these Acts, and the negotiations and treaties which surrounded them, had upon domestic law in the United Kingdom.[25]

The Reshaping of Domestic Law

The first and most obvious consequence of the so-called 'laws of international copyright' was that they led to direct changes in domestic law. This was because the agreements were 'based on the principle of extending the works of foreign authors the amount of protection afforded in each country respectively to the works of the native Authors'.[26] More specifically, it was the result of the fact that the negotiations proceeded on the 'assumption that the expediency between two countries depends upon a *precise and minute equality* of advantage to be derived by each contracting party respectively'.[27] This meant that before a treaty could be completed it was necessary to ensure that the protection available in both countries was virtually identical.[28] Consequently, it became important not only that British laws bore some resemblance to the laws of the countries with which the United Kingdom wished to enter into agreements, but also that the benefits they offered were the same.

As the scope and effectiveness of the protection available in Britain tended to be less extensive than that provided in other countries, and there was no consideration given to a reduction in protection, this meant that in order to bring about an 'approximation of laws' changes had to be made to British law. A situation where we can see the impact that the bilateral agreements had upon domestic law is in relation to the 1846 Anglo-Prussian treaty. Initial discussions aimed at establishing a treaty between the United Kingdom and Prussia began in the mid-1830s. In 1840, however, the Prussian government decided to discontinue their negotiations with Britain because they 'considered the reciprocity which was contemplated by [the 1838 International Copyright Act] to be only an apparent reciprocity'.[29] This was because the protection offered under the 1838 Prussian *Law for the Protection of Property in respect to Works of Science and of Art against Counterfeit and Imitation*[30] was greater than that available in Britain. More specifically, it was due to the fact that the protection available in Prussia extended 'to a much greater variety of objects than in England ... over a much longer period'; that the means of 'redress in cases of infraction of copyright were much easier attained in the former country than in the latter'; and because higher duties were imposed on books imported into Britain than were charged on those imported into Prussia.[31]

In spite of the breadth of these objections, by 1843 British agents were able to report to the Prussian government that the law in the United Kingdom had 'undergone important changes which will have the effect of materially increasing the protection at present enjoyed in England by literary property'.[32] In particular, the British government was able to say as a consequence of the 1842 Copyright Amendment Act (5 & 6 Vict. c. 45) that they have the satisfaction 'of being able to intimate to the Prussian Government that a change to British law *has* taken place which will have the effect of materially extending the protection at present enjoyed by literary property, as to terms of duration'.[33] The objections raised about copyright infringement and the enforcement of remedies were rectified by changes introduced by the 1844 International Copyright Act and also by changes in the Customs House regulations.[34] The complaint that the scope of subject matter protected under the 1838 International Copyright Act was too narrow was resolved with the passage of the 1844 International Copyright Act, which extended the category of works protected from literature[35] to also include the 'fine arts'.[36] This was despite the fact that at the time fine art was not protected under domestic law in Britain.[37] In turn, the requests that the duty imposed on books imported into Great Britain be lowered were agreed to and corresponding amendments made.

As a result of these changes, the British negotiators were able to say that 'an approximation between the two countries has thus been produced, which

Her Majesty's Government trusts will have the effect of rendering the Prussian Government less averse to an arrangement'.[38] Although the Foreign Office constantly intimated that the changes which had taken place in British law had come about in order to appease Prussian objections, it is difficult to determine the extent to which this was actually the case. Certainly, there is little evidence to support this in the domestic proceedings. Nonetheless, it is clear that Prussian objections played a role in alerting the Foreign Office and in turn the Board of Trade and parliament to deficiencies in domestic law as well as offering alternatives for change. While it is difficult to determine beyond this the precise impact that the Anglo-Prussian agreement had upon municipal law in Britain, a situation where we can more readily identify the ramifications of the bilateral treaties is in association with the 1851 Anglo-French treaty. While in many respects this treaty was similar to the other treaties which the United Kingdom had entered into, it differed in that it *purported* to provide reciprocal protection for translations of literary works – before such rights existed in domestic law in Britain. While there was some uncertainty about the changes that came about as a result of the Prussian objections, there is no doubt that the introduction of translation rights into British law in 1851 was done so as to bring domestic law into line with the pre-existing Anglo-French copyright treaty.[39]

While it is clear that the bilateral treaties influenced the development of domestic copyright law, this is not to suggest that British law was dictated by the Prussian or French governments,[40] so much as that in these situations the UK government was more concerned to protect British interests overseas, and as such in establishing treaties, than it was with the fate of domestic law. The degree to which the government was willing to alter domestic laws differed according to the nature of the market in question and the number of British works (typically books) that were pirated.[41] For example, in situations where there was little interest in books written in English (as distinct from translated works, as was the case in Russia) or in English prints or designs, there was more of a concern to protect British law. In contrast, in circumstances where there was more of a market for pirated books, as in France and Prussia, the fate of domestic law was less of a priority.[42]

The Self-identity of Copyright Law

Hand-in-hand with the direct changes in municipal law that came about as a result of these forays into international copyright law was a more important change in the grammar and logic of the law: a shift in the way the law was represented and imagined. Importantly, it is this logic, or a version thereof, which operates today. While the law of the eighteenth and early nineteenth centuries was primarily a backward-looking, subject-specific law which tended to respond to specific (sometimes minor) problems,[43] the copyright law which took shape in the 1850s and 1860s was an abstract law which extended 'to *all* works of literature and art in the widest sense'.[44] Moreover, as well as being an abstract law, the copyright law was also a forward-looking law: it was formulated in such a way as to encompass new forms of subject matter, 'to those productions in which the laws … now or may hereafter give their respective subjects privilege of copyright'.[45] What occurred with the shift from a reactive, specific law to a law which was abstract and forward-looking was a change in the ontological status of the law, 'a move from linguistic patterns mastered at the practical level to a code, a grammar, via the labour of codification, which is a juridical activity'.[46] This transformation marked an important stage in the formation of the modern system of copyright law in the United Kingdom. This is because what we see with this change is not only that copyright law was given a label, but that it also came to take on an identity which was widely accepted both inside and outside law. This can be seen in the manner in which commentators increasingly began to talk both meaningfully and consistently about 'our' law of copyright as a distinct and separate entity.[47] Related to this was the fact that, for the first time, at least overtly, the law in this area became self-reflexive: it became concerned with *itself*, with the shape that it took and the image that it offered to the world.[48]

A number of different factors associated with the bilateral agreements helped to facilitate the crystallization of copyright law. Perhaps most importantly of all, in responding to the requests which were made for 'an accurate and authentic report of the present state of the law of copyright'[49] it was necessary, for the first time, to think of and conceptualize the law of copyright (as distinct from the specific forms of copyright protection which had been considered previously[50]) and to ascertain what this abstract category included and excluded. In the same way in which the production of a treatise or a textbook requires the law to be reduced to writing and in so doing to a particular format, in order to negotiate the international copyright treaties it was necessary to have a picture of what copyright law was, what its minimum standards were, and what it was that a Prussian or Saxon bookseller could expect in London or Glasgow. In short, the international copyright treaties presupposed and required a representation of domestic law. To determine whether the laws of two countries were equivalent to each other it was not only necessary to have a clear idea of what the law was, it was also important that these representations were fixed and secure. In consequence, although there was a great deal of confusion as to the nature of domestic law, in negotiating the bilateral copyright treaties this uncertainty was ignored or, perhaps more accurately, resolved.[51]

As well as helping to facilitate the crystallization of the law of copyright, the bilateral treaties also played a role in shaping the particular *form* that the law took. The abstract nature of copyright law arose in part from the need to communicate about the copyright system, from the pressure for a standardized language of communication.[52] This was because, in order to determine whether the protections available in two countries were equivalent to each other, it was necessary to find a common denominator, a basis from which this task of evaluation could be carried out. It was also necessary to find some mechanism which would enable the negotiators to move beyond the traits of national character which were said to bind the copyright laws to the idiosyncratic features of the nations involved. The process of codification and abstraction met these needs by ensuring a basic level of communication and interchangeability. In order to assist in this process there were also demands for the law to be standardized and made uniform. To this end there were frequent calls for simplicity, clearness and precision in the drafting of the treaties.[53] Again, what we see is a concern with the *form* that the law took; the law taking an interest in the *shape* of the law. Hand-in-hand with this heightened self-reflexivity was an increased desire to rationalize and order the law that dealt with intellectual labour. With France acting yet again as a role model,[54] there was a demand for the law to be made as simple, uniform and precise as possible.[55] Prompted by the idea that complicated systems were evidence of the unsoundness of the principles on which they were based,[56] there were frequent attempts to consolidate and reduce the complexity of the law, a trend which was reinforced by the more general moves towards legal codification which were taking place in Britain at the time.[57]

Another factor which explains both the abstract and the forward-looking nature of the copyright law that developed at this time, why it was that the treaties were said to extend 'in principle to those productions in which the laws in both countries do now or may hereafter give their respective subjects privilege of copyright',[58] relates to the difficulties experienced in negotiating the treaties and to the time, cost and delay that this involved. An abstract, forward-looking law had the advantage in that it decreased the likelihood of the need to reopen negotiations whenever a new subject matter was given protection in a particular treaty country.

The abstract, forward-looking nature of the copyright model can also be explained by the constitutional framework within which the negotiations proceeded. More specifically, it stemmed from the fact that, while the Foreign Office and the Board of Trade were responsible for the international copyright treaties, they did not have the authority to alter pre-existing judicial or legislative arrangements. This led to a dilemma. On the one hand, in order to ensure that the treaties entered into would be able to encompass works that might have required protection in the future and as such avoid the need to renegotiate those treaties, there was pressure on the Crown for the law to be made future-looking and abstract. At the same time, it was clear that the Foreign Office lacked the authority to extend the scope of protection beyond that already provided for under the pre-existing domestic law. The response by the Crown to this dilemma was not to limit the scope of their negotiations. Rather, it was to *pretend* that the image of domestic law used in the international agreements was an accurate representation of British law. This is despite explicit recognition that the particular image of copyright law utilized and incorporated in the international treaties differed, sometimes markedly, from British domestic law as it then was: most notably in relation to the protection given to fine art[59] and translations, and in terms of the methods of enforcement.[60] The pretence of neutrality was highlighted in Palmerston's remark in relation to the drafting of copyright treaties that it was important 'to avoid the *appearance* of an assumption by the Crown of power to alter by its own authority arrangements fixed by Parliament or to control proceedings by courts of justice'.[61] The tension created by the desire to change the law, combined with an apparent inability to do so, was also avoided by the fact that the process by which the various statutory and judicial arrangements were combined into the abstract category, 'art and literature', was described as one which was merely 'declaratory of the pre-existing law'.[62] All that was being done, so it was said, in the move from subject-specific legislation (which was primarily post hoc responses to individual problems) to a forward-looking abstract area of law capable of accommodating new forms of creativity was the process of highlighting what was implicit in the statutes and related judicial decisions; what parliament and the courts had intended but not articulated. As a result, the Crown was able to argue (at least to itself) that, since they were not creating law but merely replicating it in a different form, the treaties generated no constitutional problems.

While the process of abstraction and categorization was presented as a neutral event which was merely declaratory of the pre-existing law,[63] it is clear that it was a creative task which involved selection and exclusion.[64] In particular, in deciding that copyright protected not only literary works but also artistic works, the law came to embody a particular way of thinking about creativity.[65] Despite the fact that design protection, like that offered for books, engravings, sculptures and textiles, as well as for inventions and other objects of utility, was a right to prohibit copying (a copy-right), in putting together an 'accurate picture of the law', the subject matter of design, along with works of manufacture and utility, were excluded from the remit of copyright law. Unlike the position in France, and contrary to the views of many commentators, the abstract model of copyright which came into being at this time related 'exclusively to literature and the fine arts'. In contrast 'patterns, designs, and manufacturers' marks' were 'reserved to be dealt with by a separate arrangement'.[66] While the law adopted what could be called a 'unity of literature' approach (namely, it prima facie protected all literary works irrespective of their quality), it felt unable or unwilling to adopt a unity of art approach. With this we see, for the first time, the institutionalization of the idea that copyright law protected art and literature but excluded designs: a trait which continues to shape contemporary intellectual property law.

Another important and continuing characteristic of the model of copyright law which developed during the nineteenth century was that it came to embody the belief that copyright was beyond the remit of trade and commerce (a concept which finds resonance in the contemporary idea that books are not articles of manufacture). The non-commercial image of copyright prevailed despite the clear connection which existed between literary property and the import duties imposed on paper, and between copyright and the publishing industry more generally. The attitude adopted towards literary and artistic property is in marked contrast to the approach taken towards patents, designs and trade marks which were seen to have clear connections with commerce and trade. The contrast between the non-commercial image of copyright and the commercial nature of patents, designs and trade marks was reflected in the fact that patents, designs and trade marks were placed within the Treaties of Freedom, Commerce and Navigation whereas copyright remained in separate treaties.[67] It was further reinforced by the bifurcation in international intellectual property law that took place with the passage of the Paris and Berne Conventions later in the century. The institutional manifestation of the romantic idea that copyright works should be considered in a non-commercial light can be seen in the exchange that took place in the 1840s in relation to the proposed Anglo-Prussian Copyright Treaty. In reply to the Prussian argument that there should be 'precise and minute equality in the relief of *merchantable benefits* to be afforded to each side respectively' (that is, that the cost of books should be equivalent), MacGregor argued that it was incorrect to equate what was primarily a moral issue with matters of trade. More specifically, in an attempt to take copyright outside the scope of trade and commerce and place it in a moral framework, he said:

> Although anticipating direct benefit to both parties as an arrangement for the protection of literary property, they do not conceive that an inducement of this description is the only one that ought to operate upon their minds. Copy-right is in their view a species of property and one not less entitled to the full enjoyment of legal protection within the limits defined to it than are other descriptions; and

> although it may, in certain respects, be more open to invasion, the moral formation of the right to which it gives determinate force, is not, as it appears to them, in any degree impaired thereby.... Conversely, then, piracy is a species of robbery and as such my Lords anticipate that they will find on the part of civilised states a disposition to discountenance and relinquish it without minute calculations on the part of any of them as to the degree of pecuniary profit which in one quarter of another may be derived from the allotment and distribution of the spoil.[68]

While in MacGregor's concluding remark that 'copyright is a property; all piracy is theft' we see the rhetorical nature of his argument, his comments are useful in that they capture the non-commercial and romantic perspective from which copyright is often viewed. MacGregor's argument is also useful in that it highlights the tension that exists as a consequence of holding such a view, given the obvious connections that the subject had and continues to have with commerce and trade.

Hand-in-hand with the non-commercial image of copyright law was the idea that the works protected by copyright law were cultural, unique and local. Again, this was in contrast to the subject matter of patent (and less so design) law which was technical, neutral and universal. More specifically there was a belief that the subject-matter that fell within the international copyright treaties (namely works of literature, drama and the fine arts) was closely connected to the national culture in which it was created. Following from this, and by equating the subject-matter of international copyright with copyright more generally, it was said that the copyright laws of individual member states were, like the works they protected, inextricably linked to the culture of the particular country in question. In a period where translation rights were virtually non-existent, the localized image of copyright was reinforced by the fact that the vernacular languages acted as a barrier to the movement of literary works and as such to the perceived mobility of copyright law.[69]

Another important and enduring characteristic of the model of copyright that developed during this period was that for the first time it came to be defined *against* other legal systems: 'our' law of copyright was different from that of the French and the Russians. The idea of the difference between 'our' law and 'their' law, in particular between British law and French and Prussian law, provided the focal point against which British law was defined. In so doing it not only helped to forge the self-image of domestic law but also played an important role in shaping the identity and destiny of intellectual property law in the United Kingdom.[70]

The belief which developed in the second part of the nineteenth century that the British style of copyright was naturally and inevitably different from the approach adopted in France and Germany, that the two systems were in opposition to each other (an idea which has matured as the copyright versus *droit d'auteur/urheberrecht* debates of today) is in marked contrast to the situation in the eighteenth and early nineteenth centuries which saw much cross-fertilization between different legal cultures. Indeed, in the reports, select committees, commentaries, tracts and pamphlets of this period, references were frequently made to other legal systems, to the way they protected intellectual property and to whether elements of those systems could be imported into Britain (the primary resource for inspiration being France for copyright and design law, and America for patents). Translations of foreign materials and regular reports from foreign envoys meant that the Board of Trade as well as commentators and critics more generally had access to a wide variety of materials ranging from updates on Saxon copyright law and the nature of the Belgian textile industry to information on the book-buying habits of the residents of St Petersburg and a translation of Kant's *Was ist ein Buck*? The cross-fertilization was reinforced by the fact that foreign parties were often involved in petitioning the UK parliament for changes in British law.[71]

The move from the uncertain, open period in which British law was willing to imitate and plagiarize aspects of other systems, to a period in which French and Prussian approaches to copyright were considered alien to that adopted in the United Kingdom, marked an important stage in the conceptual closure of copyright law. In so doing, it also played a central role in the formulation of domestic law in Britain.

The model of copyright law that came to the fore in the middle part of the nineteenth century gradually became more and more inflexible. As the image of copyright law utilized in the international copyright agreements slowly made its way into and dominated domestic legal culture, as it became entrenched in the legal treaties and commentaries, in the administrative arrangements, the language and statutory framework of the law, it provided less room for manoeuvre and change. This was reinforced by the fact that the image of UK copyright law was projected to the world. When that world returned to talk to the United Kingdom, it did so expecting a particular response. This helped to create a cycle of expectation and dependency in terms of the image that was portrayed of copyright law. In addition, once a particular treaty had successfully been used as the template for agreements with a number of different countries in the (United Kingdom's case it was the Anglo-Sardinia model), the Foreign Office was reluctant to negotiate on any other basis than this standard-form treaty for fear that it would lead to pressure to reopen pre-existing treaties. As the model spread to British dominions and colonies, it proved more and more difficult to change. The rigidity of the copyright model was enhanced by the fact that, as the number of treaties negotiated increased, the United Kingdom became entrenched in a web of bilateral agreements.[72] The images of copyright law that took shape in the nineteenth century were further cemented with the passage of the Berne and Paris Conventions which marked the culmination of the logic worked out earlier in the century.

Representing Copyright Law

It is clear that the bilateral copyright agreements entered into the middle of the nineteenth century presupposed an image of domestic law. It is also clear that the image of domestic law presented in the international negotiations was *not* an accurate representation of the law at that time. Beyond the direct changes that these treaties produced, however, the impact that the bilateral copyright treaties had upon domestic law is less clear. This can be explained in part by the fact that the bilateral treaties were negotiated by the Foreign Office and not the usual legal sources: namely, parliament or the courts.[73] More importantly, the primary reason why the impact that the copyright treaties had upon domestic law may not be readily apparent relates to the epistemological assumptions commonly employed in law. In particular, it can be traced to the fact that in law it is common to say that a model or image represents something which objectively exists 'out there'. As a result, we would expect that the image of copyright used in the international treaties either represented the state of domestic law or, if not, that it was inaccurate and therefore irrelevant. If we reject the realist assumptions which force us to concentrate on what copyright law actually protects (and also ignore the related attempts to cleanse the law of legal fictions[74]), we see that the image of copyright used in the bilateral agreements played an important role in the development of the domestic law. In particular, if we suspend our realist assumptions we see that the model anticipated, possibly created, the legal reality. That is, the image of copyright law was a model *for* rather than a model *of* what it purported to represent. In effect, the laws presented during the bilateral agreements as accurate descriptions of domestic law (which they were clearly *not*) became real laws, real fictions. The image presented and used in the bilateral conventions as being representative of copyright law in the United Kingdom came to be accepted as an accurate, or at least partially accurate, picture of that law. In this sense, that 'false' picture became the law, or at least a powerful and influential representation of it.

The reorganization in the logic and grammar of the law which was facilitated by the bilateral agreements entered into in the nineteenth century brought with it a number of other changes. At a general level, the image and the empirical reality which this was said to represent had an important impact upon what was expected of copyright law, where its boundaries were drawn and consequently what was included and excluded within its remit. More specifically, once imagined, the model of copyright became an instrument for reform. In particular, the fact that domestic law failed to match up to Britain's international obligations was used as a basis to argue for reform of the law (a ploy recently used in relation to moral rights in Britain and Australia). The gap which existed between domestic and international law, which meant that British laws 'were unjust in their operation upon the Subjects of those foreign States who have entered into International Copyright Conventions with Her Majesty, inasmuch as such treaties are based upon the principle of reciprocity',[75] played an important role, for example, in ensuring the enactment of the 1862 Fine Art Copyright Act.

The image of copyright also became the ideal or standard against which reform was measured.[76] For example, the 1862 Fine Art Copyright Act, which offered protection to painters, draughtsmen and photographers, was described as 'another and most important step towards the completion and perfection of the series of parliamentary enactments of Artistic Copyright'.[77] The state of perfection spoken of was the domestic embodiment of the model of copyright which was institutionalized in the international copyright agreements. Many of the reforms instigated during the remainder of the nineteenth century, in particular the numerous attempts to consolidate the various copyright statutes, can be seen as attempts to codify this model.[78] This process of perfection was formally completed at a statutory level with the passage of the 1911 Copyright Act.[79] With one or two exceptions, much of the history of copyright law since this time has largely been a process of refinement and reintrenchment of this model, which is applied with increasing sophistication and detail.

Towards a History of Copyright Law

The international copyright treaties not only brought with them changes in the way the law was imagined and consequently the way its future career was organized, they also saw a change in the way the history of the subject was organized. Perhaps more accurately it was not so much that in reconceptualizing or 'creating' copyright law that there was a change in the way the history of the subject was written, as that the official history was written for the first time.[80] The process which saw the beginning of a history of copyright law did not occur in isolation, however, but was part of a more general transformation that took place at the time. This was a consequence of the fact that 'profound changes in consciousness' such as that brought about by the formation of the modern law of copyright, 'bring with them characteristic amnesias. Out of such oblivions, in specific historical circumstances spring narratives.'[81] More specifically, it was a result of the fact that the copyright law which developed in the nineteenth century brought with it new ways of thinking and talking which not only provided a history, but also a biography of the subject. Importantly, this narrative played an central role in constituting and reinforcing the identity and self-image that copyright law has of itself.

A key feature of the explanatory narrative which developed at this time was that it presupposed a closed and insular copyright law. As we saw earlier, as well as defining British law in opposition to French and Prussian law, we also saw a tendency to deny the impact of foreign jurisdictions on British law. This process of denial played an important role in reinforcing and constituting copyright law's identity.[82] Hand-in-hand with this was the fact that the model of copyright law which developed at the time was read back into the history of the subject. As a consequence of presuming that the abstract, forward-looking copyright law which developed in the mid-nineteenth century already existed in the law (albeit in a nascent form), the law of the eighteenth century was reinterpreted. We see, for example, the 1711 *Statute of Anne* (or, at it was then known, *An Act for the Encouragement of Learning, by vesting the Copies of printed Books in the Authors and Purchasers of such copies*) change from a literary property act to become the first copyright statute. As a consequence of retaining only those commentators whose views confirmed and supported the official story, authors such as Thomas Turner and William Kenrick were read out of the history of copyright law. In order to rewrite legal history in this manner, it was also necessary to ignore the fact that during the eighteenth and nineteenth centuries the image of copyright law that came to prominence was only one of numerous ways of organizing the law.

Another notable feature of the post-identity memory which developed at the time was that there was a change in the way the law was explained, or more accurately in *what* was explained. While in the eighteenth century the central focus of debate was on whether it was appropriate and possible to grant property rights in mental labour, during the nineteenth century this question was taken as a given. Instead, the main focus for discussion was upon the manner in which the law was organized. Importantly, in addressing this question we see the resort to principle; to the abstract ideas which were said to underpin copyright law. Once identified, it was believed that these principles would solve the problems of organization; they would explain the shape that the law should take as well as enabling commentators to 'reconcile apparent inconsistencies and to arrange the whole in a logical manner'.[83] Only then would it be possible to replace the 'uncouth, incongruous, and mendacious hash, forming the common law; together with the mongrel empiricism of the statute law of England'.[84]

Although the principles of copyright played an important role in ensuring that the law was made more manageable, their use tended to be restricted to the internal organization of copyright law. When it came to distinguishing copyright law from patent and design law a different logic was employed: one which drew heavily on an image of a closed and insular law. While in the eighteenth and early nineteenth centuries the intangible property granted in books (literary property) was distinguished from that offered in clocks (patents) in terms of the nature of the labour that was used in the creation of the product in question, in the nineteenth and twentieth centuries this was replaced by a new rationale. More specifically, we see a move away from any attempt to explain the differences between the categories. Instead of focusing on *a priori factors* which were said to have give rise to the particular form that intellectual property took, there was a gradual acceptance of these categories; they were taken as givens. What we see in place of this was an increased reliance on obvious external differences that existed between the categories. Copyright was different from design law in that it arose automatically on creation and was not dependent on registration. Copyright was different from patents in that patents provided an absolute monopoly whereas copyright protection was limited to the copying of the work. Gradually, these external differences came to be treated as if they were causes of the separate categories. Copyright was different from design law *because* it arose automatically on creation and was not dependent on registration. Copyright was different from patents *because* patents provided an absolute monopoly whereas copyright protection was limited to the copying of the work. In modern law, this mode of analysis has become the primary basis for explaining and distinguishing the different categories of intellectual property.[85] One of the consequences of a narrative which teaches us that within a historical context copyright law is timeless, natural and inevitable, and that it is driven by principle, is that it leads us away from the changes that occurred in the middle of the nineteenth century. As the histories of copyright law move from the 1711 *Statute of Anne* through to the twentieth century, with occasional detours along the way, with the exceptions of the Berne and Paris Conventions it is as if the nineteenth century did not exist. However much we may wish to ignore the developments that took place during the nineteenth century, the copyright law which came to be imagined at this time continues to play an important role in shaping present-day copyright law.

At a general level the image of copyright law that took shape in the nineteenth century has become ingrained in the architecture within which copyright law operates: it shapes the way copyright textbooks are organized (which have remained fairly static since the 1860s) and is reflected in the statutory framework, the language and arguments employed by legal academics and practitioners. In short, the image of copyright which came to prominence as a result of the international copyright treaties has become the organizing logic of the law. More specifically, a number of the traits associated with the copyright law that was imagined in the nineteenth century continue to shape modern law. The romantic image of a copyright law which is beyond the remit of trade and commerce manifests itself, for example, in the discussions about how applied art should be protected and in terms of the debate as to how the overlap between copyright and designs law should be managed. It also plays an important role in shaping the arguments which focus on the question of the proper place for computer programs within intellectual property law. As the recent GATT/TRIP negotiations have shown, the notion of the vernacular and localized nature of copyright works also continues to have an important impact.

The cultural dimension of copyright law has also been highlighted in relation to the question of indigenous intellectual property rights which was raised, for example, as a consequence of the Australian High Court decision in *Mabo*.[86] While the perceived neutrality of science, trade and commerce made it easier for patents to escape the confines of local culture,[87] the idea that copyright law (or more accurately the works that copyright law protects) is inextricably linked to the idiosyncratic features of national culture has recently been perceived as creating a stumbling block to the harmonization of copyright laws in Europe.[88] The image of a vernacular copyright can also be seen, without too much cynicism, to underpin (or at least to have influenced) the recent moves to treat intellectual property as a human right.[89] By simultaneously trading on the pathos and the perceived neutrality and universality of human rights, this approach can be seen as an attempt to escape the confines of local culture. Another technique which has been adopted to this end is to reconfigure copyright in economic terms.[90] This provides both a means to speak to the commercially minded and also a standardized basis from which copyright and moral rights can be translated.[91]

An awareness of the manner in which copyright law developed during the nineteenth century can also help to explain the perplexed position that design law occupies in many countries today. The fact that design law is at once trade-related and therefore neutral and universal, yet at the same time artistic and therefore local, cultural and unique means that it occupies an ambivalent half-way position between these two extremes. Design law also suffers from the fact that, unlike copyright and patent law, it was never *directly* the subject of international treaties (or some equivalent event) which precipitated the need for it to be imagined or represented. As a consequence, design law has never been forced to create an identity or a readily identifiable image. Design has been defined, if at all, as the product the 'stepchild' of copyright and patents (which historically it clearly is not).

The image of copyright law that developed during the nineteenth century and the narrative of identity which this engendered not only play an important role in influencing the way we think of copyright law, they also restrict the questions we ask of the subject. Perhaps most importantly of all, the image of copyright also limits what we imagine is possible and consequently what we demand of the subject. While much energy in this field is taken up with the reform and harmonization of copyright law and as a result is constantly concerned with the future, there are many reasons why time should be taken to consider the image of copyright law that shapes and informs such discussions. In particular, if the law is to achieve what we demand of it, it is not only necessary to recognize the power that the image and the narratives that accompany it have concerning the law, it is also important that we set about reinventing new narratives. A possible starting-point for this which is suggested from an examination of the bilateral treaties is the need to reconsider the way we think about different legal cultures. Indeed, one of the most interesting points highlighted by a study of the international copyright treaties is the complex networks of influence which exist between different legal systems.[92] Perhaps more importantly, it may also force us to rethink what we mean by comparative law and in so doing lead us to question the traditional view of legal culture either ours, yours or theirs – as a closed physical space united and distinguished by language, habit and practice.

Notes

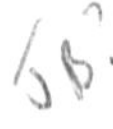

1 The first modern system of registration established in the United Kingdom was the designs registry, which was set up in 1839. This was used as a guide for the reform and modernization of the patent and trade mark administrations which took place later in the century. The 'modern' centralized system of registration is in contrast to the various local systems of registration (such as at Stationers Hall or that organized by textile manufactures in the north of England). I would like to take this opportunity to thank Lionel Bently for his helpful comments.

2 Richard Godson, *A Practical Treatise on the Law of Patents for Inventions*, London: Joseph Butterworth, 1823, viii.

3 As Turner said, the 'subject has till lately only occupied the attention of legislators and jurists at uncertain intervals … it has been but little studied by the jurist or statistician; and information respecting the subject is widely scattered, and must be sought for under any head rather than its own' (Thomas Turner, *On Copyright in Design in Art and Manufactures*, London: F. Elseworth, 1849, 12).

4 'Thus, adopting at an early period, a correct principle, the French extended the appli-

cation of copyright to all production of industrial art, and at this time, France affords, at a small cost, protection of sufficient duration, with effectual and speedy redress for the infringement of copyright. In no other country is there so comprehensive a copyright, and in the markets of every civilised country the elegant productions of France are esteemed in preference to those of all other nations' (G. Brace, *Observations on Extension of Protection of Copyright of Design, with a view to the improvement of British Taste*, London: Smith, Elder and Co, 1842, 10).

5 That is, it prima facie protected all artistic works (including industrial works), irrespective of their application or use.

6 'The first are produced principally to satisfy an appetite ever craving novelties, and excitement. They soon "play their part", and rapidly disappear' (Anon, 'Law of Literary Property and Patents', *Westminster Review*, **10**, 1829, 444, 465).

7 Montague R. Leverson, *Copyright and Patents: Or, Property in Thought, Being an Investigation of the Principles of Legal Science Applicable to Property in Thought*, London: Wiley, 1854.

8 For example, see Richard Godson, *A Practical Treatise on the Law of Patents for Inventions*, London: Joseph Butterworth, 1823.

9 The decision of *Jefferys* v. *Boosey* (1854) 4 HLC 815 is interesting in that it reflects the transition from copyright as a right to copy to copyright as a distinct area of law.

10 Design legislation well into the twentieth century habitually spoke of copyright in designs. A late example in relation to patents is the definition of copyright to mean 'the exclusive right to work, make use and vend an invention' contained in art. IV of the 1851 *Inventions Registration and Protection Bill*, appended to the (1851) *Select Committee on the Patent Law Amendment*, PP IIXX, 410.

11 As Webster said in 1853, there are now three 'separate and distinct branches of jurisprudence, which may be treated of as copyright of literature and fine arts, of design in Arts and Manufacture and of letters patent for inventors' (T. Webster, *On Property in Designs and Inventions in the Arts and Manufacturers*, London: Chapman and Hall, 1853, 10).

12 Although legal treatises and textbooks played an important role in shaping copyright law, they seem to have been less important than in other areas of law. Cf. A.W.B. Simpson, 'The rise and fall of the legal treatise: Legal principles and the forms of legal literature', in *Legal Theory and Legal History: Essays on the Common Law*, London: The Hambledon Press, 1987.

13 This attitude is summed up in Ladas' comment at the end of his chapter on bipartite conventions, treaties and agreements that 'The net outcome of the bipartite conventions entered into by the various countries before 1883 for the protection of industrial property rights was not important' (Stephen P. Ladas, *Patents, Trademarks, and Related Rights: National and International Protection*, Vol. 1, Cambridge, Mass.: Harvard University Press, 1975, 54).

14 In 1832, it was reported to parliament that there was 'already an interchange of public and parliamentary documents between UK and France' (Spring Rice, 30 July 1832, *Hansard*, **XIV**, 897). A proposal was made by the French representative, Count Mole, that 'some arrangement should be entered into between [the UK] and France calculated to remedy the inconvenience resulting from the reprinting in England of French books and English books in France'. The Foreign Office reported 'that the matter has been referred to the proper department and that the question raises so many important considerations that the government must postpone any express opinion on it. The French ambassador asked for relevant Acts of Parliament' (22 Nov. 1836, FO/27/518

No. 207). (All references to Foreign Office (FO) and Board of Trade (BT) materials refer to records held at the UK Public Records Office at Kew.)

15 In April 1837, Le Marchant (of the Board of Trade) reported to Backhouse (Foreign Office) that 'strong representations on the part of some of the most Eminent writers of this country and of the principal publishers, that from want of an International law of Copyright the interests of literature are seriously affected'. The Board of Trade had found these representations to be well founded and that this was indeed a 'case which calls for the active interference of government'. The Board of Trade noted that this issue was already under consideration by the governments of France, Prussia and America so that there was every possibility that negotiations might be successful. As a result it was suggested that Palmerston might make overtures, for 'it would be unbecoming to the position of this country, to be slow to further so important an object to the advancement of its moral rank and the deserved claims of our men of letters and men of science who have contributed so largely to exalt the character of the nation.' Furthermore, it would contribute to 'extending and cementing the friendship of nations, by subduing the prejudices and widening the sympathies of the most intelligent and influential classes of their respective populations'. The Board of Trade forwarded papers to Lord Palmerston and asked him to 'enter into any general arrangement for effecting the purposes to which this letter refers' (14 April 1837, FO/27/551). For a history of the negotiations, see FO/27/860.

16 Reprints in Brussell were frequently so hasty that 'serious misprints take place and the public is inundated with incorrect editions' (14 April 1837, FO/27/551). Lytton Bulwer sent Poulett Thompson papers on international copyright saying that such a law 'would indeed effect for English literature advantages greater than any government in any age has ever conferred upon authors' (14 April 1837, FO/27/551). On the problem of international piracy (especially in France) see Lytton Bulwer, 14 Dec. 1837, *Hansard*, **39**, 1091.

17 'The grievances suffered by authors and their publishers from spurious publications printed in other countries, have greatly increased during the last few years, and they have no power at present to protect themselves against the evil and the loss it occasions to them. Every work written by a popular author is almost co-instantaneously reprinted in large numbers both in France, Germany and in America and this is done now with much rapidity, and at little expense, generally less than one eighth of the price at which the original editions bearing the cost of the copyright can be furnished. All the works of Sir Walter Scott, Lord Byron, Messrs Robert Southey, Thomas More, Thomas Campbell, Rogers, Milman, Hallam, Wordsworth, Bulwer, James, Chamier, Monyatt, The Countess Blessington and indeed most popular authors are so reprinted and resold by Galignani and Bardens at Paris' (14 April 1837, FO/27/551).

18 There was some uncertainty in Britain at the time as to the manner and extent of copyright protection given by British statutes. For example, Talfourd said in 1837, 'if a recent decision on the subject of musical copyright is to be regarded as correct, the principle of international copyright is already acknowledged here' (Talfourd, 18 May 1837, *Hansard*, 878). For a detailed examination of the question of whether foreigners could get copyright protection in Britain (whether as resident or not) see Lord Brougham, *Jefferys* v. *Boosey* 4 HLC 681, 738 (discussing the conflicting decisions of *Tonson* v. *Collins* 1 Sir W Bl 301; *Bach* v. *Longman* Cowp 623; *Chappell* v. *Purday* 14 M and W 303; *Delondre* v. *Shaw* 2 Sim 240; *Bentley* v. *Foster* 10 Sim 329).

19 Earl of Westmorland, 25 Jan. 1843, FO/64/244.

20 Referring to the address made by British authors to the US Congress, it was said that 'the government of Britain should also assist in endeavouring to bring about one great

system of international law for the protection, in all European countries, and in America, of Literary Property, convinced that the result will be beneficial; to the authors of all countries and the interests of literature in general' (14 April 1837, FO/27/551).

21 Poulett Thompson, 20 March 1838, *Hansard*, **XLI**, 1110.

22 After initial discussions with France, meetings were planned in Berlin, Brussels, Washington and the Hague (30 Sept. 1837, BT/1/337).

23 Memo by J. Bergue on the history of the Anglo-French negotiations (19 Dec. 1849, FO/27/860).

24 Another problem with the 1838 International Copyright Act that the 1844 Act remedied was that it did not enable Her Majesty's Government to extend protection to prints and engravings made overseas.

25 Another factor which contributed to the development of copyright law was the question of Imperial Copyright. As was said, 'it is probably not too much to say that, were it not for the difficulty arising from the constitution of the Empire, the Copyright Law [of the UK] would have been remodelled long ago' (Anon, 'Copyright Law Reform', *Quarterly Review*, **CCXIII,** (1910), 483, 486).

26 Letter from Earl of Westmorland to Board of Trade (25 Jan. 1843, FO/64/244).

27 Emphasis added (25 Jan. 1842, FO/64/242).

28 'It is desirable that copyright laws, whatever they may be, should be as nearly as possible the same in all English speaking countries, and should be extended throughout these countries to all authors, without distinction. In this way the author would get the largest possible market' (T.H. Farrier, 'The Principle of Copyright', *Fortnightly Review*, **24**, 1878, 836, 850).

29 25 Jan. 1843, FO/64/244.

30 Published in Berlin, 18 Dec. 1837. Translated 15 Jan. 1838 (BT/1/337/no 6169/32a). Occasionally, there were attempts to argue that that this was not a rejection so much as a call for modification: 'At the same time, as regards the [Prussian] objections, the Prussian memorandum intimates that although the protection accorded in Prussia to Prussian Authors can by the Prussian law be granted to the same extent only to such foreigners as are subjects of a country in which the protection to Prussian authors could be shown to be in every respect the same, still that there is nothing in that law which prevents the Prussian Government from granting a more limited protection to other Foreign Authors, and the Prussian Government accordingly admits the possibility, by which Great Britain should on the one hand be bound to afford to Prussian Authors the same protection afforded to British Authors in England, while Prussia would on the other hand afford to British Authors the same extent and classification of protection which is, or may hereafter be afforded to British Authors by British law. Thus, the reply can be seen not as a rejection, but as a modification.' This logic was not, however, extended to complaints about remedies. (Earl of Westmorland, 25 Jan. 1843, FO/64/244).

31 Prussian booksellers who had been consulted on the 'proposed arrangement with the Great Britain government had requested that import duty on books into Great Britain be lowered in the same manner as duty on prints had been, and they attached great importance to this point and it would contribute especially to dispose favourably of feelings of the German people towards the projected Treaty, which was hurtful to some private interests' (Earl of Westmorland, 25 Jan. 1843, FO/64/244).

32 FO/64/242. Encloses copies of Acts of last session (5 & 6 Vict. cap 45 July 1 1842: 5 & 6 Vict, cap 47, 9 July 1842). Lord Westmorland requested attention be drawn to sections 23–25 of the late Customs Act re pirated editions in this country. He hoped that this would be 'sufficient to reach an agreement re Literary Property' (ibid.). Since

earlier legislation, 'the position of international copyright has materially changed' (15 March 1852, BT/491/343/52).

33 FO/64/241.

34 Section 17 of Copyright Act (5 & 6 Vict c 45) allowed for the destruction of pirated copies of books when seized on importation.

35 Even with the extension of international copyright to include artistic works in 1844, the primary concern in the UK was with literature.

36 FO/64/241. Unlike the 1838 International Copyright Act, the 1844 Act took into account the 1833 Dramatic Literary Property Act (3 & 4 Will 4 c. 15).

37 The Law Offices of the Crown advised the Board of Trade that, with some exceptions, fine arts were not protected by municipal copyright law (16 April 1847, BT/1/502/402). As they said, 'so far as I have been able to learn, the law of copyright in pictures is open to doubt. I cannot find any law which prevents my having any man's pictures copies if I gain access to it; and I have some doubts whether there is any express prohibition against engraving it, though the exclusive right of engraving is so universally admitted that I suppose it would be maintained in court' (Stafford Northcote to Bowring, 3 Oct. 1850, BT/1/478/2076). The Law Officers of the Crown also advised the Board of Trade that there is no law which restrains any person from copying or engraving from any picture or engraving (there was protection for prints and engravings and busts and sculptures) (ibid.). This is in contrast to the situation in 1839 where a treaty proposed by the Saxon government (which offered protection to works of art) was rejected by the Board of Trade. The reason given for this was that UK law did not extend to protect 'art' and artists. The pre-emptory nature of the 1844 International Copyright Act was admitted in section xii of the 1862 Fine Art Copyright Act which said that 'This Act shall be considered as including the provisions of the Act passed in the session of Parliament held in the 7th and 8th years of Her present Majesty, intituled "An Act to amend the law relating to international copyright" in the same manner as if such provisions were part of this Act'.

38 FO/64/242.

39 This was achieved with the passage of *An Act to enable Her Majesty to carry into effect a Convention with France on the subject of copyright, to extend and explain the International Copyright Acts, and to explain the Acts relating to copyright in engravings* (1852) (15 Vict. c12).

40 In the same manner in which the French were said to have shaped copyright law in Belgium. On this see Paul Geller (1994), 'Legal Transplants in International Copyright: Some Problems of Method', *UCLA Pacific Basin Law Journal*, **13**, 199 at 200.

41. For example, in Russia, the 'reproduction of English engravings, other works of art or design for earthenware stuff, papers etc does not take place to any extent worth mentioning; artists as well as manufacturers chiefly use French models which are preferred by the public' (from Robert J. King (in Moscow) to Lord Napier, 5 Aug. 1861, BY/556 1092/61). On 'the share which English thought and art may acquire in the demand and supply of their intellectual products of the Russian Nation' see the letter sent to Lord John Russell from Napier (St Petersburg) (14 June 1861), FO/65/576 no 166). 'No instance of reproduction of English engravings in Russia .... Those who have the taste for English engravings having the means to purchase the original prints ... English patents and designs are extensively imitated in the manufactures of cloths, stuffs and cotton prints, as well as in papers and on earthenware and china, the latter trades are however still more indebted to French and German patents for their designs' (report on English Book Trade in St Petersburg, to Napier from Saville Lumley, 12 Aug. 1861, FO/65/578/296).

42 Similar pragmatic motives were also at work in France: 'Their letters have always pressed for the conclusion of the Treaty as gaining an object of importance for this country by putting a stop to the French piratical reprints of English works; and in order to accomplish this, they have always given way on points not essential to or incompatible with their main object' (memorandum by J. Bergue, 19 December 1849, FO/27/860). This willingness to dispense with principle can also be seen in the Prussian treaties. It was reported that, 'by its treaty with England, the Cabinet of Berlin evidently recognised the justice of the claims of foreign authorship; it has not yet consented to conclude a similar convention with France, cheap French books (ie pirated editions from Brussels and Leipsic) being more necessary to Prussian enjoyment than English works of the same illegitimate origin' (Anon, 'A few words on International Copyright' *Edinburgh Review*, **95**, (1852), 148).

43 On the idea of backward-looking, reactive law (that 'took little interest in directing economic affairs and acted only when spurred by the initiatives of interested groups and individuals'), see L. Davison and T. Keirn, 'The reactive state: English governance and society 1688–1750; in L. Davison, T. Hitchcock and R.B. Shoemaker (eds), *Stilling the Grumbling Hive: The Response to Social and Economic Problems in England, 1688–1750*, Stroud, Glos. and New York: Alan Sutton and St Martin's Press, 1992, xi–liv; J. Brewer, *Thee Sinews of Power: War, Money and the English State, 1688–1783*, London: Century Hutchinson, 1988, esp. ch. 8. Cf. However, J. Innes, 'Parliament and the shaping of eighteenth-century English social policy', 5th series, *Transactions of the Royal Historical Society*, **40**, 1990, 63–92 (a critique of the traditional view of the eighteenth-century House of Commons as an inefficient and unsystematic legislative body).

44 BT/1/476/3065. Literature was defined to include dramatic and musical works. In turn, 'copyright of a picture is understood to be the right of allowing it to be engaged or made public. Copyright in a picture, or a right to permit or forbid its being made public by a copy, is a right prior to and distinct from copyright in any particular copy or engraving in it. This is what the expression artists or possessor of the picture ... means' (18 Sept. 1850, FO/27/889). In the care taken over the language used in the treaties more generally, see Foreign Office to Lord Normanby (10 Nov. 1851, FO/27/897). By 1855 the position was so well established that British law protected 'art' as an abstract category that the absence of equivalent provisions was seen as a weakness of other treaties. On this, see the criticism made of the suggestion that the Holland–France treaty, which was limited to 'oeuvres scientifiques et littéraires', be used as a model for an Anglo-Dutch treaty: 'The UK treaty was wider than that between Holland and France' (to Lord Tennent from Lord Hobart, 24 Nov. 1858, BT/1/548/1741).

45 BT/1/476/3065.

46 P. Bourdieu, 'Codification', in *In Other Words: Essays Towards a Reflexive Sociology*, trans. Matthew Adamson, Cambridge: Polity Press, 1990 80. This is reflected in the 1844 International Copyright Act whereby '4 several Acts' were reduced to a category of 'fine art'.

47 In response to a letter from Russia asking for a similar treaty with the UK as Russia had with France, the Foreign Office said that 'this was at variance with the British law on copyright' (Foreign Office to Lord Napier, 24 July 1861, FO/65/572, No. 134).

48 This was reinforced by the consolidation in legal publishing which played a role in establishing the proper shape of the legal text and, in turn, copyright law.

49 13 Jan. 1837, FO/27/538, 'which contained a memorandum on the state of the law of England relative to the protection of literary property'.

50 The nearest judicial equivalent to this was *Donaldson* v. *Becket* 4 Burr. 2408, 98 Eng

Rep 257 (1774) and *Millar* v. *Taylor* 4 Burr. 2303, 98 Eng Rep 210 (1769) and the associated tracts and pamphlets that made up the literary property debate. These focused almost exclusively on literary property (although in other respects they were clearly important).

51 In 1837, Earl Granville sent a letter to the Foreign Office which was to be forwarded to the French government in which he said, 'I herewith transmit to Your excellency a Copy of a note which I have addressed to M de Bourguenay enclosing copies of 6 acts of Parliament together with a memorandum on the state of the law of England relative to the protection of literary property and I have to instruct your excellency to apply to Count Mole for an accurate and authentic report of the present state of the law of copyright in France both as regards natives and foreigners, in return for the information thus furnished to M de Bourguenay. Her Majesty's Government still reserves for further consideration the proposal for negotiation between the two governments' (13 Jan. 1837, FO/27/538).

52 See generally Earl of Westmorland (25 Jan. 1843, FO/64/244).

53 Duchy of Brogher to Lord Palmerston (26 Oct. 1847, BT/1/476/3065).

54 The superior protection of French artists was partially attributed to 'the better definition of the law' (George Foggo, (1836), *Select Committee on Arts and Manufacture*, PP IX, 53).

55 In a similar vein, it was said, 'it is one of the evidences of the unsoundness of the principle upon which patents are based, that a complicated system of jurisprudence and of legislative machinery is specially required to maintain it' (William Hawes, 'On the Economical Effects of the Patent Laws', *Transactions of the National Association for the Promotion of Social Science*, 1863, 830, 831).

56 One of the problems with then existing law was that 'calico printing had so many different branches, varying in so many different degrees and from each other that it was impossible that one system of copy right for designs could apply to them all. If then uniformity could not be established, it would be far better to let all legislation on the subject alone' (Edmund Potter, *A Letter to Mark Phillips Esq MP in reply to his speech in the House of Commons, Feb. 9th 1841 on the Designs Copyright Bill*, 3).

57 One of the best examples of this can be seen in Sir James Fitzjames Stephen's attempt to codify copyright law, which was appended to the 1878 Copyright Commission Report.

58 BT/1/476/3065.

59 See above, note 37.

60 The Law Officers (Dodson, Cockburn and Wood) wrote to Palmerston advising him that the 'Crown does not have power to implement Article 10 on duties' and that it 'cannot bind Parliament not to raise rates during the continuance of the treaty, nor that any reduction for another country should apply to France' (13 Dec. 1851, BT/1/484 1342/51).

61 In the drafting of treaties, Palmerston warned of the need 'to avoid the appearance of an assumption by the Crown of power to alter by its own authority arrangements fixed by Parliament or to control proceedings by courts of justice ... to limit engagement of the Crown with regard to stipulations which require legislative sanctions by confining it to that recommended to Parliament'. This was especially the case in relation to the seizure of works and the registration and deposit of copyright works (Lord Palmerston (Foreign Office to Board of Trade) 18 Sept. 1850, emphasis added).

62 Ibid.

63 The idea of neutrality, which was compounded by the aesthetic agnosticism and fear of

judgement which developed in the later part of the nineteenth century, remains a central trait of contemporary intellectual property law.

64 There were occasions on which the Board of Trade acknowledged the role they were playing in prioritizing a particular view of copyright over others. See reply to letter from M. Girgot (16 Feb. 1846, BT/1/476/3065).

65 In turn, this reflected legal attitudes towards the value and nature of the works protected by copyright law.

66 See Anon, 'A few words on international Copyright', *Edinburgh Review*, **95**, 1852, 151. The law's attitude in this respect is clear in the amendments that Lord Palmerston made to a copyright treaty which had been drafted by the Foreign Office: 'The word "composer" has been substituted for the words "inventors and designers" because the latter words seem applicable rather to works of manufacture and utility, which are in this country protected by the Patents laws and by the Acts for the Registration of Designs, than to works of literature and the fine arts, to which alone, as [article 1 of Treaty] expressly states, the provisions of the convention are intended to apply' (13 Dec. 1851, BT/1/484 1342/51). The Foreign Office amended a draft convention sent to them by the Board of Trade by deleting the term 'design' and replacing it with 'drawing'. (31 Dec. 1849, FO/27/860/1069). See also 29 April 1850, FO/27/887 (from Board of Trade to Addington).

67 This can also be explained by the fact that in many jurisdictions it was possible for foreigners to obtain design and patent protection, so long as they satisfied the requisite conditions of registration.

68 To Lord Canning from MacGregor, 14 Oct. 1842, FO/64/241. In doing this, MacGregor reversed the caricatures of the two countries: 'It would be with very great regret that my Lords would find their expectations in that respect disappointed and the more so because they are most anxious to keep the question of International Copyright entirely apart from other less satisfactory matters and to show the anxiety of the two governments even while they appear unfortunately to differ in their commercial views, to unite in rendering an important service to the cause of literature' (30 Oct. 1844, MacGregor to Canning).

69 That is, the market appeal of the book was limited, at least insofar as it was protected as literary property, by the popularity of the national language. In this sense, commentators spoke of the problems British texts had in Russia because the English language was still only a 'foreign guest', whereas French had been 'naturalized' (Robert J. King, 5 Aug. 1861, from Moscow to Lord Napier, BT/1/556 1092/61). In a similar way, Anderson discusses the limited market appeal of the Czech book which can only be read by readers of the appropriate language and the Czech car, which can be used by all: Benedict Anderson, *Imagined Communities: Reflections of the Origin and Spread of Nationalism*, London: Verso, 1983, 34. In highlighting the artistic rather than the commercial nature of designs (and in so doing the ambivalent status of design law more generally), the Registrar of Design said in 1862 that the design systems in each country in Europe 'depends on the national feelings and the modes of thought peculiar to each and that unless a total change were made in the system peculiar in one country and adopted in toto by the other little satisfaction could be expected from any partial change' (31 Dec. 1861, BT/557 212/62).

70 See Benedict Anderson, *Imagined Communities: Reflections of the Origin and Spread of Nationalism*, London: Verso, 1983, 14–15; Peter Goodrich, 'Sleeping with the enemy: An essay on the politics of critical legal studies in America', *New York University Law Review*, **68**, 1993, 403.

71 See, for example, the evidence of Daniel Lee before the Select Committee on Copy-

right of Designs who was questioned as to the country of origin of the petitioners for reform (*Select Committee on Copyright of Designs* (1840) 6 PP 287: 4966 ff). On the impact of Prussia on the development of British trade mark law, see W.R. Cornish, *Intellectual Property*, 2nd edn, London: Sweet and Maxwell, 1989, 392 ff.

72 This was also the case with other treaty countries. For example, in discussions about a proposed Anglo-Russian treaty, Napier reported that he said to Prince Gottschalk, who was negotiating on behalf of Russia, that 'foreign authors would be admitted to all the rights enjoyed by a native in each country and also possess for a moderate period an interest in the translation of his work'. Napier said that Prince Gottschalk 'stopped me here and said that he regretted he could not hold out the least hope of any conception on the subject of translations. The right of authors in translations of his work was a principle which he had given much thought and he had *declined* to adopt it in the convention with France. The treaty with France was the basis of his model for other countries, and once it had been established "with much difficulty" he could not overturn it. He could not begin again' (to Earl Russell from Napier, 16 Aug. 1861, FO/65/578/274). See also Lord Napier to Lord Russell, commenting on a letter from Mr Tolstoy (BT/1/556/1092/61). It was also said that it was 'inadvisable to change clauses that have already been agreed with Prussia and Hanover' (18 Sept. 1850, FO/27/889).

73 This is reflected in Lord St Leonard's remark that 'nothing could be more improper than to consider the state of international law in deciding a question upon our own municipal law' (*Jefferys* v. *Boosey* (1854) 4 *HLC* 681, 749).

74 See, for example, L.R. Patterson and Stanley W. Lindberg, *The Nature of Copyright: A Law of Users' Rights*, Athens, Georgia: University of Georgia Press, 1991, esp. 134–43.

75 26 March 1858, *Journal of the Society of Arts*, 294.

76 Scrutton's text on copyright law sets out to deal with the 'leading ideas upon which an Ideal Copyright should be based'; a copyright which closely follows the model adopted in the bilateral treaties: Thomas Edward Scrutton, *The Law of Copyright*, London: William Clowes and Sons, 1896, xx.

77 E.M. Underdown, *The Law of Artistic Copyright: The Engraving, Sculpture and Designs Acts, the International Copyright Act and the Artistic Copyright Act 1862*, London: John Crockford, 1863, 5.

78 See, for example, Lord John Manner's Copyright Bill for consolidating and amending the law relating to copyright 1879 (Aug. 22 1879, *Journal of the Society of Arts*, 879–80). Perhaps the most interesting example was Sir James Fitzjames Stephens' attempts to codify copyright. On this, see his digest of copyright appended to the 1878 Copyright Royal Commission.

79 The law at the time, which was 'incomplete and often obscure', was 'governed by no fewer than twenty-two Acts of Parliament, passed at different times between 1735 and 1906; and to those should be added a mass of Colonial legislation, frequently following blindly the worst precedents of English law ... The new Copyright Bill [which became the 1911 Copyright Act] makes a clean sweep of all these enactments and proposes to set up in their place a homogenous code of Copyright Law, drafted on the whole on sound and generous lines' (Anon, 'Copyright Law Reform', *Quarterly Review*, **CCXIII**, 1910, 483, 489.

80 As Underdown said, as a consequence of the 1862 Fine Art Copyright Act, it was 'now possible to write histories of the law of artistic copyright (E.M. Underdown, *The Law of Artistic Copyright: The Engraving, Sculpture and Designs Acts, the International Copyright Act and the Artistic Copyright Act 1862*, London: John Crockford, 1863, 5).

81 Benedict Anderson, *Imagined Communities*, London: Verso, 1983, 204. 'After experi-

encing the physiological and emotional changes produced by puberty, it is impossible to 'remember' the consciousness of childhood .... How strange it is to need another's help to learn that this naked baby in a yellowed photograph ... is you. The photograph, fine child of the age of mechanical reproduction, is only the most preemptory of a huge modern accumulation of documentary evidence (birth certificates, diaries, report cards, letters, medical records, and the like) which simultaneously records a certain apparent continuity and emphasizes its loss of memory. Out of this estrangement comes a conception of personhood, *identity* (yes, you and that naked baby are identical) which, because it can not be "remembered", must be narrated' (ibid., 205).

82 The English doctrinal tradition has consistently defined itself against that of Europe and, most specifically, France. Here intellectual property is no exception (indeed it is an example *par excellence*): 'In both a literal and metaphoric sense France is the "foreign will" within and without the domestic constitution, and the destiny of English legal scholarship is far closer bound to its historic memory and continued presence of the continental tradition' (Peter Goodrich, 'Critical Legal Studies in England', *OJLS*, **10**, 1992, 195, 231.

83 Richard Godson, *A Practical Treatise on the Law of Patents for Inventions*, London: Joseph Butterworth, 1823, ix.

84 Montague R. Leverson, *Copyright and Patents: Or, Property in Thought Being an Investigation of the Principles of Legal Science Applicable to Property in Thought*, London: Wiley, 1854, 54.

85 This attitude has also influenced the approach taken towards design law. For example, in explaining why little progress had been made at the Third Congress of the Industrial Property Treaty in Brussels it was said there 'are in fact two different currents of opinion; the first wishing to assimilate the laws protecting designs with the laws concerning the right of reproduction; the second, on the contrary, insisting on the maintenance of a system of deposit' (*Industrial Property: Texts Adopted by the Third Congress*, Brussels, 21–27 June 1925, 11).

86 See K. Puri, 'Copyright Protection for Australian Aborigines in the Light of Mabo, M.A. Stephenson and Suri-Ratnapala (eds), *Mabo: A Judicial Revolution: The Aboriginal Land Rights Decision and Its Impact on Australian Law*, Brisbane: University of Queensland Press, 1993. Similar problems may arise with the drafting of the new South African Constitution.

87 This is because of the belief that patents are more readily translated into a language or form that can cross boundaries.

88 The EC has decided to defer harmonizing the originality requirement in copyright law because it is a cultural and local matter. As the Commission said 'the harmonisation of the originality criterion [would] prove to be extremely difficult task, because the different applications of the criterion are based on different legal and not least cultural traditions' (Green Paper on Design, para 4.2.7).

89 Cf. the *John Huston* decision (Cour d'appel de Paris, 4 chambre, sect B, 6 July 1989). On this, see B. Edelman, 'Applicable Legislation Regarding Exploitation of Colourised US films in France: The John Huston Case', *IIC*, 1992, 629. For an examination of recent attempts to treat intellectual property as a human right, see Meinhard Hilf and Thomas Oppermann, 'International protection of intellectual property: a German proposal' and Milan Bulajic, 'International protection of intellectual property in the context of the right to development: comment on the German proposal', in Subrata Roy Chowdhury, Erik M.G. Denters and Paul de Waart (eds), *The Right to Development in International Law*, Dordecht: Kluwer, 1992.

90 Cf. the attempt to rework moral rights as trade marks in Jan Ginsburg, 'Moral Rights in a Common Law System', 1990, *Entertainment Law Review*, **4**, 20.

91 Cf. Paul Geller, 'Must Copyright be For Ever Caught Between Marketplace and Authorship Norms?' and W. Grosheide, 'Paradigms in Copyright Law', in Brad Sherman and Alain Strowel (eds), *Of Authors and Origins: Essays on Copyright Law*, Oxford: Clarendon Press, 1994.

92 It is one of the oddities of modern research, which is so closed and specialized, that a company lawyer in Britain may have more contacts with French company lawyers than he may have with British criminal lawyers. Likewise, it is often the case that we have better knowledge of 'our' area of law in other countries than we may have of other areas of law within our own legal culture.

Index

Dict. mag. 2-3, 33, 66x, 72-3, 76. 100

meta-concepts

belief 84

discretion